■ THE ECONOMICS OF BARGAINING

THE ECONOMICS
OF BARGAINING ▪

JOHN G. CROSS

BASIC BOOKS, INC., PUBLISHERS
NEW YORK ▪ LONDON

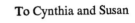

To Cynthia and Susan

FOREWORD

Martin Shubik

The behavioral sciences are entering a period of great flux and excitement. The simple behavioral models of the economist have been challenged. The power of economic reasoning has entered into psychology and political science. Mathematics and computational methods have become increasingly important throughout the behavioral sciences. Topics which at one time were regarded as belonging to the private hunting preserve of one set of specialists are now recognized to be fair game for all. Bargaining is one of these topics.

Dr. Cross has called this excellent contribution to our understanding of bargaining "The Economics of Bargaining" and *not* "The Theory of Bargaining." He has thereby avoided a major pitfall and shown that he fully appreciates the need for work in depth by individual investigators to show what their discipline can bring to a difficult subject. At the same time he has recognized that intensive work must be done in many allied disciplines before "The Theory of Bargaining" emerges.

This is a work based primarily upon economic theory, not on psychology, political science, or game theory. The closest connections are with psychology and with game theory but they are not central to the main contributions of this analysis.

The study of bargaining poses not one problem, but many. Furthermore, distinction must be made among closely related but different processes for resolving the types of conflict present in bargaining situations. Mediation may be used to modify the process; arbitration may serve as an alternative; a price system or social conventions are often utilized instead of bargaining.

The political scientist, sociologist, lawyer, or anthropologist interested in bargaining can benefit from understanding the type of approach presented here as much as the economist or psychologist. The stress in this book is upon process and the purposes, benefits, and costs associated with the bargaining process.

Psychologists deeply concerned with the complexities of learning, search, information-processing, perception, and aspiration might feel that the model of the learning process used here displays considerable naiveté, and that there is a lack of consideration of other important psychological features. Yet in any attempt to bridge the gap between disciplines, parsimony and simplicity in model building may prove to be extremely rewarding. There is a great temptation for economists, political scientists, and others to take words such as bluff, "toughness," or stubbornness and to avoid studying their implications in terms of their own discipline, by assigning them elsewhere. Unfortunately we do not know how much of a complex phenomenon such as bluffing can be explained in terms of personality, social situation, or simple economic considerations. Through investigations such as this we are beginning to find out.

Although many individuals have expected that the methods of the theory of games would yield many results in the study of bargaining, they have been disappointed for several reasons relevant to this study. The theory of games has for the most part been devoted to static analysis, while the very basis of bargaining is process. True, there has been some game theory devoted to dynamics, but neither learning nor changes in aspiration have been treated adequately.

The verbal treatment of bargaining and negotiation by economists and political scientists invariably includes features such as learning, changes in aspiration, or changes in perception. These factors are extremely difficult to treat in a rigorous game-theoretic context. An alternative but fruitful approach is to build the type of behavioristic models suggested here. By the perceptive analysis of the costs of process, the speed with which the taxi meter ticks, the phone bill mounts, or the overheads and lawyers' fees accrue, new limits on expected outcomes can be established.

In recent years political scientists concerned with the concept of power have been influenced by work in the theory of games on a type of solution known (in various forms) as the value of a game. The value may be interpreted under certain circumstances as providing an *a priori* measure of power. Although it is fundamentally a static concept, it has been given an interpretation in terms of a bargaining process. This gross oversimplification is dangerous unless used with care. However, when care is exercised, the bargaining model can be used to distinguish and analyze a few of the dimensions of the pervading phenomenon we loosely describe as power.

As John Cross points out, it is reasonable to assume that bargaining serves a *productive* as well as a distributive purpose. Bargaining is used in many parts of society: haggling in the bazaar, settling labor–management disputes, resolving conditions for arms control and deescalation, or determining tariff arrangements. Very often the productive aspect of the process is associated with the joint exploration of the complexity of the dispute at hand. Cross has stressed that one goal of negotiation is to organize cooperation. The process itself may serve to *reduce* rather than to accentuate the psychological aspects of a settlement. This can happen through the lessening of misperception and misinformation.

Although lengthy bargaining may be the most productive method known to man to settle complex diplomatic processes, it may be an inefficient procedure for selling consumer goods. What determines the "crossover point"? What are the alternative processes and the institutional factors that call for one process more than another? These are still open questions.

Most of the analysis here is carried out in terms of two parties.

Although mathematically the theory can be formally extended to more than two participants, perhaps it is here that some highly interesting further considerations are called for. As the number of parties to a bargaining process increases, how does it change qualitatively? When does it break down, and what is it replaced by if it breaks down? We must wait for the answer to these and many other related questions until further work of the type pioneered here has been completed.

PREFACE

A recent textbook in economic theory introduces the topic of bilateral monopoly "chiefly to explain the meaning of *indeterminate* in economics." * Bilateral monopoly, it goes on to explain, depends upon "bargaining skills and other personal characteristics anterior to the realm of economic analysis." This is just one example of the widely accepted proposition that there is no economic solution to the bargaining problem. Indeed, this is one of the most prominent non-existence theorems in modern economic thought.

The rather facile conclusion that the theory of bargaining belongs largely to the psychologist has always been frustrating to economists because it forces them to be satisfied with a gap in what is otherwise a very elegant theory of prices. Other gaps— such as price determination in oligopolistic markets—have been believed to be amenable to economic analysis; so that we have had at least the satisfaction of having tried. In this book, I do not intend to deny the relevance of psychological variables in influencing the outcomes of negotiations. I do intend, however, to try to show that it is possible to treat the bargaining process in terms of economic variables, and to come out with a determinate and useful theory.

The study which is reported here was first inspired in the sum-

---

*C. E. Ferguson, *Microeconomic Theory* (Homewood, Ill.: Irwin, 1966).

mer of 1962 when I attended a Social Science Research Council seminar on "Bargaining, Negotiation, and Conflict" organized by Harold W. Kuhn and John C. Harsanyi. The basic model was then conceived in my doctoral dissertation at Princeton and has since been developed and refined, especially during 1966–1968 at the Mental Health Research Institute of the University of Michigan. Over these years I have accumulated numerous debts both to those colleagues who have given me their advice and comments and to various institutions which have given me financial support for this research. Among the latter are the Social Science Research Council, the National Science Foundation, the Institute for Defense Analyses, and The Mental Health Research Institute at the University of Michigan.

I owe a particular debt to Harold W. Kuhn and to William J. Baumol who painstakingly reviewed my work while it was still in its early stages and provided me with extensive comments and suggestions. This work has benefited enormously from their assistance. I would also like to thank Martin Shubik and George E. Johnson for their valuable comments. Finally, I am grateful to the several members of the Social Sciences Seminar in the Mental Health Research Institute for providing me with an atmosphere which was very conducive to work in this area and for their willingness to devote several weeks of their meetings to discussions of bargaining and related topics.

I thank the *American Economic Review* for permission to reprint some of the material in Chapters II, III, and IV.

I am afraid that I must apologize to the reader for my unnecessarily terse and occasionally clumsy style of writing. I can assure him, however, that both he and I owe an incalculable debt of gratitude to my research assistant, Mrs. Katherine P. Rogin, without whose meticulous review of my manuscript this book would have been totally incomprehensible.

Ann Arbor, Michigan
August 1969

JOHN G. CROSS

CONTENTS

◼ THE ECONOMICS OF BARGAINING

I

▪ Introduction:
The Parameters of the Study

Negotiation may be defined as the voluntary process of distributing the proceeds from cooperation. It arises whenever the allocation of gains among participants to an agreement is subject to their own choice rather than predetermined by their circumstances. If I buy a stock on the New York Exchange, I may be more than happy to pay the price, and the seller may be more than happy to get it, but the market has already determined the distribution of benefits from the transaction; if I buy a house, however, the possible price may fall within a relatively wide range and the distribution of gains depends upon negotiation. Negotiation in this sense occurs in so many contexts—from the purchase of Manhattan Island to the distribution of its political representation—that it is surprising that such a large proportion of the literature on the bargaining process deals with specialized problem areas rather than addressing the problem as a whole. It is my belief that the selection of wage rates, the establishment of international treaties, and even the determination of income-tax legislation have enough in common to enable us to make positive statements about the bargaining process, and its probable consequences, that are relevant to all such circumstances. Dissimilar contexts may require dissimilar parameter values, but they should not lead to dissimilar theories.

The purpose of this chapter is to characterize the bargaining process in a very general way and to give the reader some indication of the problem we have in mind, our attitude toward that problem, and the kinds of questions we shall ask in subsequent chapters. Moreover, there are several situations that are frequently described using terms such as "negotiation" or "bargaining," but which are fundamentally different from that process which we intend to study here. Therefore, despite our desire to make as general an analysis as possible, it is necessary to sharpen the definitions right at the outset.

1. Negotiation as defined here will always be associated with *cooperative* enterprises, that is, situations in which all parties stand to benefit by reaching an agreement. "Zero sum" situations, in which it is necessary for one party to lose if another is to gain, are not considered in this study. Our definition does encompass cases in which the cooperation follows an act of hostility; peace negotiations after a military conflict can confer benefits upon all the parties, even though the outcome may only restore the conditions which existed before the hostilities occurred.

2. "Moves" made during the bargaining process—bids, demands, and the acceptance of a final point of agreement—are made *voluntarily*. By definition a concession would not be a part of the bargaining process if it were clear to both the parties that failure to concede would eliminate any possibility of agreement. Suppose that an automobile salesman lowers his price from $2400 to $2200 because the customer has pointed out that he can get the lower price from a competitor. This would be an example of a market force which is not a part of the bargaining process, because it is obvious to the salesman that he has no alternative but to reduce his bid if he wants any agreement at all.

3. The bargaining process is not merely a distributive device; it is *productive* as well. The distributive property is obvious: negotiation is usually thought of as a means for dividing sums of money, for selecting wage rates, and so on, all of these having the property that, were the point of agreement to appear more in the favor of one party, it necessarily would be less favorable for the other. The process is productive in that it can be used to discover

agreement possibilities which were not formerly recognized. For example, two parties might suspect that cooperation is possible, without knowing exactly what the properties of their agreement would be; the bargaining process may be used as a mechanism for discovering these properties. International negotiations are good examples of this sort of situation: the frequency with which the parties to such disputes "agree to disagree" or the negotiations "fail" may be taken as evidence that these are as much *search* operations as they are distributive ones. The bargaining process is frequently productive in a second, but similar, sense when it enables the parties to improve a present agreement by revising its terms. It may become clear through bargaining, for example, that an employer could guarantee some degree of job security in exchange for relatively modest wage increases, and the advent of this new knowledge is a benefit to both parties.

Having introduced the productive character of the bargaining process, we must admit that this study will still place most emphasis upon the distributive element as the fundamental ingredient of all negotiations. As it happens, of the two senses in which the bargaining process is productive, the first will follow naturally from this analysis. The mechanism of concession, in which each party moves toward his opponent's demands, is bound to converge upon a point of mutual benefit (if any exists) simply because no one will ever concede beyond a point which gives him a zero yield. Unfortunately, the process of improving an existing agreement through substitutions in its terms will not be given the detailed analysis which it deserves.

4. Negotiation as defined here is always characterized by some form of *communication*. Positions are taken and defended either verbally or physically (or both), and opponents are permitted to respond to these positions (or to their perceptions of them) as they choose. This characterization is not universally accepted. For example, Schelling[1] has conceived of a contrasting situation involving what he calls "tacit bargaining"—that is, a situation in which individual negotiators must select possible settlement points in isolation and in which, failing agreement (that is, failing coincidence in their choices), no cooperation is achieved at all.

In such a case, the participants necessarily will concentrate upon mutual coordination rather than upon the division of benefits, and, even more important, neither side will undergo the sequence of demand formation (or expectation formation), reevaluation, and concession which we shall take to be the essence of the bargaining process.

The communication which takes place need not be perfect, however. The accurate transfer of information is often impeded by distrust and by distorted perceptions. The frequent use of bluffing—the misrepresentation of expectations, preferences, environmental conditions, and so on—and the expectation of it from others may dramatically reduce the plausibility of verbal positions; it may even lead one party to discount the importance of more overt moves, such as the use of force or the making of concessions by the other. As a consequence, the individual's perception and evaluation of other available information will be an important parameter in our analysis.

5. A distinguishing characteristic of the bargaining process as treated in this study is the fact that there are no important benefits accruing to either party until both sides have accepted the terms of agreement: that is, the level of potential intermediate payoffs is relatively low compared to the value received from agreement itself. Thus there is no opportunity for exploiting one's partner by improving one's own return unilaterally (and at his expense), since that partner always must acquiesce to the outcome which would make the greater return possible. Again there are a number of "bargaining" models in existence which do not satisfy this condition, in that they permit important intermediate payoffs to be made. An example is the very well-known case of experimental "Prisoners' Dilemma Games" in which two or more individuals make a sequence of plays and in which each play yields positive or negative returns to each player.[2] Analysis of this kind of situation yields valuable and enlightening insights into situations in which communication is extremely poor, in which agreements are virtually unenforceable, and, indeed, in which unilateral noncooperation may actually lead to higher returns than cooperation.

However, none of these properties characterizes the process which we are considering.

6. As the title of this study suggests, we shall deal with the economic—that is, value oriented—properties of the bargaining process. Observation of negotiations in practice suggests that a variety of emotional variables may be relevant as well. The potential for cooperation that motivates the bargaining process can easily be disrupted by the conflict of personalities which frequently accompanies it. Except for a few asides, however, this facet of the problem will not be included in our study. This is so partly because the author is simply not qualified to evaluate these problems, and partly because the matter of value distribution seems to be more fundamental: without this dimension there would be no bargaining at all.

Terminology

As the reader may already have realized, we tend to use the terms "bargaining" and "negotiation" almost interchangeably in this study. When a distinction does arise, the term "bargaining" will refer to the process of demand formation and revision which provides the basic mechanism whereby the parties converge toward an agreement, while "negotiation" will refer to the whole situation within which the bargaining occurs. Thus in Chapter V we shall treat "arbitration" as a part of negotiation but as an alternative to the bargaining process.

Since we wish to keep this study as general as possible, it is desirable to leave the rest of our terminology as neutral as we can. In this respect, it is a little difficult to find appropriate terms for the participants in a negotiation. As Schelling has pointed out, individuals involved in cooperation can hardly be termed "adversaries" or "opponents"; nor, since they are taken to be disputing the division of gains, should they be called "partners." Schelling has suggested the term "mixed-motive game" for this situation, but he finds no similarly appropriate term for the individuals.[3] We are unfortunately bound to fall back on terms denoting opposition, on the undesirably abstract terms "player" and "person" which are commonly employed in game-theoretic analyses, or simply on the term "party."

There Are Really Three "Bargaining Problems"

The various bargaining models which have been put forward in the past have rarely dealt with the bargaining problem in its entirety; instead they have concentrated upon only a few of its elements at a time. Unfortunately, this has usually led to the use of highly specialized analytical techniques, so that different studies of negotiation often appear to be examining wholly unrelated phenomena rather than different components of the same thing. Here we shall distinguish three dimensions of the bargaining problem which do appear to require separate treatment, although, to be sure, they are related analytically.

The first approach is concerned solely with the outcome or settlement point of a negotiation. Models which focus upon this problem generally begin with a given state of the environment; thus, the payoff values associated with some state of disagreement, the preferences of the parties, the total benefits to be distributed, the maximum payoff each party could possibly receive, and so on, are all taken as parameters. These models then attempt to predict the distribution of payoffs at agreement, or to explain why agreement is not reached at all. Although these approaches may specify something about the nature of concessions and the factors that determine which side is expected to give in at any point, the primary emphasis is put upon characterization of the outcome itself. Most economic models of duopoly and oligopoly, for example, would fall into this category.[4]

The second approach to the bargaining problem is to deal explicitly with the *process* of concession. If this process is specified in a deterministic way, the outcome, of course, can also be specified precisely. In some recent analyses, however, the emphasis has fallen so heavily upon bargaining *behavior* and upon the multitude of variables which contribute to it that no general predictions can be made about the outcome at all.[5] The great contribution of this approach is that it clarifies the importance of different kinds of tactics and moves and makes it possible to state how changes in behavior (if they are not too complicated) can bring about changes in an outcome. For our purposes, however, the difficulties with such a microscopic analysis are substantial. Although the tactics and devices associated with the bargaining process are interesting and often entertaining, a heavy emphasis upon them tends to shift our attention away from the major forces which may be operating, and hence we gain little understanding of the long run pattern of bargaining outcomes. On the other hand, parameters related to communications, expectations, and other important features of the bargaining process, seem to derive much of their influence from their impact on the mechanism of concession. Insofar as we wish to study the dependence of the outcome upon these parameters, we must consider this intermediate process as fully as possible. Therefore, we shall use a simplified model of the concession process as a foundation stone throughout our study.

The third approach to the bargaining problem focuses upon attempts by the negotiators to change some of the basic parameters of the situation. For example, the costs to both management and labor of a protracted negotiation are heavily dependent upon whether or not there is a strike or lockout, whether or not expensive public-relations activities are engaged in, whether or not political pressures are utilized, and so on. Thus, to a great extent the costs and benefits of negotiation are themselves subject to *choice* rather than being given by the environment. There is no such thing as *"the* cost of disagreement," or *"the* cost of concession": such expressions must be defined not only in terms of the current demands of the parties,[6] but also in terms of the circumstances under which they themselves have chosen to negotiate. Since the availability, effectiveness, and cost of such environmental controls are certainly major determinants of the outcome of the bargaining process, it is possible to discuss the bargaining problem purely in these terms, relating outcomes directly to these fundamental variables. For example, we could determine the "best" values of the variables without regard to the intermediate process of concession. In this study, however, we shall argue that such a choice cannot be fully understood without first dealing with the concession mechanism. It is not always a good idea to go out on strike or to threaten to withhold foreign aid, and the proper criteria for evaluating such policies are determined by the mechanism which transforms their immediate effects into changes in the outcome. This subject will be discussed in Chapters VI and VII.

Preferences

All but the most "behavioral" of bargaining theories depend to some extent upon quantification of costs and benefits. At the very least it is necessary to specify all those settlement points at which one or the other party is indifferent between agreement and permanent disagreement (however that may be defined). This specification is widely recognized as the appropriate way of determining the extreme limits of the range of possible settlements to a negotiation. For example, the highest wage which could possibly be won by a union is taken to be that which would leave the employer indifferent between operating and shutting down (or hiring strikebreakers), and the lowest possible wage is that which would drive so much labor away as to leave the production process economically unfeasible. As we have pointed out already, even these points may in fact be subject to the discretion of the parties: the choice of retaliatory destruction of property by a union may well influence the maximum wage which would willingly be paid. The most cautious writers, as well as those who are not principally concerned with the bargaining problem itself, have tended to discontinue their analyses after these issues have been discussed, leaving a "range of indeterminateness" within which the outcome is to depend on the "bargaining skill" of the negotiators.[7] Such an approach, in effect, sidesteps the bargaining problem, often on the ground that it is a psychological rather than an economic question. In some cases, this does not seriously weaken the analysis, for even in only moderately competitive economic environments the bargaining range may be relatively small. It is not improbable, for example, that despite the attention frequently given to labor negotiations, the range of possible wage settlements is actually quite limited.

Many situations remain, however, in which the range of indeterminateness may be substantial, and those who have attempted to narrow it further have had to make more explicit use of some notion of measurable utility. The simplest recourse is to consider only the dollar figures which may be associated with various outcomes. Such an approach is appealing in its simplicity, but it is dependable only for the most purely economic situations. For example, theories of duopoly and oligopoly can be treated in this fashion because, at least in the simplest theories, profits are taken to be the primary if not the only objectives of the firm.[8]

Occasionally, dollar costs are treated as the major variables in labor–management negotiations as well. Cartter, for example, carefully defines the cost to the union of disagreement with the employer as "the probable loss of wage income during the period of the strike," and the cost to the employer as "the probable loss of profit during cessation of production." [9] (Here "probable" may be taken to mean "anticipated.") Considering the variety of noneconomic factors which seem to influence the negotiators' preferences, this certainly is an extreme simplification. Besides substantive nonwage issues, more or less psychological factors such as the attitude of a union toward unemployment and toward nonmembers, the relationship between union members and their leaders, the relationship between union leaders and management, and the importance of political and social factors can influence the wage negotiation process to such an extent that the observer is tempted to discount the monetary variables heavily. It is presumably just this type of reaction that has led to the more extreme behavioral work on wage negotiation which we mentioned earlier. Nevertheless, such a response may be too pessimistic: the labor–management relationship is still primarily an economic one, and thus, over the long run, such simplifications as Cartter's may prove to be quite fruitful. They certainly do increase the chances of constructing useful operational and descriptive theories in this area.

Such economic examples as bilateral monopoly and labor negotiations unfortunately fall far short of exhausting the entire set of possible bargaining relationships. Modern social science has not yet progressed far enough to suggest simple unidimensional measures which would serve to represent the preferences of those involved in international or political negotiations. Here we must fall back on the conviction that at least the individuals who do the bargaining—those who decide upon the concessions and accept agreements—must have some consistent notion of their own relative preferences, and that these preferences are representable (at least in principle) on a unidimensional scale.[10] It is thus a pure utility measure which has been used in the most general bargaining models. Pen, for example, makes use of an "ophelemity" function in describing wage negotiations,[11] and Nash and the game theorists make explicit use of the von Neumann–Morgenstern utility function in their models.[12] The latter function often appears to be especially satisfactory because, at least in principle, it could be constructed empirically in terms of just those alternatives which are subject to the negotiation.[13] On the other hand, we are left with the unpleasant requirement either of knowing the values of this function in advance (which is impossible without a crystal ball) or of making positive statements *a priori* about its nature, a procedure which leads us closer to an *ad hoc,* neoclassical approach anyway. It is not appropriate here to discuss the more technical characteristics of the utility functions which have been employed in bargaining models. With very few exceptions, they all appear to be translatable into the terms of Hicksian ordinal preferences.[14] The outstanding examples of models for which this is not the case will be outlined in the next chapter, and a much more detailed examination of these properties and their significance will appear in Chapter III.

Time

The most important characterization which we, in this study, will apply to the bargaining process is that it is fundamentally time dependent. It is widely appreciated that the passage of time has a cost in terms of both dollars and the sacrifice of utility which stems from the postponement of consumption, and it will be our position throughout this study that it is precisely this cost which motivates the whole process. If it did not matter *when* the parties agreed, it would not matter whether or not they agreed at all. We will discuss three different ways in which time can influence a negotiation. First, time appears naturally in a discounting function if the players discount future benefits. (Note that agreement must always offer some potential benefit; otherwise there would be no bargaining.) Second, the utility of agreement may change with the calendar date (the cake gets moldy before we agree on how to cut it, and so on). Finally, there is a fixed cost of bargaining which recurs in each time period. This last cost may vary from the simple personal inconvenience of having to spend time in this rather than other occupations, to the immense cost in terms of loss of profit and fixed cost of a temporarily unproductive plant which is faced by a strike-bound firm.

In our interpretation, a predominant concern of each negotiator must be how long the disagreement will last. This attitude, moreover, introduces a new and difficult problem into the analysis, because surely the relevant variables must represent the length of time which each party *expects* the negotiation to last rather than how long it actually does last. Given the significance of this factor, it is surprising how few models have explicitly taken it into account. The problem seems to have been treated in detail first by Hicks[15] and more recently in a text by Cartter,[16] but otherwise its apparent centrality seems to have been ignored. Even these two authors, however, have not studied the determinants of expectations with much thoroughness. The reason may be that this question seems at first to be too far removed from the main problem: Why should we concentrate upon those factors which lead negotiators to believe that the process will take a certain amount of time, when we are primarily interested in the characteristics of the outcome itself? The answer is that each negotiator must believe the expected date of agreement to depend to some extent upon the magnitude of his own demands, and hence these demands (and the outcome which depends on them) must be strongly influenced by the costs of waiting for a given payoff. This observation will provide our point of departure for most of the issues discussed in this study.

■ NOTES

1. Thomas C. Schelling, *The Strategy of Conflict* (Cambridge, Mass.: Harvard University Press, 1960), pp. 54–80.

2. A thorough discussion of experiments with such games appears in Anatol Rapoport and Albert Chammah, *Prisoner's Dilemma* (Ann Arbor, Mich.: University of Michigan Press, 1965).

3. Schelling, *op. cit.*, p. 89.

4. Examples may be found in K. J. Cohen and R. M. Cyert, *Theory of the Firm: Resource Allocation in a Market Economy* (Englewood Cliffs, N. J.: Prentice-Hall, Inc., 1965), pp. 229–261.

5. An example is the recent book by Richard Walton and Robert McKensie, *A Behavioral Theory of Labor Negotiations* (New York: McGraw-Hill Book Co., 1965).

6. Chamberlain, for example, measures all costs and benefits from the player's current demands. See Neil Chamberlain, *Collective Bargaining* (New York: McGraw-Hill Book Co., 1951), pp. 220–222.

7. This term originates with A. C. Pigou, *The Economics of Welfare* (4th ed.; London: Macmillan and Co., 1951), pp. 451–461.

8. See, for example, William Fellner, *Competition Among the Few* (New York: Alfred A. Knopf, 1949).

9. Allan M. Cartter, *Theory of Wages and Employment* (Homewood, Ill.: Richard D. Irwin, 1959), pp. 117–118.

10. We would argue here that some consistent ranking of preferences defined over the set of known possible alternatives is crucial for "successful" negotiation. Otherwise the making of concessions, for example, would be impossible on anything but a random basis. In fact, this ranking does not even need to be transitive to enable us to get a determinate solution for the bargaining process itself. It needs only to exist.

11. Jan Pen, *The Wage Rate Under Collective Bargaining*, tr. T. S. Preston (Cambridge, Mass.: Harvard University Press, 1959), pp. 47–60.

12. John F. Nash, "The Bargaining Problem," *Econometrica*, XVIII (1950), 155–162.

13. An exposition of the von Neumann–Morgenstern utility index may be found in William J. Baumol, *Economic Theory and Operations Analysis* (2nd ed.; Englewood Cliffs, N. J.: Prentice-Hall, Inc., 1965), pp. 512–528.

14. J. R. Hicks, *Value and Capital* (New York: Oxford University Press, 1946), pp. 11–25.

15. J. R. Hicks, *The Theory of Wages* (New York: Macmillan and Co., 1932), pp. 136–147.

16. Cartter, *op. cit.*, pp. 118–119.

II

• Models of the Bargaining Process: Some Background in Theory and Experiment

The discussions on the theory of the bargaining process which appear in the literature are not particularly extensive. Even so, most of the properties of negotiations which we deem to be important have been touched upon elsewhere, at least informally. The purpose of this chapter is not to review the entire literature, but only to bring its relevant portions into a perspective which will make them most useful for our subsequent discussions. In general, comments and criticisms which could be made on the various models will be disregarded unless they have a direct bearing on this study.

The Problem of "Power"

It is very tempting to try to approach the bargaining problem by making reference to "the fundamental power relationships" which are supposed to underlie it. Indeed, such phrases as "he did better because he was more powerful" come so naturally to us that one might suspect that we already have intuitively a perfectly reasonable theory of bargaining right at our fingertips. Moreover, it is true that a predominant fraction of current writing on negotiation does make use of some notion of "bargaining power." [1] Unfortunately, despite the widespread use of the term, there does not appear to be anything approaching consensus as to what "power" is. The apparent concreteness of the term is belied by the enormous diversity of interpretations which have been applied to it. One may still feel compelled, however, to seek for some consistent definition; in the words of one author: "if so many people at so many different times have felt the need to attach the label power, or something like it, to some Thing they believe they have observed, one is tempted to suppose that the Thing must exist; and not only exist, but exist in a form capable of being studied more or less systematically." [2] In part, the profusion of conflicting definitions is due to a failure to distinguish clearly enough between a bargaining outcome and the bargaining process which leads to it. Many definitions may be taken to make "power" synonymous with "the ability to get a better outcome"; that is, a "favorable" bargain for A reflects A's greater power. This approach is used by Harsanyi in defining the amount of A's power as A's "ability to get B to do something that B would not otherwise do." [3] subject to "the opportunity costs to A of attempting to influence B's behavior." [4] Similarly, Pen calls power "the capacity of a subject to carry through his will against another subject." [5] A definition of power, however, cannot contribute anything to an analysis if it is simply taken to be synonymous with or descriptive of the outcome. Moreover, this would not seem to reflect our intuitive notion of the "Thing": such definitions, for example, prevent us from considering both negotiators to be powerful (and yet, surely both General Motors and the UAW are "powerful"). Or, they would force us to say that a labor union is weak because, due to a wage which is already near the maximum obtainable, the next contract must contain a relatively small increase in benefits!

A proper definition of "power" should be directed at the *determinants* of the outcome and not the outcome itself. For example, definitions emphasizing the discretionary ability to impose heavy costs on others coupled with insensitivity to costs imposed on oneself,[6] or definitions emphasizing the legitimacy or durability of one's cost-imposing ability[7] might be more to the point. The problem then becomes one of selecting those elements which are appropriate for a fruitful definition. This task will be attempted in Chapter VI. Unfortunately the formulation of a consistent definition of this sort proves to be so difficult that here we are compelled to avoid the term altogether, except in the case of models reviewed in this chapter, for which it is explicitly defined.

Game-Theoretic Solutions and the Model of Nash

Game-theoretic models of social situations are characterized by their emphasis upon the specification of the outcome rather than the process whereby it is achieved. This approach has been shown to have a great advantage in that it enables one to simplify, at least in principle, enormously complex social situations.[8] Unfortunately, as a general rule game-theoretic models have been unable to narrow the range of possible solutions far enough to provide much explanatory or predictive power; and indeed, they usually cannot confine the expected outcome any further than the usual "range of indeterminateness" which we have already discussed. Recently there have been attempts to improve upon this deficiency in classical game theory ("classical" because the *Theory of Games and Economic Behavior* was published long ago in 1944) by adding new constraints upon the character of possible outcomes in hopes of achieving a determinate theory. It is the author's belief that by far the most important as well as the most plausible of the resulting models is that of Nash.[9]

Nash conceived of the bargaining problem in the usual game-theoretic terms; that is, he considered as relevant data only the utilities which each alternative point of agreement would provide to the players. Thus, in the case of two person bargaining, we can draw the set of possible utility combinations (the "outcome" set) on a graph with U_1, the utility of player 1, on one axis, and U_2, the utility of player 2 on the other; we can treat this as though no other data were necessary to deal with the problem. This outcome set, or, as we shall frequently call it, the "utility possibility set," is drawn in Figure 1. Nash assumed this set to be closed and bounded, and used the linear utility combinations made possible by the von Neumann–Morgenstern index to achieve convexity.[10] In Figure 1, the origin has been placed at that utility combination which corresponds to total disagreement.

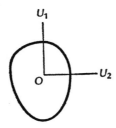

Figure 1

Nash suggested that it is reasonable to expect the outcome of a bargaining process to satisfy the following three conditions:

1. Pareto optimality—the outcome will lie on the northeast boundary of the outcome set.

2. Independence of irrelevant alternatives—consider two different bargaining situations with the same origin, and in which all the possible outcomes of one are included in the other; then, if the actual outcome of the larger game is also a possible outcome in the smaller, it will be the final outcome for the smaller game as well.

3. Symmetry—if the set of possible utility outcomes happens to be symmetric (that is, if for every point $U_1 = a$, $U_2 = b$ in the outcome set, the point $U_1 = b$, $U_2 = a$ is also in the set), then the outcome of the bargaining will give $U_1 = U_2$.

Finally, the outcome is assumed to be independent of any interpersonal utility comparisons, even if they are possible. Thus, even if one negotiator is replaced by a different person who in some sense rates each outcome as just twice as valuable as did his predecessor, the actual point of agreement will remain unchanged. This assumption also makes possible the use of such utility indices as the von Neumann–Morgenstern index, whose units of measurement are essentially arbitrary. Thus, we have a fourth rule:

4. The model must predict the same actual outcome despite any linear transformations of the players' utility functions.[11, 12]

On the basis of these four conditions, Nash came to the remarkable conclusion that the only function which can consistently describe the outcome of the bargaining process as he conceived of it is the one which maximizes the product of the players' utilities (the utilities being measured from the point of disagreement).[13] For the sake of future reference, it is useful to point out that in the case of a continuous outcome set, for which the first order derivatives on the northeast boundary of the set are always defined, the utility product is maximized at the point for which $U_1/U_2 = dU_1/dU_2$, where dU_1/dU_2 is the slope of the boundary.[14] Nash originally took the position that his model constituted a positive theory and that it would describe actual bargaining outcomes, but it is now much more common to give a normative interpretation to the analysis and to treat the Nash solution as a "desirable" outcome of the bargaining process.[15]

This model, with all its elegance, has been subjected to extensive criticism.[16] Unfortunately, two important properties of the model are often overlooked, with the result that many of these criticisms, if not wrong, are misdirected. First, we reiterate that Nash assumed that the only relevant data are the payoff utilities; that is, *any two bargaining situations which yield the same set of payoff utility possibilities will yield the same solution* (again in terms of utilities). This assertion is crucial to the result and should be stated on an equal footing with the other four conditions listed above. Objections that variables other than pure utilities should be taken into account may be well founded (indeed, we shall introduce several such variables later on), but it should be recognized that Nash has not really *forgotten* them, he has formulated a principle that explicitly dismisses them. Second, there is a tendency to read too much into the utility functions themselves. For example, Robert Bishop has criticized the independence of linear transformation of utility assumption on the grounds that (1) "in conjunction with the symmetry axiom, it actually involves an *ad hoc* interpersonal comparison of utilities" and (2) "it derives knowledge from ignorance, since it is only through a denial of any substantively valid interpersonal comparison that Nash feels free to establish, by an implicit appeal to the dubious 'principle of insufficient reason,' whatever *ad hoc* interpersonal comparison is needed to bring his symmetry axiom into play." [17] Both of these criticisms rely upon an overstrict interpretation of the axiom. The linear transformation assumption does not assert that comparability of utility functions is impossible, but rather that interpersonal comparisons are *irrelevant*. In effect, it states that the outcome of the bargaining process can be specified in real terms without regard to the relative utility levels of the players—that is, whether valid comparisons can be made or not. This point can be made more clearly if we restate the model in terms of the set of actual payoff alternatives rather than in terms of the utility combinations associated with them. The model will be less elegant, but its components may be more comprehensible.

We begin with a special case: Suppose two men are negotiating over the division of a homogeneous good which is fixed in supply. Let the total quantity available be defined as X. If the first party obtains X_1, then the second may receive some quantity X_2 which is no greater than $(X - X_1)$. Let the marginal utility of X be positive for each man. The Nash model now translates into the following terms:

1. The Pareto optimality assumption states that $X_2 = X - X_1$.

2. Symmetry: If marginal utility of X over the relevant range is positive and constant for each man, then final agreement will have $X_1 = X_2$. With regard to this assumption, we should note that, first, it is implied by Nash's system,[18] and, second, interpersonal comparisons are neither made nor denied. Indeed, no reference at all is made to the utility functions except for the qualification that X is not subject to diminishing marginal utility (and this qualification will be disposed of later). The substance of this axiom, when combined with Pareto optimality, is that when diminishing marginal utility is not a prominent factor, any homogeneous good which is fixed in supply will be divided evenly.

3. Independence of irrelevant alternatives is expressed just as before, with "outcome" now interpreted as physical payoff rather than utilities.

4. All bargaining problems which yield the same outcome possibility set in utility space have the same (utility) solution.

If we have no diminishing marginal utility, the counterpart of the second axiom in utility space is a straight line with agreement at its midpoint. The slope of this line is negative but otherwise it is not specified. Note that we could generate *any* such straight line in $U_1 \times U_2$ space we wished, simply by finding (or hypothesizing the existence of) some good with the same properties as X but with different marginal utilities for the two players. By assumption 4, any bargaining situation which produces such a straight line, *whether or not marginal utilities are constant,* must now contain the expected outcome of the relevant negotiation as its midpoint. From this point on we may follow the same proof as that in footnote 13 to obtain the Nash result.

The crucial assumptions for the Nash model, then, are Pareto optimality, independence of irrelevant alternatives, symmetry (as we have defined it here), and dependence upon utilities alone. For our purposes, one of the least defensible of these is the independence of irrelevant alternatives assumption. Our concern for the process of bargaining as well as its outcome will lead us to treat nonsolution alternatives as the "stepping stones" of concession and certainly changes in these stepping stones can lead to changes in the nature of the settlement. The dependence of the Nash model upon utilities alone is also quite difficult to justify for a positive model. If the solution depends upon *anything* besides utility, even if only the mathematical form of the utility functions themselves, this axiom will be violated. Nash's symmetry axiom is subject to similar criticism, but our modification of it appears to stand up somewhat better, primarily because it is taken to apply to much narrower circumstances. It states simply that in cases in which marginal utility is positive and constant, homogeneous commodities will tend to be divided evenly; cakes will be cut "fairly," money will be divided 50:50, and so on. Moreover, this is the only axiom which really makes an attempt at a description of behavior.[19, 20]

It is easy to construct economic examples in which the Nash point is not a valid description of what actually happens. For example, consider the familiar offer curve diagram of international trade theory in which, however, the "social indifference curves" of one country are linear. In free market trading, such a nation gains nothing over the utility which it would have received from the initial distribution of commodities, and hence if we compute the product of the two nations' utility gains after the trade, we will get zero. This is certainly not the maximum product which could have been obtained from any possible redistribution of goods. In this example, we have introduced both utility functions and price ratios as determinants of the solution, with the result that both the Nash symmetry and the independence of irrelevant alternatives assumptions have been violated.

The major deficiency of the Nash model for our purposes, however, does not rest in the weakness of its assumptions but rather in its fundamental character as a piece of game theory. As a consequence of its concern only for the specification of an outcome, it can offer us no analysis of the dynamic process of disagreement–concession–agreement which constitutes the very essence of bargaining. We are given only a solution criterion with no insight into its *raison d'être*. The model does not even attempt to answer the question that often is most interesting to us: Under what conditions will the solution *deviate* from the idealized condition, and how will that variation take place? On the other hand, as an ideal solution, Nash's construction is extremely compelling, and its relevance may be extended to almost any kind of division problem, be it normative or descriptive. It is therefore desirable that when a theory or model does not satisfy the Nash criterion, the analysis be extended to show why the deviation has come about.

The Bargaining Model of Zeuthen

A model of negotiation which was formulated by Zeuthen in 1930 has recently aroused a good deal of interest because of a demonstration by Harsanyi that it predicts a point of agreement which corresponds to that of Nash.[21, 22] Moreover, Harsanyi states that this model offers the further advantage of being based on a utility maximization principle. Zeuthen's is a two person model cast in the framework of labor–management wage negotiation in which the possibility of a conflict (strike or lockout) is taken as the motivation for concessions. He assumes that a state of conflict will yield a known payoff utility to each of the parties and that these utility values are unchanged throughout the bargaining process; that is, they depend neither upon time nor the demands made by the parties. For simplicity, we will transform the utility functions (as we did in the Nash case) so that the utilities of the conflict payoffs are defined to be zero for each party. Suppose that each player associates with each possible outcome a number between 0 and 1 which represents the probability that insistence upon that outcome will result in conflict. For example, player 1 expects that a demand x will be accepted by player 2 with a probability $(1 - p)$ and rejected (there will be a conflict) with a probability p, where, naturally, p is a function of x. Thus the expected payoff utility which player 1 receives from a demand for an outcome x is given by the expression $U_1(x)[1 - p(x)]$. Define x^0 as the outcome which is already being offered by player 2. Player 1 is certain of being able to obtain x^0 if he wishes it; that is, $p(x^0) = 0$. Thus the gain in expected payoff utility from a demand for x instead of x^0 is given by the expression

$$\Delta U_1 = U_1(x)[1 - p(x)] - U_1(x^0) \tag{1}$$

Suppose that he is considering a demand for a payoff x'; it follows that the greatest probability of conflict $\bar{p}$ which does not impose a loss on player 1 if he demands x' instead of x^0 is the value of p for which the net gain, ΔU_1, is zero. Thus, we can solve for $\bar{p}$ from expression (1):

$$\bar{p}(x') = \frac{U_1(x') - U_1(x^0)}{U_1(x')} \tag{2}$$

Zeuthen argues that if a demand for x' involves a probability of conflict which exceeds $\bar{p}(x')$, then player 1 will concede from this point.

If there are only two alternative outcomes, x^0 and x', player 2 will formulate a similar expression to describe the maximum probability of conflict $\bar{q}$ for which he will still be willing to insist upon outcome x^0.

$$\bar{q}(x^0) = \frac{U_2(x^0) - U_2(x')}{U_2(x^0)} \qquad (3)$$

If insistence upon x^0 involves a probability of conflict greater than $\bar{q}(x^0)$, player 2 will concede to x'. Zeuthen calls the expressions $\bar{p}(x')$ and $\bar{q}(x^0)$ the "risk-willingness" of players 1 and 2 respectively, and he maintains that the player who concedes will be the one whose risk-willingness is the smaller of the two. The basis for this conclusion is rather vague, but, in general, it seems that Zeuthen associates the risk-willingness of player 1 with the actual or objective risk of conflict that faces player 2 if he continues to insist upon the outcome x^0. Harsanyi attempts to make this conclusion more concrete by posing five postulates from which it follows that if $\bar{p}(x') < \bar{q}(x^0)$ then player 1 will concede, and vice versa. Basically, however, these postulates serve only to formalize the structure without appreciably strengthening it.

There appear to be two deficiencies in this system which interfere with its operation as a positive or descriptive model. The first of these is made explicit in Harsanyi's second postulate[23]:

"Perfect Knowledge: Each party can estimate correctly the probability that the other party will definitely reject a certain offer."

This assumption is not really a simplification of the bargaining process; indeed, we take it to be a rejection of one of its most fundamental properties. It is precisely the *lack* of knowledge that permits two individuals to form differing opinions as to how a situation which requires agreement will turn out. Without these differing opinions, there would be no need for the bargaining process to take place at all. An assumption of perfect knowledge will reduce the whole process to a set of mechanical rules from which we cannot possibly gain any insight into the dynamic mechanism of concession, or into the process whereby the parties formulate and change their expectations. It is the changing of opinion that causes a bargainer to change his demands, and "perfect knowledge" makes opinion change impossible. More will be said on this matter in Chapter III.

The second basic weakness in the approach of both Zeuthen and Harsanyi is that this model depends on an unjustified association between the risk-willingness expressions and the actual probabilities of conflict. For example, the risk-willingness of player 2 is equated with the probability of conflict that player 1 associates with an insistence upon his own demand. That is, $\bar{q}$ from equation (3) is equated with p in equation (1). In fact, however, the perceived conflict probabilities must be subjectively determined by the parties; even "perfect knowledge" does not justify any association between p and $\bar{q}$. Moreover, the actual conflict probabilities are dependent upon the players' *behavior,* and not upon either the perceived probabilities or the risk-willingness. Thus, given his perfect knowledge assumption, conflict is impossible in Harsanyi's model, even if only one of the players can be counted upon to concede in order to avert a conflict situation. On the other hand, if each were to underestimate the other's risk-willingness, this model would make conflict inevitable. How the values of risk-willingness are to be converted into actual conflict probabilities is as unexplained as the association between them is implausible.

In the light of these weaknesses, it seems appropriate to characterize the Zeuthen model as one concerned with bargaining outcomes rather than with the process of concession. It is true that the nature of concessions (how much and by whom) is specified, but as long as the motivation for these steps is missing and we can only identify the "loser" as the one with lower risk-willingness, we might as well take the risk-willingness expressions as solution criteria without considering the process at all.

Both Zeuthen and Harsanyi do not hesitate to use this model in bargaining situations in which more than two alternative outcomes are possible; in fact, Zeuthen's treatment is presented in terms of many outcome alternatives. Thus, if player 1 is demanding an outcome x^i and player 2 is demanding an outcome x^j, the player to concede is the one with the smaller risk-willingness as defined by the expressions below:

$$\bar{p}(x^i) = \frac{U_1(x^i) - U_1(x^j)}{U_1(x^i)}$$

$$\bar{q}(x^j) = \frac{U_2(x^j) - U_2(x^i)}{U_2(x^j)}$$

According to Zeuthen, the player to concede does not give in to the other player's demand, but only concedes to the next feasible outcome (for example, player 1 might shift from x^i to x^{i-1}). After this concession, new risk-willingness expressions are formulated using the players' new demands (e.g., the expressions above with x^{i-1} substituted for x^i), and the process is repeated. This formulation, however, does not seem to be correct. The expression for $\bar{p}(x^i)$, for example, describes the willingness to demand x^i instead of x^j, not the willingness to demand x^i instead of x^{i-1}. In considering a shift from x^i to x^{i-1}, player 1 would surely consider something like the following expression:

$$\bar{p}(x^i) = \frac{U_1(x^i) - U_1(x^{i-1})[1 - p(x^{i-1})]}{U_1(x^i)}$$

where $p(x^{i-1})$ is the probability of conflict which player 1 associates with a demand for outcome x^{i-1}.[24]

It is easy to show that the Zeuthen model yields the Nash solution. For example, player 1 will concede from a demand for x^i if and only if $\bar{p}(x^i) < \bar{q}(x^j)$. Applying the definitions of these expressions, this condition reduces to:

$$U_1(x^i) \, U_2(x^i) < U_1(x^j) \, U_2(x^j)$$

Thus, we always move from outcomes with lower utility products to outcomes with higher utility products. If marginal utility is not increasing at any value of x, this procedure will lead to a unique maximum.

The Zeuthen model has been still further modified by J. Pen.[25]

Pen introduces subjective functions which represent the risk-willingness of the parties as general functions of the expressions $\bar{p}(x)$ and $\bar{q}(x)$. He greatly strengthens the relationships between these functions and the actual concessions by introducing the players' *estimates* of one another's risk-willingness. Unfortunately, the price for these developments is high; now we must deal with a series of subjective and relatively ill-defined estimation functions, where we had depended only upon utility functions before. Moreover, our more fundamental objections to this model are left unanswered, especially the point that it is unclear how risk-willingness is to be transformed into an objective probability of conflict.

Other Bargaining Theories

The economist has been faced with the bargaining problem in two different contexts: first, in the analysis of wage determination, and second, in market situations involving very small numbers of firms. From the standpoint of our conception of the bargaining problem, these are comparable situations differing only with regard to their respective institutional characteristics. We will feel free to draw from work which has been done in either of these areas. From our point of view, however, by far the most valuable insights have been derived from discussions of labor negotiations. Bilateral monopoly and duopoly models rarely go beyond the "range of indeterminateness" mentioned in the last chapter (such as the familiar "contract curve"). For example, Bishop, in a recent article on duopoly, states that within the framework of his model "we cannot predict just what the outcome of this conflict of interest will be; for it will depend on the tempers of the two men, including their subjective assessments of one another's attitude." [26] Bishop's study is convincing in its interpretation of the duopoly problem as a bargaining problem, but it is representative of work in this field in that it brings us no nearer to a determinate solution.

Most studies of the general problem of labor–management relationships have included a chapter or two on the theory of bargaining. Except for the previously discussed work of Zeuthen, these usually do not go much beyond a review of the literature and a few variations upon existing models and theories. It is not generally recognized, however, that virtually all the models which are put under review in such discussions, as well as their adaptations, satisfy Nash's axioms, so that, like the Zeuthen model, they contain the Nash solution as their predicted outcome. For example, consider Neil Chamberlain's familiar definition of bargaining power.[27] "If the difference to [player 2] between the costs of disagreement and agreement on [player 1's] terms is proportionately greater than the difference to [player 1] between the costs of disagreement and agreement on [player 2's] terms" then player 1 is said to have greater bargaining "power" than 2. As this definition is constructed, "costs of disagreement and agreement on 1's terms" can only be measured *from a player's current demand.* Thus, in the notation which we utilized earlier, the costs to player 1 of agreement on player 2's terms is given by the difference $U_1(x') - U_1(x^0)$ while the cost of disagreement is $U_1(x') - 0$. Now the "difference to 1 between the costs of disagreement and agreement on 2's terms" is given by $U_1(x') - [U_1(x') - U_1(x^0)]$. Similarly, this difference to 2 is $U_2(x^0) - [U_2(x^0) - U_2(x')]$. The word "proportionately" is unfortunately rather vague; analytically, however, the expression is meaningful only if we interpret it to mean that if the difference to 1 *in proportion to 1's demand* is smaller than the difference to 2 *in proportion to 2's demand,* then 1 is more powerful than 2.[28] In sum, we interpret Chamberlain's statement to mean that 1 has more "bargaining power" than 2 if and only if

$$\frac{U_1(x') - [U_1(x') - U_1(x^0)]}{U_1(x')} < \frac{U_2(x^0) - [U_2(x^0) - U_2(x')]}{U_2(x^0)}$$

This reduces to

$$U_1(x^0)\, U_2(x^0) < U_1(x')\, U_2(x')$$

Since Chamberlain takes bargaining power as an indicator of which bargainer is more likely to concede, this expression is consistent with a concession on the part of player 2 from x^0. As in the Zeuthen model, this is seen always to tend to maximize the product of the negotiators' utilities! We are back to the Nash solution.

A. Cartter has also constructed an explicit model which, like the Zeuthen model after which it is patterned, has a strong relationship to the Nash solution.[29] Cartter defines the "bargaining attitude" of player 1 as the cost of disagreeing with 2, divided by the cost of agreeing on 2's terms. In our notation, this is simply

$$\frac{U_1(x')}{U_1(x') - U_1(x^0)}$$

Similarly, the bargaining attitude of player 2 is given by

$$\frac{U_2(x^0)}{U_2(x^0) - U_2(x')}$$

If these two expressions are less than 1, neither concedes and we have disagreement. Cartter indicates, however, that "the passage of time will make each party's attitude more favorable, for each will actually suffer losses which were only probabilities previously, and as the strike progresses, its probable length will appear longer. Thus the costs of disagreement will rise for both parties."[30] The one to concede will be the one whose bargaining attitude first exceeds 1 (although, of course, he need not capitulate completely to the other's terms). These bargaining attitude expressions, however, are simply inverses of Zeuthen's "risk-willingness" expressions [equations (2) and (3)]; thus the party whose bargaining attitude first exceeds 1 must also have the lower risk-willingness. The system, therefore, is analytically identical to Zeuthen's and hence it must also yield the Nash solution.

These reductions do considerable injustice to the authors of the above mentioned models. We have excluded a good deal of comment and interpretation which lends much greater substance to their constructions. Nevertheless, they do serve to demonstrate our point that in the literature on negotiation, the Nash axioms have already been widely accepted, although never explicitly.[31]

Both the Chamberlain and Cartter models treat the negotiators symmetrically; they depend in no way upon interpersonal utility comparisons; they are independent of intermediate outcome alternatives; and they satisfy Pareto optimality. This is true for the great bulk of the work which has been done on models of labor bargaining.

Some of these models have added dimensions that are difficult to reduce to the terms of Nash's theory. Cartter, for example, as the quotation above implies, has the costs of disagreement changing over time. This naturally changes the origin from which the outcome utilities are measured, and leaves the interpretation of our "Nash solution" rather uncertain, unless we have some means of specifying the players' final estimates of their disagreement costs. It is just this sort of difficulty which we shall approach in subsequent chapters.

Most of these wage negotiation models are unclear when it comes to an explanation of the process of concession. We have already commented upon the difficulty encountered when we try to transform Zeuthen's notion of "risk-willingness" to a prediction of a player's concession. Similarly, Chamberlain does not give us an explicit connection between his "power" definition and concession behavior. For this reason we are again led to characterize these models as primarily concerned with bargaining outcomes rather than the process itself. Cartter, on the other hand, is quite sensitive to the problem of distinguishing outcome from process, and it is a consequence of this concern that the relationship between his model and that of Nash is much harder to discover.

Finally, we reiterate a point made with respect to the Zeuthen model. Since most bargaining theories have been concerned with some notion of "power," emphasis has frequently been concentrated upon the whole difference between the two sides' demands. If we wish to consider concession behavior, however, the values of payoffs *adjacent* to a player's demand must surely be of equal importance. Movements are generally made to nearby positions, and we maintain that utility differences associated with *capitulation* [e.g., $U_1(x') - U_1(x^0)$] are not relevant in the consideration of a *concession*.

Hicks' Model

Hicks' theory of wage negotiations, though widely presented to students in labor courses, is just as widely rejected in those courses on the grounds that it is totally unrealistic.[32] This model characterizes the wage negotiation in terms of two functions: an "employer's concessions curve" which relates the wage which the employer would be willing to pay in order to avoid a strike to the *expected* length of the strike, and the "union's resistance curve" which gives the wage which the union will accept rather than call a strike, also expressed as a function of the expected length of the strike. These functions have opposite slopes and Hicks looks upon their intersection as giving the maximum possible wage.

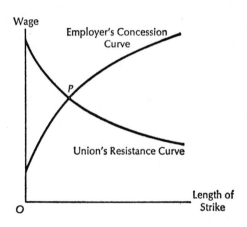

Figure 2

This model has been criticized for too much concern for the intersection in a scissors diagram,[33] for failure to deal with the negotiators' behavior in the area *between* the concession curves,[34] for failure to deal with the bargaining *process*,[35] and finally for treating the union and the employer asymmetrically.[36] This last point is of particular interest to us because, due to the asymmetry, this is one of the few models in the literature which clearly could not be expected to lead to the Nash solution. The asymmetry stems from Hicks' position that the labor leaders are attempting to get the best wage they can subject to (1) their estimate of the employer's concessions curve and (2) their own ability to sustain a strike. Similar behavior on the part of the employer does not arise: the union is the active element in the process, while the employer is largely passive.

Another important feature of Hicks' model is that there is no requirement that the parties' decisions actually fall *on* the "concessions" or the "resistance" curve: these are meant primarily to provide boundaries to the possible wage rather than to discover precisely what it will be. The union, not knowing the employer's concessions curve, might try to get too low a wage (in which case it has not obtained all that it could) or too high a one (in which case there is a strike). Thus Hicks' model is not really intended to be a deterministic one, but rather it is designed to associate the "range of indeterminateness" with the occurrence and the possible length of a strike. Within this range, the outcome depends, as is so often the case, on the "bargaining skill" of the respective negotiators.

Most criticisms of Hicks' theory seem to rest on the supposition that it is meant to be deterministic, and it is true that as a predictive model it is subject to a wide variety of objections on both logical and descriptive grounds. On the other hand, Hicks appears to have been first to introduce into his theory two elements which are absolutely fundamental to the bargaining process. First, he has recognized the importance of a relationship between the amount of time which a negotiator *expects* to lapse before agreement is reached, and the magnitude of his payoff demand. Furthermore, this relationship has been made into an integral part of the model.[37] Second, Hicks has suggested that a strike reflects a *mistake*—that is, it is the consequence of an error in the union's attempt to estimate the employer's concessions curve.[38] Although this position seems to have been generally disregarded, the point is well taken: after all, if both parties *knew* what the outcome would be, there would be no reason for bargaining at all (except possibly for the sake of form). As an aside, we might suggest that the danger of making such a mistake is partly responsible for the widespread use of "pattern bargaining"—a phenomenon in which extended negotiations are necessary to obtain the first wage contract in an industry, but in which other contracts in that or related industries are quickly and easily settled along the same general lines. The use of precedents in this way will certainly reduce the likelihood that an "error" in demands will precipitate a strike.

R. L. Bishop has made use of the first of these two contributions of Hicks and has formulated a Zeuthen-type model which substitutes for the Zeuthen concept of "risk-willingness" the maximum duration of a strike which a player would be willing to bear in order to obtain a given outcome.[39] Technically, this model is virtually identical to that of Zeuthen (and hence is subject to the same comments), but its interpretation has a great advantage in that it does emphasize the time dependence of the bargaining process.

Empirical Conclusions on Bargaining

Some excellent experimental work on bargaining has been conducted recently by Siegel and Fouraker.[40] They have performed a series of two person bargaining experiments set in the context of bilateral monopoly (one player a "seller" and the other a "buyer"). Each player of a bargaining pair was given a table on which were printed his "profits" associated with various price–quantity combinations, and the two bargained by means of price–quantity "bids" written on slips of paper which were delivered from one to the other by the experimenters (in order to avoid personal contact between the bargainers). Besides studying the actual point of agreement, Siegel and Fouraker compared bargaining outcomes under various controlled conditions, studying the effects of complete versus incomplete information,[41] variations in the structure of the payoffs, and variations in the "level of aspiration." This last concept, which is fundamental to Siegel and Fouraker's discussion, would be regarded by an economist as something of a cross between expected payoff and the utility of payoffs. By definition, "the level of aspiration is associated with the higher of two goals between which the rate of change of the utility function is a maximum." [42] In other words, suppose that a player expects a payoff x. All payoffs less than x have lower utility not only because of the reduced physical payoff, but because of "psychological feelings of dissatisfaction" which result simply from the failure to achieve expectations, and payoffs greater than x have higher utility, both because of the greater payoff *per se* and because of the psychological satisfaction associated with achieving more than x. Since the psychological factor varies most strongly in the vicinity of x, we obtain a utility function with a form similar to that in Figure 3.

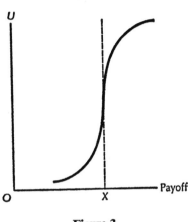

Figure 3

This construction involves the assumption that "expected payoff" has a subjective importance to an individual above and beyond its immediate utility. For our discussion, we would prefer to break this concept into its component parts (expected payoff, utility of payoff, and the assumption of subjective importance of expected payoffs), and so, in presenting (and using) Siegel and Fouraker's results, we will use whichever aspect of the concept of "aspiration level" seems to be the appropriate one. [43] The following are those conclusions of the Siegel–Fouraker study which seem to be the most relevant for our discussion of the bargaining process.

1. There is a tendency for bargainers to negotiate contracts that are Pareto optimal.[44]

2. Increasing the amount of relevant information available to the bargainers strengthens the tendency toward Pareto optimal agreements.[45]

3. "Increasing the amount of information available to the bargainers tends to lead to a more equal division of the joint payoff." [46]

4. Supplementing the higher payoffs to only one player so as to increase the utility to him of these outcomes tends to increase his payoff at agreement.[47]

5. If both bargainers have complete information, they tend to be more modest in their initial demands than they are in cases of incomplete information.

6. "Occasionally an opponent would offer an unexpectedly generous bid (this might be unintentional—the opponent would be maintaining a constant payoff plateau or concession rate, but moving toward the Paretian optima in his bids). The subject's usual reaction was to raise his own payoff request—make his next bid one which would yield a higher profit to him than would have been yielded by his own previous bid." [48] In other words, his usual reaction was to raise his expected payoff.

7. There is some evidence that increasing the information to one player alone tends to decrease his payoff at agreement.[49]

Siegel and Fouraker conclude their study with a bargaining model which may be characterized with the following expression:

$$\alpha_i = \max E_1 - \frac{\max E_1 - \min E_1}{1 + s_1 r_2}\left(1 - \frac{1}{(t_i)^{r_1}}\right)$$

where:

$\max E$ = a player's maximum payoff expectancy.

$\min E$ = a player's minimum payoff expectancy.

r = an index of a bargainer's rate of concession.

s = an index of a bargainer's ability to perceive his opponent's concession rate.

t = duration of negotiations, in terms of either units of time or number of bids exchanged, so that t_i indicates the stage of the negotiations in a session which will last N units, where $i = 1$, $\ldots, N$.

α_i = level of aspiration of a bargainer at time of ith bid.[50]

Unfortunately, this model is not derived from anything; it is apparently introduced only because it fits their data fairly closely. Consequently, we are led to look upon this more as an exercise in curve fitting than as any sort of explanation of the bargaining process. The choice of variables is significant, nevertheless, as many of them are similar to those which will appear later in our own model.

Summary

In conclusion, we believe that despite a few very imaginative pioneering efforts in this field, a satisfactory theory has yet to be developed which can simultaneously describe the dynamic process of concession, point out at least a likely candidate for the point of agreement, and be used to derive empirically testable conclusions. As yet we have only parts of a theory—an idealized outcome criterion, the principle that expectations may dominate a negotiation, and a number of empirical results. In the following chapter we will offer a theory of the bargaining process which may help to fill the gaps in the existing body of theory. Insofar as possible, the work will build upon the theoretical and empirical results which have been discussed in this chapter.

■ NOTES

1. A good example is found in H. M. Levinson, *Determining Forces in Collective Wage Bargaining* (New York: John Wiley and Sons, 1966), pp. 18, 272–276.

2. Robert Dahl, "The Concept of Power," *Behavioral Science*, II (1957), 201.

3. *Loc. cit.*

4. John C. Harsanyi, "Measurement of Social Power, Opportunity Costs, and the Theory of Two-Person Bargaining Games," *Behavioral Science,* VII (1962), 68–70.

5. Jan Pen, *The Wage Rate Under Collective Bargaining,* tr. T. S. Preston (Cambridge, Mass.: Harvard University Press, 1959), p. 98.

6. These items are important elements in Chamberlain's definition. Neil Chamberlain, *Collective Bargaining* (New York: McGraw-Hill Book Co., 1951), pp. 220–222.

7. Boulding has emphasized the legitimacy of one's ability to influence (threaten) another subject, in a paper to American Political Science Association, September 1965.

8. The simplification is known as a reduction from the extensive to the "normal" form of a game. See John von Neumann and Oskar Morgenstern, *The Theory of Games and Economic Behavior* (Princeton, N.J.: Princeton University Press, 1944), pp. 79–86.

9. John F. Nash, "The Bargaining Problem," *Econometrica,* XVIII (1950), 155–162.

10. Since the von Neumann–Morgenstern index is defined for lotteries, we can obtain any convex combination of the payoffs associated with the outcome X and Y by constructing the lottery $L = PX + (1-p)Y$ where $0 \leq p \leq 1$.

11. Note that this assumption also strengthens condition 3. To state that whenever there exists any linear utility transformation which can make the outcome set symmetric, then we must have $U_1 = U_2$ with the utilities expressed in terms of the same utility transformation.

12. The foregoing description of the Nash theory is a very slight modification of the material in R. Duncan Luce and Howard Raiffa, *Games and Decisions* (New York: John Wiley and Sons, 1957), pp. 124–128.

13. We may sketch a simple proof of the theorem as follows: Consider a utility payoff set bounded by the straight line $U_1 + U_2 = k$. The symmetry assumption requires the outcome, $U_1{}^*$, $U_2{}^*$ to obey the condition $U_1{}^* = U_2{}^*$, and the addition of the Pareto optimality assumption further constrains the outcome to $U_1{}^* = U_2{}^* = k/2$. Thus the point of agreement must be at the midpoint of the (straight) boundary line of the set. Through shifts in the units in which one or both players' utilities are measured, however (holding the origins constant), *any* straight boundary line in $U_1 \times U_2$ space can be given the same form as our original line $U_1 + U_2 = k$. Moreover, the midpoints of such lines always refer to the same actual outcomes under such transformations. Thus, the independence of linear transformations of utility assumption implies that all utility sets bounded by straight lines have the midpoints of those lines as expected outcomes. We now need only recall a plane geometry theorem which states that the largest rectangle (in area) which may be inscribed in a right triangle bisects the hypotenuse, and conclude that, indeed, the product U_1U_2 is maximized at the point B. (This is, incidentally, the same condition that

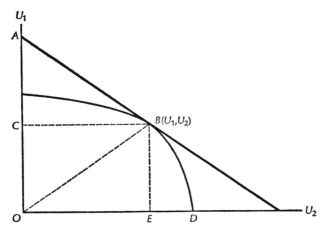

Figure F-1

leads to maximum total revenue from the midpoint of a straight line demand curve.) Now consider any convex outcome set bounded by $U_1 = f(U_2)$. In our continuous example, we can always find a straight line which is tangent to $U_1 = f(U_2)$ such that a point of tangency, U_1', U_2', includes the midpoint of the straight line (rotate the tangent line around the boundary—at some point our condition must be satisfied). Independence of irrelevant alternatives now ensures that U_1', U_2' is the outcome of the smaller game, and it is obvious that if this point maximizes the product U_1U_2 on the straight lines, U_1', U_2' must also maximize the possible utility product of the game bounded by $U_1 = f(U_2)$.

14. The boundary is defined as $U_1 = f(U_2)$; we want to maximize P where $P = U_1U_2$; $dP/dU_2 = U_1 + U_2dU_1/dU_2$; so for a maximum: $U_1/U_2 = -dU_1/dU_2$.

15. For example, Luce and Raiffa, *op. cit.*, prefer to characterize the Nash model as an "arbitration scheme."

16. Reviews of the criticisms of the Nash model may be found in Luce and Raiffa, *op. cit.*, pp. 128–134 and in Robert L. Bishop, "Game Theoretic Analyses of Bargaining," *Quarterly Journal of Economics*, LXXVII (1963), 559–602.

17. Bishop, *op. cit.*

18. The payoff possibilities, by constant marginal utility, map into a straight line in utility space. Hence (see footnote 14) the Nash solution divides the payoff equally.

19. Even yet we have not enumerated all the implicit axioms in the Nash system. One might argue, for example, that there is no single mathematical function which can describe bargaining outcomes; that the relationship which applies when marginal utilities are constant is different, in fact *inconsistent*, with that which applies at other times. Homogeneous com-

modities might be divided evenly because of a traditional notion of "fairness" which does not apply otherwise.

20. An important technical point regarding the Nash utility functions may also become apparent from our reinterpretation. Nash asserted that he was using von Neumann–Morgenstern utility in the construction of his model. It is true that this utility construction works, but its use obscures the fundamental requirement of the Nash utility function. The von Neumann–Morgenstern index is an ordinal index (that is, it reflects only a ranking of preferences) which is limited to linear (rather than monotonic) transformations because it also must satisfy the expected utility construction. That is, the utility of a lottery L which pays x with a probability p and y otherwise must be expressible in the form $U(L) = pU(x) + (1 - p)U(y)$. The Nash utility function is also ordinal, but it too must satisfy an additional requirement: that the division which maximizes the product $U_1 U_2$ remains unchanged under changes in the utility functions, and this restricts us again to linear transformations (if we change origin, we simply measure U as a utility difference between a payoff and disagreement). The outcome set may not contain any lotteries at all, in which case we could drop the need to satisfy the expected utility construction, but our functions are still subject only to linear transformations because of Nash's solution requirement.

21. Frederik Zeuthen, *Problems of Monopoly and Economic Warfare* (London: G. Routledge and Sons, Ltd., 1930), pp. 104–150.

22. John C. Harsanyi, "Approaches to the Bargaining Problem Before and After the Theory of Games: A Critical Analysis of Zeuthen's, Hicks', and Nash's Theories," *Econometrica*, XXIV (1956), 144–157.

23. Harsanyi, *op. cit.*, 149.

24. In the two-alternative case, we know $p(x^{i-1}) = 0$.

25. Pen, *op. cit.*, pp. 120–149. Pen's model also appears in his article, "A General Theory of Bargaining," *American Economic Review*, XLII (1952), 24–42.

26. Robert L. Bishop, " 'Duopoly' Collusion or Warfare," *American Economic Review*, L (1960), 933–961.

27. Chamberlain, *op. cit.*, pp. 220–221.

28. This interpretation is virtually forced upon us by the necessity of a "power" definition which does not depend upon the units with which we measure the players' utility functions.

29. Allan Cartter, *Theory of Wages and Employment* (Homewood, Ill.: Richard D. Irwin, 1959), pp. 117–120.

30. *Ibid.*, p. 120.

31. As we shall see, a notable exception is the model of Hicks. See Robert Bishop, "A Zeuthen–Hicks Model of the Bargaining Process," *Econometrica*, XXXII (1964), 410–417.

32. J. R. Hicks, *The Theory of Wages* (2nd ed.; New York: St. Martin's Press, 1963), pp. 136–158.

33. George L. S. Shackle, "The Nature of the Bargaining Process," in John Dunlop, ed., *The Theory of Wage Determination*, Proceedings of the International Economic Association (New York: St. Martin's Press, 1957), p. 303.

34. Pen, *op. cit.*, pp. 114–117.

35. Cartter, *op. cit.*, pp. 128–129.

36. Bishop, "A Zeuthen–Hicks Model of the Bargaining Process," *op. cit.*

37. Hicks, *op. cit.*, pp. 144–147.

38. *Ibid.*, pp. 140–144. In this connection, Hicks even hints at the importance of the learning process, which we shall treat later.

39. Bishop, *op. cit.*

40. Sidney Siegel and Lawrence Fouraker, *Bargaining and Group Decision-Making* (New York: McGraw-Hill Book Co., 1960).

41. Experimentally, this was done by permitting one player to see the other's profit table in cases in which he was to have complete information.

42. *Ibid.*, p. 62, where it is quoted in turn from Sidney Siegel, "Level of Aspiration and Decision-Making," *Psychological Review*, LXIV (1957), 257.

43. For example, the generalization: "experiences of success generally lead to a raising level of aspiration, and experiences of failure to a lowering" (p. 62), becomes "experiences of success generally lead to raising of *expected payoff* and experiences of failure to a lowering," while the raising of level of aspiration through supplementing the returns of certain payoffs will be interpreted simply as raising the utility of those payoffs.

44. *Ibid.*, p. 41.

45. Unfortunately, Siegel and Fouraker use payoff tables in which all the Pareto optimal points also represent the joint maximum; so that from their experiments it is impossible to tell whether the tendencies are specifically toward the joint maximum, or just toward Pareto optima. Siegel and Fouraker seem to use these expressions interchangeably; we have substituted "Pareto optima" simply because it seems more plausible to us that this is the correct interpretation. It may be, however, that conclusions 1. and 2. could be put much more strongly.

46. *Ibid.*, p. 70.

47. *Ibid.*, pp. 62–70.

48. *Ibid.*, p. 81.

49. *Ibid.*, pp. 57–58.

50. This all appears in Siegel and Fouraker, *op. cit.*, pp. 90–91.

III

▪ The Bargaining Process and Its Outcome

The bargaining process can be characterized in terms of two limiting cases: (1) the pure bluffing case: each participant plans to give in as the other does, expecting ultimately to achieve agreement at some intermediate point (which may even go beyond the point to which the other expects to concede);[1] (2) the pure intransigence (or asymmetrical expectations) case: each expects to obtain agreement at his initial demand, anticipating that the other player will make all of the concessions. A negotiation involving pure bluffing alone would not provide a very interesting example of the bargaining process because it would represent no real disagreement at all. Admittedly, it is likely that such negotiations occasionally do occur; this can be inferred from the fact that in many labor–management disputes, just before strike time, each party sends behind-the-scenes envoys to the other hoping to discover that their true expectations are sufficiently below expressed demands to permit immediate settlement.[2] Nevertheless, it is the case of asymmetrical expectations that underlies the bargaining problem in its predominant form, since only in this situation does the disagreement represent more than a simple communications failure. Most bargaining situations, of course, are best represented as a mixture of the two components—the players demand more than they expect to obtain (bluffing), but the expectations them-

42

selves are not initially compatible (asymmetry). Because of the importance of the intransigence component, we shall base our simple model upon this aspect alone and leave further discussion of bluffing to a later chapter.[3]

Notation

The formal analyses of negotiations which were discussed in the last chapter were all conducted in terms of utility units rather than physical "payoff" units although, as in Cartter's model, dollar costs are sometimes used as proxy variables for utility. In general, however, people do not bargain over utilities: "You take two utiles, and I'll take three"; they bargain in terms of more objective quantities: states of their mutual environment or the division of goods. Moreover, unless utilities are perfectly proportional to physical payoffs, this distinction will have an effect on the properties of our model. We must therefore have some means of relating preferences to payoffs, and for this reason we shall define and use a relatively naive form of a utility function.

There are two alternative means for measuring the physical payoff demands of the parties, the choice depending upon the nature of the circumstances under discussion. In cases in which a fixed quantity M of some homogeneous good is being divided into smaller quantities, we can indicate player j's demand by means of a quantity variable q_j; here, we shall have disagreement whenever the sum of the players' demands exceeds the total amount available, whenever

$$\sum_j q_j > M.$$

If we are simply dividing a sum of money, this notation would be appropriate. For other cases in which the available amount of the good is variable, unknown, or perhaps not even defined, it is more appropriate to consider an ordering index P which ranges over the various outcome alternatives, taking, for example, large values for outcomes which are very favorable to player 1 and small values for outcomes which are very favorable to player 2.

In labor–management wage negotiations, for example, we would simply associate P with the wage rate.[4] In a two person negotiation of this type, we would have disagreement whenever P_1, the demand of player 1, exceeds P_2, the demand of player 2; in our example, whenever the wage demanded by labor (P_1) was greater than that offered by management (P_2). It does not matter which of these schemes we choose for the formulation of our model if M is constant; but if M is variable, we must use the P-notation if we wish to avoid undue complication in the model (see footnote 8). The only analytical difference between the two measures consists of a reversal of sign in some of our expressions using the P-notation (player 2 prefers *higher* q_2, but *lower* P_2). Simply to avoid possible sign confusion we shall generally adhere to the quantity notation except where the other is clearly required.

Naturally if the negotiators are to be able to evaluate the progress of the negotiation for themselves, they must make use of variables or indices such as we have described. Furthermore, if the goods to which the variables refer are homogeneous, or if they are completely discrete, so that the q_j's can only take on integer values, we are justified in assuming that for any commodity, the bargainers will choose indices which differ by no more than a linear transformation. For instance, if the objective is in money terms, one player may measure the outcome in dollars, while another measures the same good in pennies.[5] As it happens, such transformations leave the outcome of our model unaffected, and so, purely for expository convenience, we shall assume that the bargainers all employ the same units of measurement over the possible outcomes. Furthermore, we shall assume that each player has a utility function reflecting the value to him of his share of the payoff, and that these utility functions display positive but diminishing marginal utility with respect to increasing quantities of payoff.

In this chapter we shall consider the simplest case of a bargaining process—two persons negotiating over the division of a fixed quantity M of a single good which is continuously divisible. We may write utility functions for players 1 and 2 in terms of the payoff quantities that they may receive: $U_1 = f(q_1)$ and

$U_2 = g(q_2)$, and we shall adjust the origins of our functions so that $f(0) = 0$, and $g(0) = 0$. Assuming that the first two derivatives of the utility functions always exist, we have:

$$f(0) = 0 \qquad f'(q_1) > 0 \qquad f''(q_1) \leqslant 0 \tag{4}$$
$$g(0) = 0 \qquad g'(q_2) > 0 \qquad g''(q_2) \leqslant 0$$

Time and Expectations

Perhaps the greatest weakness of most formal models of negotiation lies in the general failure to introduce a time variable explicitly into what is fundamentally a dynamic problem. Even Hicks' "expected length of strike" variable is not really a dynamic one—almost any other cost-imposing variable could have been put on his horizontal axis to generate his model. Nevertheless, we will use a dynamic version of this same variable in the construction of our own theory.

The costs which time imposes on the negotiators can assume three different forms: (1) future agreements may be discounted to the present, (2) the value of the agreement may (primarily for technological reasons) change over time, and (3) there may be a fixed cost which recurs in each time period and which can be associated with the bargaining process itself. All three of these have the consequence that the more distant the agreement, the less its present value. It is an important property of our utility functions that they are defined as the utilities of the payoffs *at the time of agreement,* and therefore that these time costs are not included in them. Since the value of any anticipated outcome is dependent upon the time at which it would be obtained, it is necessary for each party to estimate the time required to reach agreement. For example, player 1 must estimate the delay necessary to obtain a payoff quantity q_1 by observing the current demand of player 2, q_2, and considering the amount of time that it will take 2 to concede over the difference $(q_1 + q_2 - M)$. In general we expect that the greater this difference, the more time would be required for the negotiation. Player 1, however, can have no specific knowledge of player 2's relative rates of conces-

sion over various payoff demands.[6] Thus player 1 is forced to
make some general estimate of his opponent's concession behavior, and specifically of the rates at which he can be expected to
move from one demand to another. A variety of models could be
constructed to describe these expectations, although it is unlikely
that alternative formulations would affect the qualitative implications of the theory.[7] We shall therefore choose the simplest possible expectations model and assume that player 1 expects concession to take place at a constant rate which we shall call r_2. By
restricting our simple model to bargaining situations in which
bluffing does not occur, we have already assumed that player 1
does not think of r_2 as a function of his own behavior. The expected time necessary to reach agreement such that player 1 receives a quantity q_1 is then given by the expression $(q_1 + q_2$
$- M)/r_2$, which we shall represent by w.

We have defined our utility functions so as to express preferences at the time of agreement and hence we must adjust them
back to the present. First, we will make use of a discounting function $\phi(w)$ such that, neglecting other time costs, the present
value of a demand for a quantity q_1 is given by the expression
$f(q_1).\phi(w)$. Moreover, we shall let this discounting function be
written in exponential form (ke^{-aw}). Second, suppose that player
1 must pay a fixed cost C_1 in each time period, where C_1 is expressed in utility units. The sum of these costs Z, extended to the
expected time of agreement, may be expressed in present value
terms as:

$$Z = C_1 e^{-a} + C_1 e^{-2a} + \ldots + C_1 e^{-aw}$$

or, in continuous terms:[8]

$$Z = C_1 \int_0^w e^{-ax}dx = \frac{C_1}{a}(1 - e^{-aw})$$

For the purposes of this simple model, we shall neglect any dependence of the outcome upon calendar date.

Now the total present value to player 1 of insisting on a return q_1 is:[9]

$$U_1^* = f(q_1) e^{-aw} + \frac{C_1}{a} e^{-aw} - \frac{C_1}{a} \tag{5}$$

To decide what outcome to demand, player 1 chooses the quantity which satisfies these preferences—that is, the q_1 which maximizes U_1^*. Differentiating U_1^* with respect to q_1 and noting that $\delta w / \delta q_1 = 1/r_2$, we obtain the first and second order conditions for a maximum:[10]

$$\left[f(q_1) + \frac{C_1}{a} \right] \frac{a}{r_2} = f'(q_1) \tag{6}$$

and $f'(q_1) \dfrac{-a}{r_2} + f''(q_1) < 0$, or since $f'(q_1) > 0$, and $r_2 > 0$:

$$\frac{f''(q_1)}{f'(q_1)} r_2 - a < 0 \tag{7}$$

The content of equation (6) is not difficult to put into intuitive terms. Whenever a party increases his demand, he increases the payoff which he expects to receive at the time of settlement, but he also delays the date of that settlement by an amount of time determined by his opponent's rate of concession. His demand is optimized when the utility increase is exactly offset by the time delay which results from a marginal increase in demand. Measuring these two at the date of agreement, for example, player 1 will lose a per cent of his total expected return for every further time period of delay. Thus, since an increase in his demand Δq_1 will put off agreement by $\Delta q_1 / r_2$ units of time, such an increased demand will cost him $(\Delta q_1)(a/r_2) U_1$ "utiles" where U_1 is the *undiscounted* gain in utility which player 1 expects to receive from his current demand. This utility gain includes the benefit of no longer paying the recurring costs of bargaining, and therefore $U_1 = f(q_1) + C_1/a$. On the other hand, his return at the date of settlement is increased by $\Delta U_1 = \Delta q_1 (dU_1/dq_1) = \Delta q_1 f'(q_1)$. It follows that so long as $f'(q_1) > (a/r_2)[f(q_1) + C_1/a]$ (that is, so long as the marginal return from an increase in his demand is greater than its marginal cost), player 1 will be better off if he increases his demand. He will have maximized his return from equality holds.[11]

This explanation may help to clarify a very important property of our model: The optimal value of player 1's demand depends upon r_2, but not at all upon q_2, his opponent's specific demand! The reason for this is that player 1 is concerned with balancing the marginal time cost with the marginal benefit of an increase in demand, and the total time cost associated with q_2 is irrelevant to this calculation.[12] Of course, this result is qualified by the possibility that q_2 is so large that even the optimal demand, q_1, is not sufficient to give a positive value to the discounted utility, U_1^*, in equation (5), and in this case the first party will refuse to negotiate altogether.[13] Moreover, this independence is really only a very short run phenomenon; in the longer run, r_2 is itself determined by q_2 through an important dynamic relationship which is described below.

Finally, condition (7) simply requires that if q_1 is to provide a utility maximum, the expression $f'(q_1)$ must be decreasing relative to $(a/r_2)[f(q_1) + C_1/a]$ as q_1 is increased. Positive and diminishing marginal utility are obviously sufficient to satisfy this condition. Since we have assumed that the bargainers do not engage in bluffing, player 1 demands that q_1 which satisfies (6) and (7) and no other.

Learning

The first party demands a payoff quantity q_1 on the basis of an *expected* rate of concession from the other player; if player 2 in fact does not concede at that rate, then clearly 1's expectations will alter—that is, r_2 will change—and, as a consequence, he will demand a different q_1. At this point we are naturally led to examine a process of *learning*. Most generally, a learning model is a time dependent relation which must satisfy at least the following conditions:

$$\frac{dr_2}{dt} > 0 \quad \text{if} \quad -\frac{dq_2}{dt} > r_2$$

$$\frac{dr_2}{dt} = 0 \quad \text{if} \quad -\frac{dq_2}{dt} = r_2 \tag{8}$$

$$\frac{dr_2}{dt} < 0 \quad \text{if} \quad -\frac{dq_2}{dt} < r_2$$

That is, if player 2 concedes faster than is expected, player 1 will increase his estimate of 2's concession rate; if player 2 concedes just as rapidly as is expected, player 1 will retain his original estimate of r_2; and so on.

Furthermore, it is reasonable to assume that the magnitude of dr_2/dt varies positively with the discrepancy between $-dq_2/dt$ and the expected rate of concession: the greater the error in player 1's expectations, the faster his expectations will change. Thus we will require:

$$\frac{d\dot{r}_2}{d(-r_2 - \dot{q}_2)} > 0 \tag{9}$$

where $\dot{r}_2$ is defined as dr_2/dt, and $\dot{q}_2$ as dq_2/dt. Later, a more specific characterization of learning behavior will be used, but for the present we shall be content with just the conditions (8) and (9).[14, 15]

The Process of Concession

Due to the learning process, the expected concession rate r_2 is likely to change over time. As a consequence, player 1's outcome demand q_1 will also be a function of time. Analytically, we can find $\dot{q}_1$ simply by differentiating (6) with respect to t and solving for dq_1/dt, obtaining:

$$\dot{q}_1 = \frac{-1}{\dfrac{[f''(q_1)}{f'(q_1)]}r_2 - a} \frac{dr_2}{dt} \tag{10}$$

So, if r_2 changes by some amount Δr_2, the cost, $(a/r_2)[f'(q_1) + C_1/a]$, of a unit increase in player 1's demand is changed, and hence q_1 will be adjusted until the marginal return $f'(q_1)$ is equal to the new marginal cost $(a/[r_2 + \Delta r_2])[f'(q_1) + C_1/a]$. Expression (10) simply represents Δr_2 and the resulting change in q_1 in terms of time.

In the light of our second order conditions, expression (10) requires that q_1 should vary in the same direction as r_2. In other words, if player 1 discovers that his opponent is yielding more rapidly than was expected, he will increase his demands. Conversely, he will reduce his bid if he discovers that player 2 is not giving in as fast as he formerly thought. Thus expressions (7) and (10), in conjunction with our learning theory, would already lead us to expect Siegel and Fouraker's intuitively appealing conclusion that sudden large concessions from one player tend to encourage increased demands on the part of the other.

Expressions similar to those derived for player 1 can be obtained from the point of view of 2. In this case, the expressions corresponding to (6)–(10) are obtained simply by reversing the subscripts and substituting b, player 2's discount rate, for a.

So far no restrictions have been imposed on the possible signs of the $\dot{q}$'s. Often, retraction of an offer during negotiation is thought to be either unethical or at least undesirable because of the unfavorable psychological impact which such behavior may induce in the other player. In fact Siegel and Fouraker, in their study, deliberately formulated their rules so as to eliminate this possibility (they stipulated that any price–quantity bid, once made, was always good). Nevertheless, such retractions do occur in practice. We shall, therefore, retain the analytical possibility that demands will be increased over time, but we recognize that if this ever does happen, the resulting psychological forces (such as resentment) might disrupt the whole process and hence weaken the explanatory power of our simple model.[16]

The Bargaining Process

The essential character of the bargaining process can now be described. In the first place, we observe that if r_1, for example, were less than or equal to zero (that is, if player 1 were expected to hold out forever), the other player would give in immediately or abandon the entire negotiation. Thus we must have both r_1 and r_2 positive if the bargaining process is to take place at all. Suppose each bargainer's learning pattern follows some general form such as that which we outlined earlier [conditions (8) and (9)]. So long as the negotiators are at all able to learn, it is impossible that neither negotiator will shift. If player 1 is not conceding, for example, his opponent will come to appreciate it, r_1 will fall, and player 2's demand q_2 will decrease along with it. If q_2 declines precisely as player 1 expected (if $-\dot{q}_2 = r_2$), then player 2 will eventually make the entire concession himself. If player 2 gives in at a rate less than that expected, then r_2 will fall as well, reducing player 1's demand, q_1. This is the general case of a convergent bargaining process—whenever both actual concession rates are less than the expected rates, both parties will converge to an agreement.

We should also stress the existence of a potential instability in this bargaining model. Suppose that player 2, for example, is a very sensitive learner, and he finds that player 1 is conceding at a rate significantly below his expectations. If he tends to respond to such information with large concessions, he may be found to be giving in at a rate even greater than player 1 expects. Player 1 will naturally increase his demands in response, the extent of the increase depending upon the value of expression (10) and his learning capacity. If this increase in demands is sufficiently marked, r_1 will again fall (depending upon 2's capacity to learn), and 2 may give in even more rapidly than before.[17] This sequence may still converge so long as player 2 concedes faster than player 1 reneges, in which case the conditions characterizing the point of agreement will be found to be no different from those of the previous case. It may be, however, either that the sequence does not converge or that it does not converge soon enough, so that the point of "agreement" will simply be at or arbitrarily close to the best possible outcome for player 1.

According to expression (10), the rate of concession varies inversely with the expression $[f''(q_1)/f'(q_1)]r_2 - a$ or, in the case of linear utility functions, with the value of the discount rate itself. Thus both high learning rates and low discount rates will tend to increase instability in the model. The stringency of the necessary stability condition, however, cannot be evaluated without some information as to the actual form of the learning functions in bargaining situations. An example of such a derivation will be given in the next chapter. One might infer from many widely publicized negotiations that in practice learning rates are quite low, so that we need not worry about the problem. On the other hand, it is the author's impression that in certain relatively minor cases (as in negotiating with a salesman over the price of a car) instability is by no means an unusual event. While it is true that Siegel and Fouraker's experiments provide no evidence that instability ever arises, their results are unfortunately not conclusive on this point. In the first place, they made retraction of bids illegal, and this would tend to suppress instability. (Note that the above-mentioned psychological forces would do the same.) Moreover, they provided no means for distinguishing bluffs from actual payoff expectations, and bluffing will tend to conceal instability (see Chapter VIII).

The Convergence of Expectations

According to equation (6), a player's demand is independent of his opponent's bid, and we can obtain q_1 in the absence of any knowledge of the value of q_2. In the last few sections, however, we have reintroduced such an interdependence by pointing out that *changes* in demands (or the absence of changes) will operate through the learning process to influence the values of the expectations variables r_1 and r_2. The resulting dynamic interaction between the parties has some remarkable and perhaps unexpected properties of its own, and these are worth discussing further.

Suppose we have two players who are relatively similar in that their abilities to learn and their discount rates are virtually equivalent. Further, suppose that r_2, player 1's expectation of 2's rate of concession, is greater than r_1, and finally, consider the situation at the start of the bargaining process when neither is giving in.[18] According to our assumption that large errors in expectations bring about more rapid changes in expectations [expression (10)], r_2 will fall faster than r_1. This, however, implies that as long as the second order terms $f''(q_1)$ and $g''(q_2)$ are not large, player 1's demand will fall *faster* than that of player 2 [by equation (10)].[19] This, in turn will reinforce the tendency for r_2 to fall faster than r_1. *Thus we observe a tendency for the two expected concession rates to approach one another.* Whenever $r_2 > r_1$, player 1 will change his expectations more rapidly (for a given rate of concession from his opponent) than will player 2, and the magnitude of the resulting changes in q_1 and q_2 will strengthen the tendency for r_2 to fall relative to r_1. In the case in which the two players have equivalent learning abilities and equal discount rates and in which the utility functions are linear (to eliminate the second order effects), we will have a tendency for r_2 to approach r_1. Thus whatever the players' initial expectations, if the above process has time to work itself out (that is, if the sequence of concessions does not get us to agreement first), we will expect equivalent expectations at the end of the bargaining process.

These conclusions may be obtained more rigorously by means of a graphical device. Suppose that player 2 is conceding, but at a rate below that expected by player 1. From our assumptions regarding a player's learning behavior, we conclude that player 1 will reduce his expectation r_2 at a rate which depends upon the discrepancy between r_2 and player 2's actual concession rate $-\dot{q}_2$; the larger this discrepancy, the more r_2 is reduced. Furthermore, player 1's outcome demand q_1 depends upon r_2, so that as r_2 is reduced, q_1 will be reduced as well. Thus the greater is $-\dot{q}_2$, the concession rate of player 2, the smaller the concession rate of player 1 will be, and *vice versa*. When $-\dot{q}_2 = r_2$, the expectations of player 1 are realized, and he retains his previous demand $(-\dot{q}_1 = 0)$. This relation is represented by the curve labelled F

in Figure 4. Placing $-\dot{q}_1$ and $-\dot{q}_2$ on the axes, we have drawn a line with negative slope which intersects the $-\dot{q}_2$ axis at the point $-\dot{q}_2 = r_2$. This line represents player 1's reaction to any concession rate $-\dot{q}_2$, given his expectation r_2, and may be represented by the function $-\dot{q}_1 = F(-\dot{q}_2, r_2)$. This relationship, of course, is derived analytically from our equations (6), (10) and some explicit learning function which satisfies our conditions (8) and (9). In exactly the same fashion, the curve G represents the function $-\dot{q}_2 = G(-\dot{q}_1, r_1)$ relating player 2's rate of concession to his expectation r_1, and his opponent's concession rate $-\dot{q}_1$. Figure 4 is deliberately constructed to show the special case in which utility functions are linear [to eliminate the second order effects in equation (10)], the players have identical learning capacities and discount rates, and current expectations are the same ($r_1^o = r_2^o$).

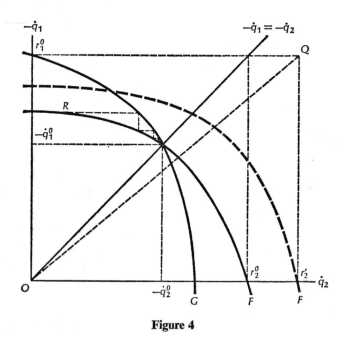

Figure 4

Under these special circumstances the two rates of concession will be given by the point $(-\dot{q}_1^o, -\dot{q}_2^o)$, which is the intersection of the functions F and G (by symmetry of the situation, $\dot{q}_1^o = \dot{q}_2^o$). This is the case because when we consider the situation from the point of view of a period analysis, the parties will move from any point R to the point of intersection as described by the dotted example on the diagram. Now suppose r_2 is increased *ceteris paribus* to r_2'. This will *shift* the line $-\dot{q}_1 = F(-\dot{q}_2, r_2)$ to the right to a position such as that shown by the dashed curve F on the graph. The effect of this shift is to increase $-\dot{q}_1$ immediately and to move the point of intersection of F and G up and to the left. Now, however, $-\dot{q}_1$ is greater than $-\dot{q}_2$, which, in our symmetrical example, implies the condition $-\dot{r}_2$ is greater than $-\dot{r}_1$. Thus, r_2 will fall faster than r_1, tending to *shift* the function F down faster than the function G, until equality is restored.[20]

Of course, it could be that r_1 and r_2 approach equality only because they are both approaching zero, so for our purposes it is important to show that the *ratio* r_1/r_2 tends toward a value of unity. Suppose that when r_2' is greater than r_1^0 this ratio does *not* increase. This could occur only if the intersection of F and G fell on or below the dashed line OQ. Since the function G has a negative slope, this is clearly impossible if, as r_2 rises, the slope of the function F does not decrease so rapidly as to permit an intersection below and to the right of the old one. It is sufficient for this condition that every point of F move upward as r_2 is increased. We must be certain, therefore, that the response functions F and G always satisfy the conditions $\delta F/\delta r_2 > 0$ and $\delta G/\delta r_1 > 0$ (in the positive quadrant): we must be certain, for example, that a *ceteris paribus* increase in r_2 will always induce a higher concession rate from player 1. The second learning condition, $d\dot{r}/d(-\dot{q}-r) > 0$, guarantees that this restriction will be satisfied so long as the second order terms [such as $f''(q_1)/f'(q_1)$ in the denominator of (10)] do not increase rapidly as r_2 or r_1 are increased.[21] In our special case in which the utility functions are linear, of course, this condition must be satisfied. In any case it is not likely that our conditions are violated at *all* points on the functions F and G. There may be, at worst, a limited number of values of r_2 and r_1 for which the ratio r_1/r_2 may be expected to display equilibrium properties (r_1/r_2 is a constant). Thus, our conditions may be taken to be uniqueness conditions; if they are violated over only limited ranges, our equilibrium analysis is valid and we are only prevented from pointing to one single expected outcome.

When the players are not identical in terms of their learning abilities and discount rates, these differences can be easily introduced into the model. For example, if player 1 is a more able learner than player 2, he will concede more rapidly for every value of $-\dot{q}_2$ which is less than r_2 than in the previous case. Thus the slope of F, $d\dot{q}_1/d\dot{q}_2$, will be steeper than before, and our diagram now has the form (for $r_1 = r_2$) which is drawn in Figure 5.

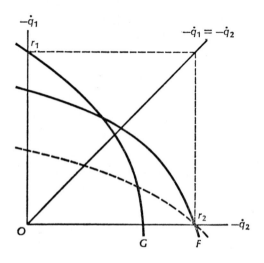

Figure 5

When $r_1 = r_2$, we expect to find player 1 conceding *more* rapidly than player 2. It follows that r_2 will tend to fall faster than r_1, and thus the equilibrium state must have r_2 *smaller* than r_1.

If player 1 has a higher discount rate than player 2, the function $-\dot{q}_1 = F(-\dot{q}_2, r_2)$ has a form similar to the dotted curve F' in Figure 5. Through reasoning similar to that used in the paragraph above, we conclude that in this case r_2 will tend to be larger than r_1.

We have drawn the graph in such a manner that the response of each player to a discrepancy between his expectations and reality is not too great: this represents the case of a stable bargaining process. In fact, we can see from the graph that whenever the function G intersects the function F from lower right to above left, we will have a stable bargaining process. If we define the slope of the function F, $\delta F/\delta(-\dot{q}_1)$ as $-A$, and the slope of the function G, $\delta G/\delta(-\dot{q}_1)$ as $-B$, then the stability condition is $1/B > A$ or $AB < 1$.

If two lines had intersected in the opposite fashion, we would have had instability on *two* counts: we would not expect to find the actual rates of concession at the point of intersection of F and G (a period analysis now takes us away from that point, as can be observed from the dotted time path in Figure 6, and the condition $r_2 > r_1$ tends to make r_1 fall faster than r_2). In this case we are unable to make any prediction concerning the outcome of the negotiation.

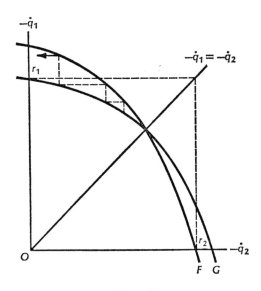

Figure 6

The Point of Agreement and the Nash Solution

Agreement is defined by the situation in which the sum of the players' demands is equal to the available supply, that is, $\bar{q}_1 + \bar{q}_2 = M$. Let us divide the left and right sides of equation (6), the utility maximization expression for player 1, by the left and right sides of a similar utility maximization expression for player 2 as follows:

$$\frac{f'(\bar{q}_1)}{g'(M - \bar{q}_1)} = \frac{f(q_1) + C_1/a}{g(M - \bar{q}_1) + C_2/b} \frac{a}{b} \frac{r_1}{r_2} \tag{11}$$

If we follow Nash's example and shift the origins of our utility functions so that a point of permanent disagreement is represented by the origin, and if we consider the utilities only at the time of agreement, neglecting the time discounting factors, we obtain the following utility functions:

$$U_1 = f(\bar{q}_1) + C_1/a$$
$$U_2 = g(M - \bar{q}_1) + C_2/b \tag{12}$$

That is, the utility of agreement to each player is equal to the utility of his payoff $f(q_1)$, *plus* the cost saving which results from the existence of a state of agreement rather than a state of disagreement, C_1/a. If we transform expression (11) into utility terms according to this definition of the utility functions, we obtain:

$$\frac{dU_1}{dU_2} = -\frac{U_1}{U_2} \frac{a}{b} \frac{r_1}{r_2} \tag{13}$$

where dU_1/dU_2 is the slope of the Pareto optimum curve in $U_1 \times U_2$ space, at the point determined by $\bar{q}_1$.

We can now apply the conclusions of the previous sections in the special linear and symmetric situation. In the case of similar players—players with equal discount rates ($a = b$) and equivalent learning abilities—we concluded that we had an equilibrium relationship between expectations when $r_1 = r_2$. In this case, expression (13) becomes simply

$$\frac{dU_1}{dU_2} = -\frac{U_1}{U_2}$$

the expression which characterizes the Nash solution to the bargaining problem! Thus we obtain the rather satisfying result from our model that in the special case of identical players, the bargaining outcome can be expected to be the Nash solution.

We need not rely on linear utility functions for this conclusion. Suppose we devise a version of the Nash condition of "symmetry" which is compatible with our formulation of the bargaining problem. Assume that if $q_1 = q_2$, then there exists some linear utility transformation such that:[22]

$$f(q_1) = g(q_2)$$

It follows by differentiation that, for q_1 always equal to q_2,

$$f'(q_1) = g'(q_2)$$
$$f''(q_1) = g''(q_2)$$

We may conclude, therefore, that at the point where $q_1 + q_2 = M$ (and, of course, $q_1 = q_2 = M/2$):

$$\frac{f''(q_1)}{f'(q_1)} = \frac{g''(q_2)}{g'(q_2)}$$

Making our assumption of "similarity" between the players ($a = b$, and the learning abilities are identical), then [by equation (10)] the preceding relations ensure that the actual concession rates become equal and we again have an equilibrium state at $r_1 = r_2$. Thus, by equation (13) we have the Nash point as the solution, and since $dU_1/dU_2 = -1$ at q_1, $U_1 = U_2$.[23]

Even given our "similarity" assumption, however, the solution to our model as given by (13) is *not* generally the Nash solution. The dependence of our results on second order derivatives as well as first is sufficient to show that the two solutions will be different in all but fortuitous cases. This difference is due to the introduction of explicit utility functions into the model, and this violates the Nash assumption that the utilities alone are sufficient to determine the outcome. Furthermore, due again to the dependence upon real payoffs as well as utilities, the model will not satisfy the independence of irrelevant alternatives assumption. Nevertheless, given identical players, our symmetry assumption *is* satisfied and, of course, this simple one dimensional model meets the Pareto optimality condition because, given utility maximization, there are no demands made which are not Pareto optimal.

The Effects of the Parameters

We concluded earlier that if player 1 is a more sensitive learner, the bargaining process will tend to yield the condition $r_2 < r_1$ (player 2 expects player 1 to concede more rapidly than player 1 expects player 2 to concede). Referring to equation (13), it is clear that a decrease in r_2 relative to r_1 at agreement results in a smaller value of U_1 relative to U_2 and probably a larger dU_1/dU_2 than before. Hence the better a learner he is, the more the outcome will go against a player! It does not follow that such a player is made worse off by his superior ability since it may be that the saving in time which results from his more rapid concession outweighs the loss in present utility of the outcome. Naturally, the other player gains, and he probably gains more than the faster learner.[24] There is a striking resemblance between this conclusion and Siegel and Fouraker's observation to the effect that increasing the information available to a player tends to reduce his payoff. It is possible that, in their experiments, increasing one player's information concerning the other player's payoff utilities may have sharpened the first player's awareness of the other's rate of concession and simply made him a better learner.[25]

We also concluded earlier that if player 1 used a higher discount rate than player 2, the bargaining process would tend to yield the condition $r_2 > r_1$. Nevertheless, referring to equation (13) we find the consequences of the high discount rate to be ambiguous. Compared to the symmetrical case, a higher value of a tends to decrease the ratio r_1/r_2 because it reduces player 1's concession rate, and this alone would increase player 1's outcome utility. However, a high discount rate also leads player 1 to sacrifice some payoff units at the start of the negotiation in order to hasten agreement [see equation (6)]. The net effect of these two forces is uncertain, and so we shall have to wait for more specific cases of our model before we can derive any definite conclusions.[26]

High values of the bargaining costs C_1 and C_2 will have the effect of reducing the time required by the bargaining process. An inspection of equation (6) coupled with positive and diminishing marginal utility supports the intuitively reasonable hypothesis that high bargaining costs will induce the players to reduce their payoff demands. The time saved by this initial reduction in demands may be somewhat offset by a decrease in the magnitude of the concession rates if the values of the second order expressions $f''(q_1)/f'(q_1)$, $g''(q_2)/g'(q_2)$ are much affected by the different q_1 and q_2, but it is clear that on balance we have a saving of time simply because agreement can be reached with higher values of r_1 and r_2 than before. In most cases, of course, changes in C_1 and C_2 will change the solution as well as bringing about an earlier settlement. This point will be discussed in a later chapter.

Intuitively, it is fairly clear that an increase in the costs of bargaining will tend to hasten agreement through a consequent reduction in payoff demands; this may be taken, for example, as a major explanation for the vastly different amounts of time which are taken by different kinds of bargains. A housewife normally spends only a few minutes bargaining over the price of a household item (on the rare occasions when she bargains over them at all) simply because the inconvenience which accompanies such a bargaining process is so large relative to the value of the good. A labor dispute, however, may last for months, and international negotiations in which the physical costs of bargaining are virtually nil (relative to the importance of the outcome) may last for years (test ban talks, talks over Berlin, trade negotiations, and so forth).[27] *Rising* costs during negotiations will also bring about additional concessions. For example, in pre-strike labor–management negotiations, the costs are very low compared to costs during the strike. Thus as long as the expected date of agreement comes before the strike deadline date, a bargainer will make relatively large demands, but he will make significant concessions before he will permit the expected time of agreement to extend beyond the strike date. If the strike comes nevertheless, his rate of concession will be reduced because he is no longer faced by a deadline beyond which bargaining costs are again made higher.

Thus we would expect labor negotiations to follow a pattern of relatively stable and low concession rates at first, rapid concession as the strike deadline approaches, and lower concession rates afterward—a sequence which in fact is commonly observed.[28]

Furthermore, rising costs can bring about a semblance of negotiation without any changes in expectations (and thus without any equilibrating process) taking place at all.[29] For example, as public officials bring increasing pressure upon unions and employers, concessions—the symbols of "responsible collective bargaining"—will be made, even to the point of bringing about an agreement. In the extreme case the outcome depends only upon the initial conditions and the relative pressures imposed on the two sides, and hence it is essentially arbitrary, having no relationship to the Nash point or any other theoretical solution. A more appropriate analysis might treat this case as a three way bargaining process taking place among management, labor, and government.

We must still be extremely cautious in discussing "the" solution of the bargaining process. For example, the "Nash solution" which is determined before a strike takes place is by no means equivalent to the "Nash solution" relevant to a negotiation after the strike. Only if the discounted stream of bargaining costs which appear after the strike are the same for both parties [$C_1/a = C_2/b$ so that in equation (9) U_1 will equal U_2 whenever $f(\bar{q}_1) = g(M - \bar{q}_2)$] will the "Nash solution" be the same in both cases. This ambiguity is a consequence of our procedure which classifies any state in which agreement does not prevail as a disagreement point (the origin of Figure 1). Nash certainly meant his solution to be constant over time, and for this reason it might be desirable to define the disagreement point in terms of the worst possible outcome—a complete failure of the parties to retain any amount of cooperation. On the other hand, such a procedure would obscure the fact that the bargaining process is heavily influenced by current conditions and that the costs of such possibilities as strikes or lockouts may never even be relevant in arriving at a settlement. To evaluate the agreement in terms of the worst possible form of conflict would not seem to be realistic; it would be much more appropriate to treat strikes and lockouts as variables rather than as foreordained parameters of the negotiation.[30]

Comments on Two Empirical Points

Our simple model may also help us to understand two more of Siegel and Fouraker's observations. Consider first their conclusion that increasing (utility) information to both players tends to increase the equality of the payoffs. This result may be taken as an indication that such information (simply that of having a table of the opponent's monetary returns as well as one's own) tended to make expectations more realistic as well as more symmetric. That is, when presented with a relatively symmetric bargaining situation, one would tend to expect a symmetric outcome—as we mentioned earlier, the symmetry assumption may well have become a matter of social habit. Furthermore, if both players were in possession of an important common source of information, we would expect this to make their learning abilities relatively more equal. If we have no reason for believing the players' discount rates to be very different and if the monetary payoff functions are fairly symmetric, this would all tend to place the Nash point where $U_1 = U_2$.

Siegel and Fouraker's conclusion that adding to the utility of higher payoffs for one player tended to increase his physical payoff at agreement is easy to treat with this model. Their method was to supplement the utility to one player of any payoff above some q' by a fixed amount, making q' his "level of aspiration." Thus if player 1 is the favored player, his utility function can be written:

$$U_1 = f(q_1 + \rho)e^{-aw}$$

where $\rho(q_1, q')$ is defined as

$$\left\{ \begin{matrix} k & \text{if} & q_1 > q' \\ 0 & \text{if} & q_1 < q' \end{matrix} \right\}$$

The condition for a utility maximum is

$$f(q_1 + \rho)\frac{a}{r_2} = f'(q_1 + \rho)(1 + \frac{\Delta\rho}{\Delta q_1})$$

where

$$\frac{\Delta\rho}{\Delta q_1} = \begin{cases} 0 & \text{for} \quad q_1 \neq q' \\ +k & \text{for} \quad q_1 = q' \end{cases}$$

(over the concession from q' to $q' - 1$).

We may expect a player in these circumstances to behave just as we described in our previous model, except that when his payoff approaches q', he will refuse to concede for a considerable time. A concession from q' to $q' - 1$ would involve the utility loss associated with $k + 1$ payoff units while saving only as much time as is associated with one payoff unit. This reluctance can be expected to lower his opponent's estimate of his concession rate and cause player 2 to concede instead (probably fast enough to reduce the usual decline in r_2). Thus even if player 1 does eventually go below q', the outcome may be expected to favor him. The fact that in several of Siegel and Fouraker's cases the payoffs to the favored players were significantly above q' would indicate that there was some bluffing taking place as well, causing a player to balk at an inflated demand and forcing the other player to concede much more rapidly than before.

These comments are not meant to imply that this theory has explained Siegel and Fouraker's results—no empirically untested model could do so—but it is significant that results so similar to theirs can be obtained from our model.

■ NOTES

1. The term "bluffing" is commonly used in several distinct ways. The meaning which we have in mind refers to a player's deliberate misrepresentation of his outcome expectations in order to influence his opponent. That is, he demands x while he expects (or would otherwise expect) to receive y ultimately. This definition corresponds to that used in game

theory [see John von Neumann and Oskar Morgenstern, *Theory of Games and Economic Behavior* (2nd ed.; Princeton, N.J.: Princeton University Press, 1947), pp. 188–189].

2. A case in which management clearly harbored such hopes appears in Raskin's description of the 1962–1963 New York newspaper strike (A. H. Raskin, "The New York Newspaper Strike," *The New York Times*, April 1, 1963).

3. This assumption implicitly eliminates for now the possibility that one player may expect his behavior to influence the other.

4. If there are many dimensions involved in measuring the possible outcomes, we would require an equal number of indices.

5. Even if the goods are not homogeneous, this may be true. Schelling has ascribed considerable importance to "prominences" or "focal points" inherent in the objectives of any bargaining situation—certain of the objectives which, for psychological or historical reasons, possess enhanced interest to all the bargainers. If such points are used to construct the measuring scales, the latter will not differ (for each good) by more than a linear transformation. See Thomas C. Schelling, *The Strategy of Conflict* (Cambridge, Mass.: Harvard University Press, 1960).

6. Player 2 may greatly prefer an outcome q^o over q', and be nearly indifferent between q' and the inferior quantity q'', even where $q^o - q' = q' - q''$. In this case, if we knew his utility function, we would expect 2 to concede more slowly from q^o to q' than he does from q' to q''.

7. A more general concession function could be substituted for our constant rate. See Alan Coddington's "Comment" on this model and my "Reply," *American Economic Review*, LVI (1966), 522–533. Professor Coddington has expanded further on this subject in Chapter VI of his *Theories in the Bargaining Process* (Chicago: Aldine Publishing Co., 1968).

8. This may be conceived of as an infinite stream of costs originating at the present time minus an infinite stream of costs originating at the time of agreement. In present value terms, this is $C_1/a - C_1e^{-aw}/a$.

9. Our notation will always use U^* to represent present values of utility, and U to represent undiscounted utility.

10. We can see here why M must be constant to permit us to use our simple quantity notation—if M varied with the outcome, then M would be a function of q_1—changing the maximization conditions. If instead we used the P-index notation, $w = (P_1 - P_2)/r_2$, we would not be disturbed by a variability in M since it no longer appears in the utility function which is to be maximized. Of course, such a transformation would be reflected by changes in the other parameters, and in partciular our assumption that r_2 is constant requires that we use some care in defining the units of P sensibly.

11. It may appear peculiar at first that an increase in costs C *increases* U_1, that is, increases the utility of agreement. It becomes clear once we

realize that this expression measures the *gain* in utility which player 1 obtains from agreement compared to permanent disagreement. This gain is certainly increased as the costs of disagreement are increased.

12. This result is completely analogous to the conclusion that fixed costs do not enter into the calculation of the profit maximizing output of a firm. Thus, the utility which player 1 would receive from granting q_2 immediately to his opponent is basically an origin from which all further gains must be measured.

13. This will be discussed further in Chapter V.

14. Expressions (5) and (6) do seem to correspond to a very general characterization of existing learning theory. Although work attempting to define mathematically the time path of a learning process such as the one with which we are concerned is decidedly in the minority in the otherwise extensive literature on the psychology of learning, some useful models do exist. Most notable are those of Hull [see E. Hilgard, *Theories of Learning* (New York: Appleton Century Crofts, 1956), pp. 1–115], Kenneth Spence [*Behavior Theory and Learning* (Englewood Cliffs, N.J.: Prentice-Hall, Inc., 1960)], and Robert Bush and Frederick Mosteller [*Stochastic Models for Learning* (New York: John Wiley and Sons, 1955)]. It may be argued that even our generalized learning model should follow Bush and Mosteller in making use of a statistical response theory. We do have some doubts, however, as to the appropriateness of probabilistic elements in a positive theory.

15. At this point it is interesting to paraphrase a result of Robert H. Strotz ("Myopia and Inconsistency in Dynamic Utility Maximization," *Review of Economic Studies,* XXIII (1956), pp. 165–180) and show why we are confining ourselves to the use of a discount function in exponential form. Let us rewrite this function as we did originally: $\phi(w)$. In this more general case, player 1 has maximized his expected return when he has satisfied the condition $f'(q_1)\phi(w) + f(q_1)\phi'(w)/r_2 = 0$. (We are neglecting the cost term C_1.) Suppose his estimate of player 2's concession rate, r_2, proves to be correct, and $-q_2$ does equal r_2. We naturally expect player 1 to retain his choice of q_1, and we assert that it would be irrational for him to change that decision. Observe, however, that this implies that the *same* q_1 as before must satisfy the maximization condition—that is, $f'(q_1)$ and $f(q_1)$ retain their values. Also r_2 is unchanged (from expressions 8). However, w has changed over time because of the change in q_2. To preserve the maximization condition, therefore, it must be true that $\phi'(w)/\phi(w) = -a$ where a is some positive constant. Simple integration leads to the conclusion that the only function which can satisfy this condition is the exponential ke^{-aw}. Thus individual behavior which retains decisions in the light of realized expectations implies that the time discounting function has exponential form, and since we are only interested here in such consistent decisions, we are constrained to use this kind of a function.

16. This problem will be discussed again in Chapters VI and VIII.

17. It is not sufficient for instability to have $-\dot{q}_2 > r_2$; we must also have a strong response to this condition on the part of player 1, otherwise player 2, not observing much of a change in $\dot{q}_1$, may fail to repeat the cycle, and we will have $-\dot{q}_2 < r_2$.

18. We are here implicitly asssuming a lag in the learning process. A great deal more can be said regarding initial positions of the bargainers, but this is put off to Chapter VIII.

19. The second order terms $f''(q_1)$ and $g''(q_2)$ appear in the denominator of equation (10) (and a similar expression defined for player 2). If $f''(q_1)$ is very large when q_1 is large, while $g''(q_2)$ is very small when q_2 is small, then it is possible to have $|\dot{q}_2| > |\dot{q}_1|$ even though $|dr_2/dt| > |dr_1/dt|$. See footnote 21.

20. This analysis oversimplifies the problem somewhat by neglecting the fact that curves F and G are also shifting as $-\dot{q}_1$ and $-\dot{q}_2$ approach their intersection. For the purposes of our simple diagrammatic model, we shall assume that the convergence to this point is instantaneous. A period analysis can be constructed containing both phases of the problem, and such a model gives the same results as the one used here.

21. Specifically, if the learning function for player 1 were written $\dot{r}_2 = R(-\dot{q}_2 - r_2)$, then our condition would reduce to [using equation (7)]

$$\frac{\delta}{\delta r_2} \left(\frac{-R(-\dot{q}_2, r_2)}{\dfrac{[f''(q_1)]}{f'(q_1)} r_2 - a} \right) \geqslant 0$$

which in turn can be written (calling the expression in the denominator D)

$$\frac{\dfrac{\delta}{\delta r_2}\left[\dfrac{1}{D} \right]}{\dfrac{1}{D}} \leqslant -\frac{\dfrac{R}{r_2}}{R}$$

The right hand side of this expression is positive, so the condition simply requires that the expression $1/D$ not vary so strongly "percentagewise" as does R. In less technical terms, we are asking that a change in r_2 not be accompanied by a shift in D which will change a player's concession rate so as to nullify the effect of the change in R.

22. The Nash assumption is weaker than this because it only requires that for any q_1 there exist some q_2 (not necessarily equal to q_1) such that $f(q_1) = g(q_2)$ and $q_1 + q_2 = M$.

23. It must be remembered that the condition $r_1 = r_2$ is only achieved if the bargaining process takes enough time for the initial discrepancies to be eliminated. Otherwise the solution which is derived from our model will differ from the actual results. In fact, as we shall show later, some error is almost always to be expected, although our solution will always serve as the focus toward which a stable bargaining process will tend.

24. The potential gain of a more rapid learner is only offered as a possibility—in general, he probably will not gain on balance. In Chapter IV, note 12, there is an example in which he certainly does not benefit.

25. Perhaps it should be emphasized that the Siegel–Fouraker game was two dimensional, and that in such a case it is practically impossible for a player to tell whether an opponent's movement from a point (x, y) to a point (x', y'), where $x > x'$ and $y < y'$, constitutes a concession or not. Hence possession of information about the utilities associated with these points would greatly increase one's ability to estimate a rate of concession.

26. Robert Bishop, in "A Zeuthen–Hicks Model of the Bargaining Process," *Econometrica,* XXXII (1964), 410–417, has concluded that higher discount rates always tend to reduce a player's payoff, primarily because his model does not consider the dynamics of concession and hence misses part of the influence of the discount rate. Assuming a linear learning model and assuming equal learning rates, it is not hard to show that our model also yields this result (see Chapter IV). We might expect the opposite conclusion if the learning ability is relatively high.

27. Of course, these second two examples depend upon negotiations between two groups rather than two individuals, and the reader may wish to make some qualifications here. The significance of a shift from individual to group negotiations is probably vastly overrated, however. It is perhaps conceivable that groups should have lower learning rates than individuals, but the most important characteristic of groups—the difficulty of formulating consistent preference functions—does not in itself impede the operation of our model.

28. For example, see Lloyd G. Reynolds, *Labor Economics and Labor Relations* (Englewood Cliffs, N.J.: Prentice-Hall, Inc., 1959), p. 182. We may infer from Raskin's description of the 1962–1963 New York newspaper strike (*op. cit.*) that the phenomenon appeared in that case as well.

29. In fact, it is through such increasing costs (or decreasing value of the payoff over time) that Bishop, *op. cit.*, and Lucien Foldes, "A Determinate Model of Bilateral Monopoly," *Economica,* Vol. XXXI (1964), are able to obtain determinate models.

30. This we shall attempt to do in Chapters VI and VII.

IV

■ Some Detailed Models
of the Bargaining Process

Before going on to further elaboration of the bargaining problem itself, it is worthwhile to draw out some further implications of our basic model. So far, we have been able to describe a definite solution only for a very special case in which the players, for all intents and purposes, were identical. Furthermore, the description in the previous chapter was highly qualitative in nature, and its generality prevented us from giving examples of its basic dynamic relationships. In this chapter, we will make additional simplifications with a view to obtaining more detailed descriptions of the bargaining process itself. Naturally, the resulting model suffers as we substitute special cases for more general functions, but our results should suggest some important phenomena which can occur in less restricted bargaining situations. On the other hand, as the model becomes mathematically more tractable, our discussion will become increasingly technical, and it may appear at times that we are more concerned with analysis of the *model* than of the bargaining process itself. It is very important, however, to understand to what extent an equilibrium theory such as this one can be used as a description of a dynamic bargaining process, and to be able to evaluate the errors inherent in it. These objectives alone justify a more detailed discussion.

The first step must consist of a more restrictive definition of the players' learning behavior. Ideally, a learning theory should take the form of a functional expression with its independent variable(s) taking values at all previous points of time. Unfortunately, however, there exists no convenient way to handle such a form mathematically, and we must take a much more simplified view. A simpler learning theory can be based on the fact that the expected concession rates r_1 and r_2 are constantly changing over time, depending upon the actual concession rates $\dot{q}_1$ and $\dot{q}_2$. We shall assume, then, that the current values of r_1 and r_2 already contain the appropriate weighting of all previous experiences and that a player's current observations of his opponent's concession rate merely modify his expectations through some simple weighted average. That is, we shall assume that the players modify their expectations according to a constant proportion of the *error* in their expectations:

$$\dot{r}_2 = \alpha \left[-\dot{q}_2 - r_2 \right]$$
$$\dot{r}_1 = \beta \left[-\dot{q}_1 - r_1 \right] \tag{14}$$

where α and β are parameters related to the rates at which players 1 and 2 modify their expectations.[1] Expressions (14), of course, satisfy both of the conditions for learning which we set down in the previous chapter [conditions (8) and (9)].

The Solution of the Model

In the last chapter, we defined the function F to represent player 1's concession rate as a reaction to player 2's concessions, given a certain level of expectations. We may use our specific learning model to derive this relationship explicitly. For example, if player 2 is conceding at a rate $\dot{q}_2$, then, by (14), player 1 will modify his expectations at a rate $\dot{r}_2 = \alpha \left[-\dot{q}_2 - r_2 \right]$. Substituting this into our condition that player 1's concession rate $\dot{q}_1$ is a function of the rate of change of his expectations [equation (10)], we obtain the response function F:

$$\dot{q}_1 = \frac{\alpha \, (\dot{q}_2 + r_2)}{\dfrac{f''(q_1)}{f'(q_1)} r_2 - a}$$

A similar formula applies to the response function G which was defined for player 2. It is now easy to obtain the slopes of the response functions, which we defined as $-A$ and $-B$:

$$-A \equiv \frac{d\dot{q}_1}{d\dot{q}_2} = \frac{\alpha}{\dfrac{f''(q_1)}{f'(q_1)} r_2 - a}$$

$$-B = \frac{\dot{q}_2}{\dot{q}_1} = \frac{\beta}{\dfrac{g''(q_2)}{g'(q_2)} r_1 - b}$$

Our model suggested that in the case of stable negotiation we could expect the players' concession rates to be given by the intersection of the response functions F and G. Solving these two functions simultaneously, we obtain the concession rates (and thereby the rates of change of the players' expectations) which are determined by this point:

$$\dot{q}_1 = \frac{A \, (Br_1 - r_2)}{1 - AB} \qquad \dot{q}_2 = \frac{B \, (Ar_2 - r_1)}{1 - AB} \tag{15}$$

$$\dot{r}_1 = \frac{(Ar_2 - r_1)}{1 - AB} \qquad \dot{r}_2 = \frac{(Br_1 - r_2)}{1 - AB} \tag{16}$$

Let us first consider the bargaining process when the product AB is less than one. It is clear from equations (15) and (16) that the signs of the expressions $(Ar_2 - r_1)$ and $(Br_1 - r_2)$ determine the directions of change in the expected concession rates r_1 and r_2, and hence of the payoff demands q_1 and q_2. In Figure 7, we have represented by the curve OT the locus of values of r_1 and r_2 which make $\dot{r}_1 = 0$. This locus is defined by the condition $Ar_2 = r_1$. The curve OR similarly represents the values of r_1 and r_2 which make $\dot{r}_2 = 0$. These lines are not necessarily straight:

second order effects will probably cause A and B to vary as r_1 and r_2 change. We do know, however, that the function $Br_1 = r_2$ lies above and to the left of the function $Ar_2 = r_1$—otherwise for some value of r_1 we could have $Br_1 \geqslant r_1/A$, which implies $AB \geqslant 1$, contrary to hypothesis. We also know that the slope of the function $Br_1 = r_2$ can never become permanently vertical (or turn even farther over to the left) because that would require the value of B to become indefinitely small as r_1 becomes indefinitely large. Similarly, the line $Ar_2 = r_1$ could not turn permanently horizontal.

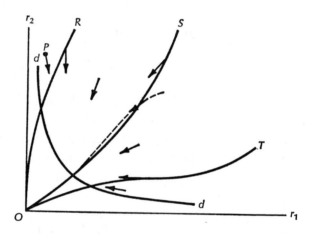

Figure 7

As time passes, expectations will be adjusted in such a way that any combination (r_1, r_2) will change in the directions indicated by the arrows on the diagram. For example, at point P, Ar_2 is less than r_1 and Br_1 is greater than r_2. Equations (16) imply that $\dot{r}_2 > 0$ and $\dot{r}_1 < 0$, and therefore the arrow through P is drawn to indicate that r_2 is rising while r_1 is falling. It is clear from the directions of the arrows that regardless of the values taken by the expected concession rates at the start of the bargaining process, *ceteris paribus,* the combination (r_1, r_2) of the players' expectations will eventually appear between the two lines OR and OT. Thus their rates of change, $\dot{r}_1$ and $\dot{r}_2$, must become negative.

As long as our model is continuous, there must exist a set of points (r_1, r_2) for which $\dot{r}_1/\dot{r}_2 = r_1/r_2$; that is, for which the arrows on our graph will point directly toward the origin. The locus of these points is the positively sloped curve OS on the diagram. Any point on this line represents a state in which the players' *relative* expectation levels, given by the ratio r_1/r_2, will remain constant. Furthermore, this particular curve describes an equilibrium relation: whenever the current values of r_1 and r_2 do not fall on OS, the bargainers will tend to move back onto it. More precisely, whenever the point (r_1, r_2) lies below and to the right of the OS, the ratio r_1/r_2 will tend to increase over time, and whenever the point (r_1, r_2) lies above and to the left, r_1/r_2 will tend to decrease.

The equilibrium properties of OS, however, must be qualified. Whenever the values of A and B do not remain constant as r_1 and r_2 vary,[2] the locus may be curved, so that the combination (r_1, r_2) will reach OS, only to have OS move right away again. This possibility is shown, for example, by the dotted time path on the diagram. Nevertheless, the condition $\dot{r}_1/\dot{r}_2 = r_1/r_2$ remains as a central state toward which the players' expectations will tend, and, whenever this state is reached, the expectations may be expressed in a ratio which is constant over time. Thus again we have obtained our fundamental theorem:

1. $\dot{r}_1$ and $\dot{r}_2$ must both eventually become negative, implying convergence: $\dot{q}_1 < 0$, $\dot{q}_2 < 0$.

2. There exists a stable relationship between r_1 and r_2 in the sense that any *ceteris paribus* shift in r_1 and r_2 will set up forces tending to restore that relation during the course of the negotiation.

Except for providing new insight into the path of the adjustment process, this model is no different from our previous one. Naturally it contains all of the same implications that we have already discussed. In addition, of course, we are now able to examine in more detail those cases involving negotiators who are not identical.[3]

As our model is formulated, the bargainers' payoff demands depend upon the expected concession rates (r_1 and r_2) in such a way that the faster a player expects his opponent to concede, the greater will be his own demand. Thus equation (6), which describes this relationship, is monotonic as well as continuous. It follows that for any value of q_1, we can find one and only one value of r_2 which will induce player 1 to make q_1 his demand. Similarly, we can find an r_1 which will induce player 2 to demand any q_2 we choose. Therefore, we should be able to find a whole set of combinations of r_1 and r_2 which will determine demands q_1 and q_2 such that $q_1 + q_2 = M$, establishing agreement. Naturally, the line in $r_1 \times r_2$ space which represents the locus of these points must have a negative slope.[4] In Figure 7 we have drawn such a line, labelling it *dd*. The most likely outcome of the bargaining process appears at the intersection of *dd* and our equilibrium locus, given as point Q on the diagram. We will call this intersection the "solution." [5]

It is still true, however, that the point Q represents a solution only in an equilibrium sense: if the bargainers start the negotiation with widely disproportionate estimates of each other's concession rates, they may reach agreement long before the equilibrium condition is achieved. Furthermore, as we have already indicated, the function $\dot{r}_1/\dot{r}_2 = r_1/r_2$ is not usually representable by a straight line, because of the second order effects of diminishing marginal utility; hence, we may reach the equilibrium and then pass it by, so that the ratio r_1/r_2 oscillates around the equilibrium. Finally, the value of the ratio r_1/r_2 which is associated with the solution is generally only approached asymptotically, so that, strictly speaking, the actual value of this ratio can only come arbitrarily close to the solution value. For all of these reasons, we are able to speak of our "solution" at Q only as a *most likely outcome* rather than as a fully determined one.

Stability

We indicated in Chapter III that when the product of the slopes AB is greater than one, the model indicates that the bargaining process is unstable. On our diagram (Figure 8) this condition amounts to a reversal of our two lines $Ar_2 = r_1$ and $Br_1 = r_2$, and the arrows which describe the course taken by the bargaining process now describe

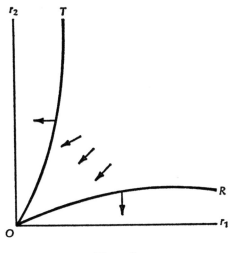

Figure 8

a tendency away from the condition $\dot{r}_1/\dot{r}_2 = r_1/r_2$.

Our model will be stable whenever $AB < 1$, and a sufficient condition for this is that the slopes of the reaction functions be less than one: $A < 1$, $B < 1$. Sufficient conditions for these, in turn, are $\alpha < a$, $\beta < b$. Thus, we are assured of stability if each individual's rate of learning is less than his rate of discounting. This conclusion corresponds to our intuitive discussion of instability in Chapter III: If the players' learning rates are high (α and β large) and if they tend to respond markedly to changes in their expectations (a and b small), then an increase in one player's demand (or a reluctance to concede) will give rise to a relatively large concession from the other which, in turn, will reinforce the first player's demands for a larger share of the outcome.

To require a player's learning rate to be smaller than his discount rate, however, may appear to be rather restrictive. After all, a player's rate of discount is not likely to be more than 15–25 per cent per year at most, and a learning rate less than that is somewhat lower than we might expect. Of course, the second order terms

$$\frac{f''(q_1)}{f'(q_1)} r_2, \quad \text{and} \quad \frac{g''(q_2)}{g'(q_2)} r_1$$

are likely to add significantly to the denominators of A and B in cases of nonlinear utility functions, and thus contribute toward stability. This property reflects the fact that diminishing marginal utility will tend to make a player less willing to compound concessions (because the losses grow more than proportionately) and at the same time less anxious to seek large increases in his payoff. Thus, his responsiveness will be reduced in both directions, providing stability. Furthermore, there are other factors which in practice will increase the likelihood of stability and which have not been introduced explicitly into our model. First, the previously mentioned "ethic" against the retraction of bids is likely to prevent the model from exploding by preventing demands from increasing. Second, most negotiations are quite unlike our simple model in that they are concerned with several issues at once, rather than with just one divisible commodity. As the number of these issues increases, it naturally becomes much more difficult to estimate a "concession rate" because there are so many different ways to concede, and as a consequence the learning rate may prove to be quite low. This point suggests, incidentally, that the likelihood of instability will be less as the complexity of the subject of the negotiation is greater. Finally, it is quite possible that the presence of "bluffing" in the bargaining process has the effect of inhibiting the learning process and hence of lowering the values of α and β.[6] More will be said on this last point in Chapter VIII.

In the last chapter the stability condition $AB < 1$ applied to *two* aspects of the bargaining process: first, it permitted the conclusion that $-\dot{q}_1$ and $-\dot{q}_2$ would be found at the intersection of the response functions $-q_1 = F(-\dot{q}_2, r_2)$ and $-\dot{q}_2 = G(-\dot{q}_1, r_1)$; and second, it implied that r_2 would fall faster than r_1 whenever $r_2 > r_1$, given similar players. By solving our bargaining equations simultaneously in this simple model, we have ignored the first of these and used the intersection of the response functions to describe the players' outcome demands. In the unstable case we are not really justified in using such a model at all, since we do not expect the bargaining variables to appear at this intersection. In general we could avoid this oversimplification if we used a lagged learning theory in a difference equation model instead of our differential equation system. Such a model behaves exactly like the one which we have been studying (in the stable case) except for the additional time lag, and even this becomes negligible if we assume that the adjustment toward the intersection of our F and G functions is rapid compared to the adjustments in r_1 and r_2.[7] Nevertheless, we will continue to use our instantaneous model simply because it is so much easier to handle.

The Impact of Changes in the Discount Rate

Naturally, all the conclusions which we derived from the model in Chapter III can be deduced from this one as well.[8] In that earlier discussion, however, we were unable to determine the effect of *ceteris paribus* change in a player's discount rate. An increase in a, for example, reduced player 1's rate of concession, causing r_1 to fall more rapidly and hence tending to favor player 1 in the outcome. On the other hand, one would expect that if a player has a higher rate of discount and strongly prefers present goods over future goods, he will sacrifice some units of payoff in order to hasten agreement and thus tend to reduce his own share in the outcome. The latter turns out to be the dominant factor once we have introduced the learning model given in equation (14). The solution point Q in Figure 7 is described by the relation $\dot{r}_1/\dot{r}_2 = r_1/r_2$, and applying equations (15) and (16) to this, we obtain the following result:

$$\frac{r_1}{r_2} = \left(\frac{A}{B}\right)^{\frac{1}{2}} \tag{17}$$

We may now apply our solution condition from the last chapter [equation (13)] and determine the impact of a change in discount rate by differentiating the product $(a/b)\sqrt{A/B}$ with respect to a. The resulting expression has a positive sign,[9] and hence if a player's discount rate rises, his share of the payoff at agreement falls; that is $dU_1/da < 0$.

A Linear Model

We have already used an assumption of linear utility functions as one means of deriving the Nash solution to the bargaining process (in the case of similar players). This assumption also simplifies the model enough to permit a complete description of the dynamic system. Suppose that player 1 has the utility function $U_1 = fq_1$ where q_1 is his share of the benefits of agreement and f is the marginal utility of q_1. (This function is deliberately chosen so that $U_1 = 0$ when $q_1 = 0$.) As usual, the process of bargaining imposes a recurring cost to the first party of C_1 utility units per time period, he has a time discount rate a, and he expects player 2 to concede at a rate r_2. The expected present value of an outcome which gives him q_1 [equation (5)] now becomes:

$$U^*_1 = fq_1 e^{-aw} + \frac{C_1}{a} e^{-aw} - \frac{C_1}{a}$$

where again w, the time player 1 expects to elapse before agreement is reached, equals $(q_1 + q_2 - M)/r_2$ where M is the constant amount of the payoff commodity to be divided. The maximum of this expression with respect to q_1 gives player 1's demand:

$$q_1 = \frac{r_2}{a} - \frac{C_1}{f}\frac{1}{a} \tag{18}$$

If r_2 changes at a rate $\dot{r}_2$, then q_1 changes at the rate given by $\dot{q}_1$:

$$\dot{q}_1 = \frac{1}{a}\dot{r}_2$$

We obtain similar expressions for player 2 simply by reversing the subscripts and exchanging a for b and using his utility function $U_2 = gq_2$.

Now that we have eliminated the second order conditions, the response functions F and G are linear and their slopes are constant with $-A = \alpha/a$ and $-B = \beta/b$. Thus we may treat (16) as a pair of first order differential equations and solve for r_1 and r_2 as functions of time alone:

$$r_1(t) = k_1 e^{x_1 t} + k_2 e^{x_2 t}$$
$$r_2(t) = m_1 e^{x_1 t} + m_2 e^{x_2 t}$$

(19)

where

$$x_1 = \frac{-\alpha - \beta + \sigma}{2(1 - AB)}$$

$$x_2 = \frac{-\alpha - \beta - \sigma}{2(1 - AB)}$$

and

$$\sigma = |[(\alpha - \beta)^2 + 4 \alpha b AB]^{\frac{1}{2}}|$$

We have chosen to define σ as the positive root in order to ensure that, provided we have our usual stability condition $AB < 1$, we will always have

$$0 \geqslant x_1 > x_2$$

The constants k_1, k_2, m_1, and m_2 are defined in terms of the initial conditions: $r_1 = r_1'$ and $r_2 = r_2'$ when $t = 0$.[10]

$$k_1 = \frac{1}{\sigma}\left[\beta A r_2' + \tfrac{1}{2}(\alpha - \beta + \sigma) r_1'\right]$$

$$m_1 = \frac{1}{\sigma}\left[\alpha B r_1' + \tfrac{1}{2}(-\alpha + \beta + \sigma) r_2'\right]$$

(20)

$$k_1 + k_2 = r_1'$$

$$m_1 + m_2 = r_2'$$

By choosing σ as the positive root, we have $(\alpha - \beta + \sigma) \geqslant 0$ and $(-\alpha + \beta + \sigma) \geqslant 0$, and hence we know that k_1 and m_1 are always strictly positive; k_2 and m_2, however, are ambiguous in sign. The sums $k_1 + k_2$ and $m_1 + m_2$ are always positive, of course, since they equal the (positive) initial expected rates of concession.

Equations (19) reproduce our conclusion that as time passes, both $\dot{r}_1$ and $\dot{r}_2$ will eventually become negative. Differentiating equation (19) for $\dot{r}_1$, we obtain

$$\dot{r}_1 = k_1 e^{\pi_1 t} x_1 + k_2 e^{\pi_2 t} x_2 = e^{\pi_2 t} \left[k_1 e^{(\pi_1 - \pi_2)t} x_1 + k_2 x_2 \right]$$

The first term of the expression in brackets is always negative, and since $x_1 - x_2 > 0$, it increases in magnitude over time, eventually becoming greater (in magnitude) than the constant term.

We can find the players' outcome demands as functions of time simply by combining equations (18) and (19) for both players.

$$q_1(t) = \frac{1}{a} \left[k_1 e^{\pi_1 t} + k_2 e^{\pi_2 t} \right] - \frac{1}{a} \frac{C_1}{f}$$

$$q_2(t) = \frac{1}{b} \left[m_1 e^{\pi_1 t} + m_2 e^{\pi_2 t} \right] - \frac{1}{b} \frac{C_2}{g}$$

(21)

Finally, it is easy to describe the solution which is "predicted" by the equilibrium model, the point Q in Figure 7. We need only solve simultaneously equations (18), (19), and the solution condition $q_1 + q_2 = M$ to obtain the payoff to player 1:

$$q_1 = \frac{M + \dfrac{C_2}{bg} - \dfrac{C_1}{af} \left(\dfrac{a\alpha}{b\beta} \right)^{\frac{1}{2}}}{1 + \left(\dfrac{a\alpha}{b\beta} \right)^{\frac{1}{2}}}$$

(22)

The Implications of the Linear Model

By making use of this model, we may, of course, derive all of the general conclusions which we obtained earlier.[11] Furthermore, it can be shown here that although r_1 and r_2 approach their equilibrium relationship only asymptotically, equations (21) indicate that a state of agreement is approached directly. This fact may be more clear from the example of equations (21) which is plotted on the graph in Figure 9. Here we have graphed player 1's outcome demand (q_1) and the residual which player 2's demand implicitly leaves to player 1, ($M - q_2$), against time. Agreement occurs when $q_1 = M - q_2$.

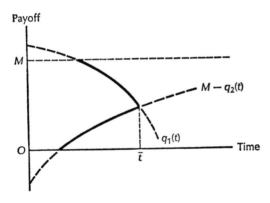

Figure 9

For certain values of t, equations (21) may yield values of q_1 and q_2 which are beyond the resources of the bargaining situation (the dashed lines in Figure 9). For an interpretation of this condition, we must pay closer attention to the nature of the problem which the model is intended to represent. If the parties are dividing a homogeneous commodity whose total supply is known to be fixed at a level given by M, then, of course, it would be absurd for either party to demand more than M, even if the expected concession rates seemed to justify it. The "optimal" demand may be $1.2\,M$, but the party can ask only for the maximum payoff which is possible. Moreover, this boundary state will affect the mechanism of our model because the rate of change of such a player's demand is zero even when his expectations are changing, and this is likely to accelerate the rate at which his opponent revises his own expectations. On the other hand, we also intend our model to apply to situations in which M is variable or unknown and in which we would have to use the P-notation which was introduced in Chapter III. In these cases, it may be extremely difficult to identify the boundaries of the situation: Who can quantify the wage demand which is "too high" or the offer which is "too low" in the sense that they leave the respective opponents indifferent between a settlement and permanent disagreement? When the negotiation is of this sort, it is possible for demands to exceed the "boundaries" and the operation of our model is unaffected by whether the demands are "realistic" or not. As a matter of fact, it is likely that this second case is the one which is by far the more frequently encountered, and, indeed, we shall argue subsequently that it may well be the only interesting case. Moreover, it is in this case that the bargaining process becomes a productive operation: no matter how narrow or how skewed the range of possible agreements relative to the parties' initial demands, a stable bargaining process will eventually lead to a point within that range.

Define $\bar{t}$ as the total amount of time necessary to reach agreement. We can determine its value by solving the agreement condition:

$$q_1(\bar{t}) + q_2(\bar{t}) = M$$

for $\bar{t}$. If we substitute equations (21) into this expression, we could, in principle, obtain $\bar{t}$. The resulting expression is too complicated for direct solution, however, and so further simplification is necessary.[12] It becomes easy to solve for $\bar{t}$ if we apply our "similarity" conditions ($a = b$, $\alpha = \beta$) to the model.[13] These conditions generate the following result:

$$\bar{t} = -\left[\frac{1}{\alpha} + \frac{1}{a}\right] \ln \left[\frac{\dfrac{C_1}{af} + \dfrac{C_2}{ag} + M}{\dfrac{r_1'}{a} + \dfrac{r_2'}{a}} \right] \qquad (23)$$

From equation (18), and the essential bargaining condition that $q_1 + q_2 \geqslant M$, at time $t = 0$, it can be shown that the expression in the brackets of equation (23) must be positive but less than 1, and therefore that the logarithm of that quantity must be negative.

From expression (23), we may again deduce the conclusion that higher values of C (higher bargaining costs) decrease the necessary amount of bargaining time. It should be remembered that higher bargaining costs hasten agreement only by reducing the player's demands at any given level of expectations. Bargaining costs in this model have no direct influence over the players' expectations of one another's concession rates, and thus, if it remains fixed, *the level of costs does not affect the rate at which concession takes place.*

Expression (23) also indicates that higher rates of learning (for both players) reduce the time required by the bargaining process, as will higher rates of discounting. However, although an increase in player 1's discount rate a reduces $\bar{t}$, it need not reduce the product $a\bar{t}$. If it does reduce this expression too, then the higher discount rate is advantageous to the two players because it increases the expected value to each of them of the whole bargaining process—that is, the discount factor $e^{-a\bar{t}}$ is nearer unity.

Knowing the total bargaining time $\bar{t}$, it is possible to determine the actual point of agreement by substituting the value for $\bar{t}$ [equation (23)] into equations (21) in order to obtain $q_1(\bar{t})$ and $q_2(\bar{t})$.

$$q_1(\bar{t}) = \frac{M}{2} - \frac{1}{2}\frac{C_1}{af} + \frac{1}{2}\frac{C_2}{ag} + \frac{r_1' - r_2'}{2a}\left[\frac{\frac{C_1}{af} + \frac{C_2}{ag} + M}{\frac{r_1'}{a} + \frac{r_2'}{a}}\right]^{\frac{1+A}{1-A}} \tag{24}$$

As before, r_1' and r_2' are the expected concession rates at the start of the bargaining process.

The first three terms on the right of equation (24) may be seen to correspond to the solution for the symmetric case which we derived in Chapter III.[14] Thus a particularly useful property of equation (24) is that the far right hand term determines the *deviation* of the actual bargaining outcome from the "ideal" solution which would appear if bargaining took an infinite amount of time. Since the condition $r_1/r_2 = 1$ is only approached asymptotically in this model, while agreement takes a finite time, the outcome will not correspond to the "predicted" solution if the initial expected concession rates (r_1' and r_2') are not equal. It is an obvious conclusion that greater discrepancies between the two initially expected concession rates result in a greater deviation of the outcome from our "ideal" solution and hence a greater error in our model in predicting actual outcomes. Moreover, equation

(24) indicates that large values of A (near to unity) tend to decrease the error in the model, as will small values of C_1 and C_2 (the bargaining costs). This last conclusion is simply a consequence of the fact that high costs tend to reduce the time taken by the bargaining process and thus give the ratio r_1/r_2 less time to adjust to its stable value. Higher rates of learning will decrease the error by increasing A, in spite of their tendency to accelerate bargaining, because they bring about more rapid adjustments of r_1 and r_2. The impact of changes in the discount rate a is ambiguous, although in most reasonable cases ($\frac{1}{4} < A < 1$) increases in the discount rate can be shown to increase the error.[15] The ambiguity comes about because increases in the discount rate tend to decrease bargaining time by reducing initial demands as well as by increasing the adjustment rates of r_1 and r_2; the first of these effects tends to increase the error, the second to decrease it.

Finally, it must be pointed out that even the error term here is really only an approximation. Even if the players' learning behavior and the utility functions actually are linear as we have assumed, our results depend upon the instantaneous learning model which was chosen for our example. We are actually studying only the behavior of the intersection of the functions F and G without regard to any time lags which may appear in arriving at that intersection. Lagged models would naturally alter our error term somewhat.

A Numerical Example

The complete solution of the model makes it possible to put some numbers which correspond roughly to experience into the theory in order to get some indications of the magnitudes of the quantities which are involved. For the sake of variety, we will assume that the total amount of the payoff commodity which is to be divided is variable or unknown, in which case the P-index measure of the players' outcome demands is more appropriate than our quantity notation.[16] Such a model is obtained simply by substituting P_1 for q_1, and $M - P_2$ for q_2 in all of our equations, where M is now to be interpreted as some (arbitrary) maximum value which the P-index is likely to reach (M is constant in this interpretation, even if the total quantity whose division is indicated by P is not). As we have already pointed out, except for a few changes in sign (which are necessary to preserve the meaning of our expressions), the model is unchanged, and as it happens, equations (23) and (24) retain their forms completely.

Imagine a labor–management negotiation in which the wage may range between 0 and 100 (100 is simply an arbitrary upper bound which is chosen to exceed the highest wage demand which the union is likely to make).[17] We only have a complete solution for the symmetrical case, so we must assume the same discount and learning rates for both parties. Suppose the discount rate is .25, and the learning rate is .20, both on a yearly basis. Neither bargainer in a union–management dispute has any illusions about being able to obtain large and rapid concessions from the other— experience has shown that this is unlikely (and analysis of a model in which the players expect rapid concessions would suffice to show how such experience may come about). Thus let us assume initial expected concession rates of $r_1' = 12.5$ and $r_2' = 17.5$, where these are also on a yearly basis.

Consider first a case with no bargaining costs. In this case, expression (23) gives us a $\bar{t} = 1.67$; that is, it takes over a year and a half to reach agreement. On the other hand, the deviation from the "predicted" solution is only -1.87, so that the wage turns out to be 48.13 instead of 50 as is predicted by the simple model. This is not a large deviation considering the large discrepancy between r_1' and r_2' [equation (18) indicates that the initial demands are given by a union demand of 50, and a management offer of only 30].

Now let us add bargaining costs to the situation. Suppose the costs to the union are fairly high: $C_1/f = 3$, while the costs to the management are lower: $C_2/g = 1$.[18] These are sufficient to shorten the bargaining time to about .3 years, or 4 months (bargaining costs which summed to 5 or more would bring about immediate agreement). In this case, however, the deviation from the predicted outcome is -7.33; that is, the union gets a wage 7.33 less than would be predicted. It should be noticed also that the disproportionate costs have shifted the expected (Nash) solution. The predicted solution is now 46, having moved in management's favor because of the higher bargaining costs to the union. In view of these results, it is not hard to surmise why international negotiations, where learning and discount rates are probably lower than in the above example, where expectations may be more optimistic, and bargaining costs are practically zero, can last for years. Nevertheless, for the same reason we would expect that the outcomes will be fairly near to the Nash solution.

The above example is fairly sensitive to changes in the data. For example, a decrease in the learning rate from .20 to .15 in the case of zero bargaining costs has the consequence of increasing the length of the bargaining time to 1.95 and of increasing the error in the general prediction to -4.83. On the other hand, more similar values r_1' and r_2' would bring about a considerable reduction in the deviation (for example, if the difference $r_2' - r_1'$ were reduced to 2.5, the deviation would be halved).

▪ NOTES

1. These really represent an exponential theory of learning: if $\dot{q}_2$ were constant over time, equations (14) would imply:

$$r_2(t) = -\dot{q}_2 + [\dot{q}_2 + (r_2)_{t=0}] e^{-at}$$

2. The line $\dot{r}_1/\dot{r}_2 = r_1/r_2$ will be straight whenever the players' utility functions are linear, and whenever they are "symmetric" as defined in Chapter III.

3. Algebraically, we can express our equilibrium condition (using equation 14) as:

$$\frac{\dot{r}_1}{\dot{r}_2} = \frac{\beta}{\alpha} \frac{Ar_2 - r_1}{Br_1 - r_2} = \frac{r_1}{r_2} \tag{25}$$

which, when solved, gives:

$$\frac{r_1}{r_2} = \frac{\alpha - \beta + \sqrt{(\alpha - \beta)^2 + 4\alpha BAB}}{2\alpha B} \tag{26}$$

4. Suppose that we are at a state of agreement; if r_1 is increased, player 2 will demand a greater payoff, and for agreement to be restored, player 1 would have to demand a smaller payoff, which in turn, can happen only if r_2 is decreased.

5. In Chapter III we discussed the existence of uniqueness conditions which in our current notation may be written: $|(\delta A/\delta r_2)| < A/r_2$; $|(\delta \beta / \delta r_1)| < B/r_2$. These conditions may be derived here by requiring that the equilibrium locus always have a positive slope; that is, equation (26), derived in footnote 3, may never be permitted to represent a line with either vertical or horizontal slope. For example, writing the right hand side of (26) as X we always want $\delta/\delta r_2 (r_1/r_2) < \delta X/\delta r_2$. Applying this condition, it is straightforward to derive the same uniqueness criteria which we obtained in Chapter III.

6. This applies to "bluffing" in both of the first two meanings mentioned in note 1 of Chapter III.

7. If the learning theory is $\Delta r_2(t) = -\alpha [q_2(t-1) + r_2(t-1)]$, for example, we get the solution:

$$\Delta q_1{}^{(t)} = Z(t) [1 - \tfrac{1}{2}(\sqrt{AB})^t - \tfrac{1}{2}(\sqrt{AB})^{t-1} - \tfrac{1}{2}(-\sqrt{AB})^t$$
$$- \tfrac{1}{2}(\sqrt{AB})^{t-1}]$$

where $Z(t)$ corresponds to the solution of the simultaneous model:

$$Z(t) = \frac{A[Br_1(t-2) - r_2(t-1)]}{1 - AB}$$

8. For example, suppose that the two players are "similar" in the sense that they exhibit equal learning rates and equal discount rates ($a = b$ and $\alpha = \beta$). Assuming the utility functions to be linear (or symmetrical—see Chapter III), then equation (25), derived in note 3, becomes $r_1 = r_2$, duplicating our conclusion that in this exactly symmetrical situation, the players tend to form identical expectations during the course of the bargaining process (and this in turn leads to a Nash solution).

To see how these results are modified when the learning abilities of the two players differ, assume a *ceteris paribus* increase in the learning rate which is exhibited by player 1. If α is increased, then the quantity A must increase as well. Whenever the players' expectations appear in the concession area of Figure 6 (i.e., the conditions $Ar_2 < r_1$, $Br_1 < r_2$ are satisfied), an increase in A will decrease the magnitude of the expression $Ar_2 - r_1$. Thus we can see from equation (26) that the increase in α will decrease the value of the ratio $\dot{r}_1/\dot{r}_2$. It follows that any combination of expectations between the lines $Ar_2 = r_1$, $Br_1 = r_2$, will tend to move more westerly (less southerly) than before. Therefore the line $\dot{r}_1/\dot{r}_2 = r_1/r_2$ must lie above and to the left of its former position. We may conclude that the solution is characterized by a higher value of r_1 and a lower value of r_2

than before. This is the same conclusion regarding the consequences of greater learning ability as that which we obtained in Chapter III.

9. Define $P = (a/b) \sqrt{(A/B)}$. Then

$$\frac{dP}{da} = \frac{1}{b} \sqrt{\frac{A}{B}} + \frac{a}{b} \frac{1}{2} \sqrt{\frac{B}{A}} \frac{1}{B} \frac{\alpha}{\left[\frac{f''(q_1)}{f'(q_1)} r_2 - a\right]^2}$$

$$= \frac{1}{b} \sqrt{\frac{A}{B}} \left[1 + \frac{\alpha}{2\left[\frac{f''(q_1)}{f'(q_1)} r_2 - a\right]}\right] > 0$$

10. These constants are determined by differentiating equations (19) with respect to t and substituting the resulting $\dot{r}_1$ and $\dot{r}_2$ into equations (16). Setting $t = 0$ in the two resulting equations as well as in equations (19) yields the constants.

11. For example, it is straightforward to show that our conclusions regarding a stable relationship between r_1 and r_2 still hold. As time passes, t becomes large, and the terms $k_2 e^{x_2 t}$ and $m_2 e^{x_2 t}$ become small compared to $k_1 e^{x_1 t}$ and $m_1 e^{x_1 t}$ as we have already shown. It follows that the ratio $r_1(t)/r_2(t)$ approaches k_1/m_1 as $t \to \infty$. That is,

$$\frac{r_1}{r_2} \to \frac{A r_2' + \frac{1}{2}(\alpha - \beta + \sigma)r_1'}{B r_1' + \frac{1}{2}(-\alpha + \beta + \sigma)r_2'} =$$

$$\frac{\frac{1}{2}(\alpha - \beta + \sigma) \left[\frac{\beta A}{\frac{1}{2}(\alpha - \beta + \sigma)} r_2' + r_1'\right]}{\alpha B \left[r_1' + \frac{\frac{1}{2}(-\alpha + \beta + \sigma)}{\alpha B} r_1'\right]}$$

Multiplying out the expressions we find that

$$\frac{\beta A}{\frac{1}{2}(\alpha - \beta + \sigma)} = \frac{\frac{1}{2}(-\alpha + \beta + \sigma)}{\alpha B}$$

and hence that

$$r_1/r_2 \to \frac{\alpha - \beta + \sigma}{2\alpha B},$$

which is the same expression that we had before in equation (26). Furthermore, if

$$r_1'/r_2' = \frac{\alpha - \beta + \sigma}{2\alpha B},$$

then k_2 and m_2 are equal to zero, and r_1/r_2 remains constant until agreement is reached. The effect of the variations in the learning and discount rates is obvious from equation (25).

12. Recall that in Chapter III, when we demonstrated that a *ceteris paribus* increase in a player's learning rate worked to his disadvantage in terms of the point of disagreement, we qualified our conclusion by pointing out that more rapid learning behavior might also hasten agreement enough to compensate for the loss in outcome utility with a substantial saving in time. It is possible to obtain at least some information about the influence of a *ceteris paribus* change in one player's learning rate upon total negotiation time by differentiating the agreement condition $q_1 + q_2 = M$ [with equation (21) substituted into it] implicitly with respect to α (i.e., we are using player 1's learning rate) and making use of definitions (19).

If we make the assumptions of "similarity," $a = b$, $\alpha = \beta$, and add the condition $r'_1 = r'_2$ (that is, if we start at the "equilibrium" ratio of r_1 and r_2), then it is easy to show that $d\bar{t}/d\alpha = 0$. Thus, in this special case, a change in one player's learning rate will not alter the time necessary for agreement. In other words, if player 1, say, increases his learning ability, he will concede faster than before (because he is now more aware of the fact that player 2 is conceding more slowly than expected), but this same higher concession rate will be observed by the other player, reducing the latter's rate of giving in. It happens that in this exactly symmetrical case, the two effects just cancel, and the amount of time required by the bargaining process remains unchanged.

13. In deriving equation (23) [and later, equation (24)] it is useful to remember that under our "similarity" assumptions, $a = b$ and $\alpha = \beta$, our constants [equation (20)] become

$$x_1 = -\frac{\alpha}{1+A} \qquad x_2 = -\frac{\alpha}{1-A}$$

$$k_1 = \tfrac{1}{2}(r'_1 + r'_2) \qquad k_2 = \tfrac{1}{2}(r'_1 - r'_2) \qquad m_1 = k_1 \qquad m_2 = k_2$$

14. That is, equation (11) becomes

$$\frac{f}{g} = + \frac{fq_1 + C_1/a}{g\,(M - q_1) + C_2/a}$$

which reduces to

$$q_1 = \tfrac{1}{2}\left[M - \frac{C_1}{af} + \frac{C_2}{ag}\right]$$

This is simply the symmetric Nash outcome which we mentioned in Chapter I (note 4). Translating the cost factors C_1/a and C_2/a into their equivalents in real outcome space C_1/af, C_2/ag, we may assert that the players would divide the "goods" equally—that is, $q_1 + C_1/af = \frac{1}{2}(M + C_1/af + C_2/ag)$ where the left side represents player 1's portion and the right side represents the total available supply. This expression reduces to the same expression as the previous one.

15. Take logarithms and compare the expressions $d(\ln a)/da$ with $d[(1 + A)/(1 - A)]/da$.

16. See Chapter III, pp. 43–44.

17. Of course, the higher we make this upper limit, the less likely we are to have linear utility functions over the whole range of P. However, we need only assume that the functions are linear in the relatively small range over which the bargaining actually takes place.

18. We have not put down the costs C_1 or C_2 explicitly; we are simply assuming the costs to be such that when they are appropriately adjusted by the utility factors f and g, they may be compared to a change of 3 and 1 units of P (in one year) respectively.

V
▪ Arbitration

The bargaining process is an extremely costly way of distributing value. Compared to the ease and efficiency of the price system,
for example, exchange via negotiation is clumsy, time consuming,
and inconvenient, and it is very likely that a large share of the
value of a transaction will be absorbed in the business of performing it. Some markets do exist (the Arabian bazaars) in which all
commodities must be purchased via the bargaining process, and,
indeed, one needs only to observe the frequent irritation and ex-
asperation displayed by Americans when they encounter such
markets abroad to appreciate the value of the low transaction
costs which are experienced at home. This irritation is not just a
matter of difference in culture or custom. We have already shown
that the high costs of the bargaining process are really an integral
part of its operation: if steps are taken to reduce these costs, the
negotiation will simply take longer to work itself out. The expense is not simply an unfortunate but frequent companion to
bargaining; it is an essential part.

It is reasonable, therefore, to expect people to seek other mech-
anisms which can substitute for the bargaining process and which
will perform its services more efficiently. This is one of the incen-
tives which leads developing economies to replace barter with a
price system. Indeed, whenever it is possible to use established
rates of exchange, even if they are only set by tradition, there is

91

much to be gained by turning to these rather than undergoing extensive haggling over every transaction. Unfortunately, these alternatives are effective only when it is impossible for any single participant (or any small group of participants) to alter the rates of exchange through unilateral action. The very frequency with which negotiations occur is evidence that this requirement often is not satisfied. There are other means for shortcutting the bargaining process, however, and it is these which we shall discuss in this chapter. Since they all seem to have fundamental similarities in their effect upon a negotiation and upon its outcome, we shall classify them all under the term "arbitration."

The Definition of Arbitration

In our definition, "arbitration" is not interpreted as a part of the bargaining process but as a *substitute* for it. We take "arbitration" to be an appropriate term for any mechanism which selects a single outcome and then proposes that it be agreed upon immediately as an alternative to *all* further discussion. We are particularly concerned with cases in which this outcome is to be accepted *voluntarily*. By this we mean that if either party decides that he prefers the bargaining process to the proposed alternative outcome, then he may reject the arbitration, and his choice will be binding for both of them.

In our interpretation, an arbitrated solution has the further property that it is proposed by some agent not associated or allied with either negotiator. To be effective, he must be a neutral party. A short paradigm may clarify this notion of the arbitration process: A third party approaches the first two and makes only the following simple suggestion: "I have identified the state X as a possible point of agreement. I suggest that both of you accept X immediately and avoid all the expense of further negotiation. This outcome is inferior to the current payoff expectations of each one of you, but I calculate that the benefits which you would receive from early agreement would outweigh any losses associated with those smaller payoffs." The outcome X must be inferior to the current demands of both parties because otherwise immediate acceptance of X by both sides would already have been an available alternative. The point is that without the arbitration, neither party could have received the payoff associated with X without waiting for his opponent to concede to it. Arbitration makes it possible to achieve X immediately.

Each party, of course, is perfectly capable of calculating the (expected) benefits which he would receive from accepting X as the outcome; hence the only service performed by our arbitrator has been to make a suggestion. If this is so, then why is it a service which the original two parties could not perform for themselves? Why is the third party required to be disassociated with them? The answer is that it is not possible for arbitration, as we conceive of it, to take place unless two conditions are satisfied. First, the outcome X must be clearly presented as an alternative to further bargaining; and second, the outcome X must not be seen as a variable which is itself subject to negotiation. If the suggested agreement point were advanced by anyone who could be associated with one of the sides, then neither of these conditions could be likely to be satisfied. In the first place, it would be very difficult to make the proposed arbitration settlement appear as anything other than a new bid, even if the proposal could be quickly retracted if unaccepted. This bid would then be treated in the same way as any other change in demands; that is, it would tend to change expectations and to determine new counterbids. Thus, if one of the negotiators or an ally of his were to suggest an "arbitrated" outcome, that party thereby would run the risk of appearing very anxious to reach agreement, and even willing to make large concessions to do so. The likely result would be a hardening of the other party's position rather than an early settlement. It is by nature impossible to make a "move" during the bargaining process without having it react upon the expectations of the opponent. Thus it would be enormously difficult, especially in the atmosphere of overstatements and exaggerated defenses which usually accompanies negotiations, for one party to convince the other that he is not making a move at all but suggesting arbitration. In the second place, if it were made clear that the arbitration suggestion is not a bid, the absence of a neutral party would leave open the possibility of bargaining over the arbitration point itself. For example, if the first party suggests a settlement X, the other party may try for some other outcome Y which is more favorable to him. (After all, the choice of X was not a disinterested one.) The parties would then have to negotiate between the outcomes X and Y. As soon as this occurred, neither X nor Y would be a possibility for immediate acceptance, and the bargainers would simply revert to their original demands.

The conclusion that an outside agent is required for arbitration is by no means based upon any premise that the first two parties are stupid, or pig-headed, or so involved emotionally that obviously rational choices are not made; we maintain rather that the very nature of the bargaining process precludes self-arbitration. Nevertheless, it is important to recognize that this outside agent need not be a specially designated third individual; this role may be filled just as well by precedent, tradition, or even by the presence of a particularly prominent solution possibility which appears naturally to the negotiation. For example, if two friends simultaneously see a dollar bill lying in the street, they will automatically divide it (or its proceeds) equally. The principle of equal division is already well established in their culture and immediate acceptance of this solution is far superior to the unpleasant process of bargaining over the division. A similar but more complex case arises when heirs to an estate are presented with a collection of family heirlooms to divide among themselves. They frequently apply market values to the items and then use a rule of equity, dividing the goods so that the dollar shares of all the participants are equal. This may take place despite a certainty that none of the items shall ever be sold. In such a case market values are completely irrelevant and, therefore, they are a highly arbitrary means for representing the values to the heirs; nevertheless, this device is preferred to the bargaining process.

The principle that prominent outcome possibilities often appear as agreement points has already been proposed several times in the literature, so there is no need for us to elaborate upon it further here. A very thorough discussion has been put forward by T. C. Schelling in his *Strategy of Conflict*.[1] Schelling proposes that "focal points"—outcomes with numerological, cultural, or physical attributes which set them apart from alternative outcomes—provide the "solutions" to a wide variety of social problems. His analysis is concerned especially with problems of mutual coordination when no communication is possible, but from this case he extends his solution concept to the bargaining process itself. We would agree that negotiations often do end with agreement at some "focal point." However, this is not because the bargaining process leads to such points, but because focal points serve as effective substitutes for what would otherwise be a very expensive debate, that is, they are natural arbitration solutions.

We stated that we are primarily concerned with arbitrated solutions which can be accepted voluntarily by both parties. At first glance, it might appear that it is always possible to propose an agreement which both sides will prefer to further negotiation, given that our arbitrator is astute enough to identify the proper outcome. After all, if the two bargainers are going to agree on some outcome eventually, one should at least be able to propose that same outcome for arbitration, pointing out that neither party would suffer any real loss of payoff and that each would save the cost of further delay of agreement. The difficulty is that if the arbitration is to be accepted voluntarily, each party will compare the value of the proposed settlement, not with what he would actually receive from bargaining but with what he *expects* to receive, and the latter naturally is the larger quantity. The very fact that bargaining is taking place is sufficient to demonstrate that the expectations of at least one party are overoptimistic, and in most negotiations, of course, both sides will have to revise their expectations downward before agreement can be achieved. The fact that expectations are too optimistic is not in itself sufficient to make arbitration impossible, because immediate settlement always provides some saving in bargaining costs which can compensate for some loss of payoff. It is possible, nevertheless, that this saving is not sufficiently large, so that, for any arbitration agreement that may be proposed, at least one party will find it to be inferior to the expected value of the bargaining process and will therefore reject the early settlement.

Although we are concerned largely with voluntary arbitration, a few comments are in order with regard to "compulsory arbitration," that is, agreement by fiat. We have just noted that there always exists an outcome possibility which will benefit both sides if it is accepted immediately. The point at which ultimately they will agree is one such settlement point. The possibility that the two parties will not perceive the benefits of accepting this settlement immediately, and therefore that the arbitration would be resisted, might be used to justify an effort by some third party to dictate the outcome. After all, he is making them better off even if they don't know it. Of course, the negotiators would display a good deal of antagonism toward such a practice, but this would be due to erroneous expectations on their part and not to any losses which they would suffer in fact. As a practical matter, however, it is likely that the arbitrator is no more able to predict the outcome of the bargaining process, were it to continue, than are the parties themselves. Even worse, his decisions may not even reflect an attempt at such a prediction, but rather they may be based upon quite irrelevant criteria—notions of justice or equity or precedent—which have little to do with the eventual agreement. There is really no way to guarantee that compulsory arbitration will not make one of the parties substantially worse off than he would be otherwise, and it is likely that fear of such a result has contributed toward the widespread aversion to compulsory arbitration which is frequently encountered, especially in the area of labor disputes.[2]

An important property of our arbitration definition is that it is concerned with a phenomenon rather than the activities of any specially designated individual. Any third party whose interests are not closely tied with those of either negotiator can perform the service of arbitration, whatever his official function may be. We are aware that any third party usually becomes involved in many more ways than we have described here. One encounters outsiders engaging in all sorts of other activities, ranging from "representing the public interest" to "establishing standards of equity and justice" to "establishing a healthy emotional climate in which bargaining can take place." It is to be feared, for example, that the public image of labor mediators is essentially the same as that accorded to marriage counselors! The bargaining process, however, is not quite the same as a personality conflict and, especially in this chapter, we wish to focus upon the main problems associated with the division of value rather than with these other, admittedly important, problems.

The Agreement Point after Arbitration

We shall discuss three aspects of the arbitration process. First, we shall define the conditions under which it is possible. It seems to be generally believed that even though arbitration is not likely to be possible in the early stages of a negotiation, after a period of time a point will be reached when this process is possible. We wish to determine whether this belief is reflected in our model, and, if so, at what point arbitration does become feasible. Second, we shall consider the leeway which is available to an arbitrator in estimating a suitable point of agreement. If there exists only one settlement which would be accepted immediately by both parties, it is very unlikely that any third party could ever pinpoint it precisely, so that, for all practical purposes, successful arbitration may be impossible. Third, we shall investigate the relation between an arbitrated agreement and the outcome which we would expect to occur were the bargaining process to continue. For example, if initial expectations are skewed, one party expecting a great deal and the other expecting very little, will arbitration tend to preserve this skewness, increase it, or reduce it?

Analytically we follow our usual practice of considering the problem from the point of view of the first party. At each point in the negotiation he is expecting some payoff q_1, and he expects some period of time w to pass before he actually receives q_1. The value to him of the negotiation as a whole is therefore equal to the utility of q_1 minus the disutility of waiting for it. The net expected utility was derived in Chapter III:

$$U_1{}^* = \left[f(q_1) + \frac{C_1}{a} \right] e^{-aw} - \frac{C_1}{a} \qquad (5)$$

Here, as usual, $f(q_1)$ is a utility function, a is a discount rate, and C_1 is an additional bargaining cost which recurs in each period of time.

Let us define q_1' as a payoff which would be just acceptable to the first party as an arbitrated settlement. That is, he is indifferent between the choice of receiving q_1' immediately and the choice of continuing with the bargaining process as he sees it. Since the time costs associated with bargaining will tend to reduce the present value of any expected payoff, the acceptable arbitration payoff q_1' must be smaller than the first party's current demand. Algebraically, we can represent q_1' as follows:

$$f(q_1') = \left[f(q_1) + \frac{C_1}{a} \right] e^{-aw} - \frac{C_1}{a} \qquad (27)$$

In accordance with our interest in voluntary arbitration, we have compared q_1' to the *expected* value of the negotiation. In the usual case, of course, each party is demanding (and expecting) more than he will receive at agreement, and each is underestimating the amount of time that the negotiation will take. Thus, q_1 is larger and w is smaller than the "facts" would justify. Figure 10 represents the situation diagrammatically for a simple example in which two parties are negotiating over a variable quantity of some commodity which is infinitely divisible. Player 1 is demanding q_1, player 2 is demanding q_2, and they are willing to settle immediately for q_1' and q_2' respectively—q_1' and q_2' are, of course, only lower bounds from the point of view of the respective bargainers. Either party would willingly accept more in an arbitrated settlement.

Figure 10a represents a case in which there is plenty of room for an arbitrated settlement; any point in the range between p_1 and p_2 would be found by both parties to be preferred or equivalent to further bargaining. In Figure 10b, however, q_1' and q_2' are so large that no such range of settlement possibilities exists, and voluntary arbitration cannot occur. Compulsory arbitration is, however, always possible. For example, suppose it were known that the negotiation represented in Figure 10b would lead ulti-

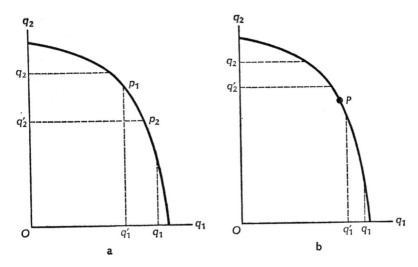

Figure 10

mately to the point P. Then that outcome could be used for compulsory arbitration, and despite the players' resistance, we would know that the result would benefit them both.

Equation (27) expresses q_1' as a function of q_1 and w. However, recall that w is itself a function of q_1. By definition, $w = (q_1 + q_2 - M)/r_2$. Thus q_1' is really determined by the variables $q_1, q_2,$ and r_2 subject to the parameters a and M. Furthermore, we already have another relation among these three variables, since q_1 was chosen so as to maximize expected utility, given q_2 and r_2. This optimum demand was given in Chapter III by equation (6):

$$f(q_1) + \frac{C_1}{a} = \frac{r_2}{a} f'(q_1) \tag{6}$$

If we use this equation to dispose of the r_2 term in equation (27), we obtain:

$$f(q_1') = \left[f(q_1) + \frac{C_1}{a} \right] e^{-(q_1 + q_2 - M)\frac{f'(q_1)}{f(q_1) + C_1/a}} - \frac{C_1}{a} \tag{28}$$

Our purpose in constructing this equation is to demonstrate that the settlement payoff q_1' can be determined from the players' current demands and the parameters M, C_1, and a. Thus we can look at any stage of the bargaining process purely in terms of the parties' demands and evaluate the potential for arbitration without having to make any specific reference to the expectations variable. This is an important result because this last variable, r_2, is virtually unobservable in practice, whereas the parties' demands are much more accessible (subject to distortions through bluffing). Moreover, these demands are comparable to the objects of our analysis, q_1' and q_2'.

As the reader may well imagine, the complexity of expression (28) makes it rather difficult to draw general conclusions regarding the characteristics of arbitrated agreements. Indeed, the best we can do here is to investigate thoroughly a very simplified example and then indicate how the implications derived from this model would be modified if we were to relax the simplifying restrictions. It should not be inferred, incidentally, that anyone who aspires to be a professional arbitrator would have to develop facility in solving pairs of equations such as expression (28). It is in fact a relatively straightforward matter to calculate whether or not a particular arbitration suggestion is consistent with a given model. The difficulty arises when we try to discover functions to represent the complete boundary lines between acceptability and nonacceptability. To obtain the boundaries which are discussed in the following sections, equation (28) has been "solved" by taking points from the graph of the function.

A Simple Arbitration Model

We shall resort to a simplification which was also used in parts of Chapter IV: that is, we let the utility functions be linear ($U_1 = fq_1$ and $U_2 = gq_2$) and we disregard any recurring costs of bargaining so that C_1 and C_2 equal 0. Using these assumptions, equation (28) becomes:

$$q_1' = q_1 e^{-(q_1 + q_2 - M)/q_1} \tag{29}$$

Similarly for player 2:

$$q_2' = q_2 e^{-(q_1 + q_2 - M)/q_2} \qquad (30)$$

Arbitration is possible whenever the two players are willing to settle immediately for payoffs which sum to no more than the total available quantity; that is, whenever $q_1' + q_2' \leqslant M$. In Figure 11 we have graphed all the combinations of expected payoffs q_1 and q_2 which, according to equations (29) and (30), make arbitration just possible: $q_1' + q_2' = M$; this is the outer frontier on the diagram. All demand pairs which fall on or within this frontier are amenable to arbitration; corresponding to each of these points, there exists some set of points on the payoff frontier which both parties will accept in lieu of further negotiation.

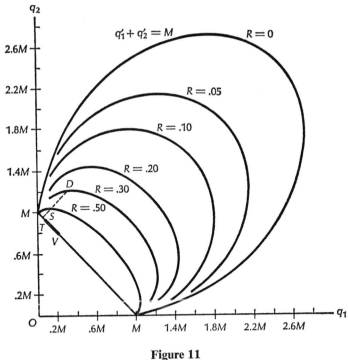

Figure 11

It is apparent from the frontier in Figure 11 that our first intuitive proposition regarding the possibility of arbitration is reflected in our model. That is, arbitration may not be possible early in a negotiation because demands are so optimistic that they fall outside the frontier, but after a period of time this will cease to be true. Concessions which bring the players' demands closer to agreement will also tend to bring them inside the arbitration frontier, and settlement points will become available for immediate adoption.

The most striking feature of the area bounded by $q'_1 + q'_2 = M$ is the enormous range of demands which appears to be consistent with early settlement, especially if the demands are fairly symmetric. For example, if they are equal to one another, they may sum to nearly five times the total amount which is available for division and still remain amenable to arbitration! Even if they are not equal to one another, the range is large and, what is especially significant, early settlement is always possible so long as neither party is demanding more than the total available supply M. Such a dramatic result as this leads one first to question the simplifications and assumptions of the model which produced it. There does not appear to be any variable, however, inside the model or out of it, which has been so grossly mistreated in principle as to generate an erroneous conclusion of this magnitude. If there are no such weaknesses in the analysis, we are next led to wonder why people ever bargain at all. Why not arbitrate all disputes? We shall discuss this issue at some length after having developed the model further.

The Ease of Arbitration

The large area bounded by the frontier $q'_1 + q'_2 = M$ in Figure 11 may be misleading if we rely on it for estimates of the ease of achieving an early settlement to a negotiation. For example, if a demand pair falls on the frontier itself, there is only one agreement possibility which both parties would accept voluntarily in lieu of further bargaining. We certainly could not expect any outside party to be able to pinpoint this outcome exactly so long as the demands are so far from agreement. Early settlement is not a practical possibility unless the arbitrator has some margin for error when he recommends an agreement point, and it is quite possible that this margin does not become large enough until the demands fall well within our frontier.

We will often use the phrase, "distance between the two negotiators" as a convenient way of expressing the difference between the sum of the two players' demands and the total available supply. In any negotiation, the distance between the parties is the amount of concession which must be made by one or both sides before agreement is possible. Now, as a first approximation, a useful measure of the ease of arbitration might be given by the range of acceptable arbitration points—the "leeway" available to the arbitrator—expressed as a proportion of this distance. For example, if the two demands sum to 10 units more than the available supply (the demands are "10 units apart"), and if the set of acceptable arbitration points are all within ±.25 units of an equal division, then a range equalling only 5 per cent of the distance between the two negotiators contains possible arbitration agreements. In practice, finding a point within such relatively close limits would probably be a very difficult matter. If we consider arbitration to be essentially impractical until the set of possible settlements fills at least 10–20 per cent of the distance between demands, then a good deal of concession beyond the frontier $q_1' + q_2' = M$ may be necessary before arbitration will be effective.

Let us use the symbol R to represent the ratio of the "leeway" available to the arbitrator to the "distance between the negotiators." In Figure 11 we have represented some typical values of R for various combinations of current demands. The diagram is drawn to scale. Each of the curves in the figure represents a locus of demand pairs which lead to the same ratio between the range of potential arbitration points and the distance between the negotiators. Curves are drawn for R equal to .05, .1, .2, .3, and .5. R is zero, of course, on the outer frontier. If, as we have suggested, arbitration is unlikely to be successful until this variable attains a value at least of the order of .1 and .2, then it is clear from the figure that a good deal of concession must take place within the outermost frontier before an early settlement will occur: the demands must be less than half those which are represented on the frontier itself. It is still true, however, that arbitration is possible while expectations are highly optimistic; for example, if the two parties' demands are equal, they can sum to almost twice the available supply and still give a range of possible arbitrations which covers 30 per cent of the distance between them.

Measures of the leeway available in locating a possible early settlement point are useful, but they are, nevertheless, only partial indicators of the difficulty which an arbitrator might encounter in proposing an early settlement. They should certainly be supplemented with a consideration of the likelihood that commonly applied principles of arbitration will lead to settlements which will be accepted by both sides. For example, if it is possible to end a negotiation simply by "splitting the difference," then the task of the arbitrator may be quite easy despite a very low value of R. On the other hand, it is quite possible for R to be relatively large and for simple symmetric arbitration rules to fail. As an example of this latter possibility, suppose that the two parties' demands are given by $q_1 = .3M$ and $q_2 = 1.2\ M$. These demands are represented by point D in Figure 11. Applying equations (29) and (30), these demands give $q'_1 = .0567M$ and $q'_2 = .7911M$, and the resulting range of possible arbitration agreements corresponding to D is TV, the heavily drawn portion of the payoff frontier. Now suppose the arbitrator suggested splitting the difference. The distance between the negotiators being $.5M$ units, this would mean that each party would give up $.25M$ units, taking them to point S on the diagram. However, this would leave the first party with a payoff of only $.05M$ units, an amount less than he was willing to settle for. Therefore the arbitration would be rejected. This is true despite the fact that the "leeway" which is available equals 30 per cent of the distance between bargainers.

Splitting the difference appears to be among the simplest and most frequently used of arbitration schemes; in fact, as we have already pointed out, it often embodies such a strong social norm that negotiators can apply it to themselves, without needing any assistance from some third party. As it happens, it is a relatively simple matter to determine the conditions under which this particular rule will provide a satisfactory candidate for an early settlement. In Figure 11 we represented an example of a case in which splitting the difference would not work; that is, if the parties' demands were found at the point D, then this rule would identify an outcome at S, and this point would be rejected as an arbitration settlement. The objection comes from the first party: although he is already making the smaller demand, the point S is even more heavily biased against him. This observation leads to the suggestion, which is confirmed by other examples, that whenever splitting the difference is rejected, it will be the party with the *smaller* current demand who is responsible for the veto. Given this result, the model can be analyzed in two parts, considering first all those cases in which the first party is making the smaller demand ($q_2 > q_1$), seeking those conditions under which he is just willing to accept the suggested settlement point, and then treating the second class of cases ($q_2 < q_1$).

Let us represent the payoffs which the players would receive from splitting the difference with the symbols q_1^o and q_2^o for players 1 and 2, respectively. Thus the arbitrator is asking the first party to reduce his demand by an amount $q_1 - q_1^o$, and the second party to reduce his demand by $q_2 - q_2^o$. By the nature of the splitting of the difference rule, $q_1 - q_1^o = q_2 - q_2^o$. Naturally, since ($q_1^o, q_2^o$) is a possible agreement point, $q_1^o + q_2^o = M$. The first party will be just willing to accept this settlement when q_1^o is equal to the smallest payoff which he is willing to substitute for the bargaining process as a whole; that is, when $q_1^o = q_1'$. Putting all of this together we have:

$$q_1 - q_1' = q_2 - (M - q_1')$$

It is convenient to rewrite this expression as follows:

$$2(q_1 - q_1') = q_1 + q_2 - M$$

We may now substitute the expression for q_1' from equation (29) and divide through by q_1

$$2(1 - e^{-(q_1+q_2-M)/q_1}) = (q_1 + q_2 - M)\frac{1}{q_1}$$

This expression is easily solved to give $(q_1 + q_2 - M)/q_1 = +1.5936$, which in turn implies:

$$q_2 = .5936q_1 + M \qquad (31)$$

Equation (31) is a linear function, and it is drawn as a straight line between the points M_2 and Q on Figure 12. A similar analysis can be applied to cases in which $q_1 > q_2$, and we then obtain another straight line between the points M_1 and Q. Thus the triangle M_1QM_2 bounds the desired area: whenever the two parties' demands identify a point on or within this triangle, the whole negotiation can be arbitrated by the simple device of splitting the difference. This same device will fail if the demands appear outside the triangle.

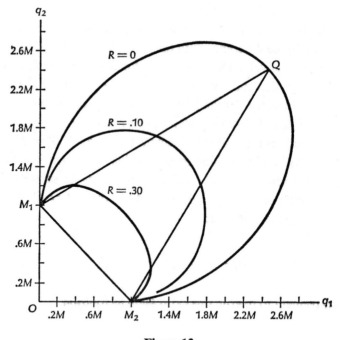

Figure 12

The triangle M_1QM_2 gives us what is probably the most useful measure of the ease of arbitrating a negotiation. The difficulty in arriving at an early settlement is not simply due to the magnitude of a disagreement—the distance between the parties' demands—but also to the technical difficulty which is encountered in locating an acceptable point for agreement. If a simple symmetric rule can be applied successfully, then even if the bargainers have enormously overoptimistic expectations, arbitration is not difficult. Of course, as the figure suggests, the more optimistic the expectations, the less likely it is that the demands will fall within the triangle and that such a simple rule will be workable.

We could apply this same sort of analysis to arbitration rules other than splitting the difference, although there do not seem to be any other rules which enjoy sufficiently widespread use to justify an extensive discussion of them here. As an example, one might consider the possibility of maintaining payoff proportions rather than requiring equal concessions. That is, defining q_1^o and q_2^o as the payoffs to be received by the two parties if they accept this suggested arbitration plan, we could require:

$$\frac{q_1^o}{q_2^o} = \frac{q_1}{q_2}$$

If we were to solve equations (29) and (30) for the set of demands under which this device will operate successfully, we would obtain an area similar to, but very slightly larger than, the triangle M_2QM_1. As it happens, however, there is a good reason for rejecting this as a useful arbitration rule: whereas the splitting-the-difference device can be applied to any negotiation in which the distance between the parties is measurable, this maintain-the-proportions rule would require that we be able to measure all payoffs from some origin. As a practical matter, this is often not possible. Negotiations over a wage rate, for example, are amenable to splitting the difference, but not to maintaining proportions, because there is no natural zero from which to measure the payoff increments. On the other hand, any negotiation for which the proportions rule is applicable can be treated equally well with our original device of splitting the difference. Thus, we would not add anything to the ease of arbitration, but only provide an alternative rule for some situations. Proposing such alternatives, moreover, may be more hazardous than beneficial. A particular advantage of the splitting-the-difference rule is that negotiators can apply it to their own dispute without any third party assistance. If there were several commonly accepted arbitration principles, the negotiators would surely start bargaining over the choice of which one to use, and thus defeat their own purpose. For this reason, it is desirable to have as *few* arbitration rules as possible.

The Nature of the Settlement

As our examples suggest, the use of arbitration does not permit the kind of equilibrium adjustment which we observed in the case of the bargaining process itself. In Chapters III and IV we discussed an important central tendency in the bargaining process, finding that even if the parties entertain widely disparate expectations initially, this asymmetry will tend to be reduced during the bargaining process, so that the agreement point appears very near to an outcome which could be predicted without any knowledge of the initial demands. Unfortunately, arbitration appears to work in just the opposite direction. Disparities in arbitrated payoffs are likely to be even greater than disparities in the demands existing before the arbitration takes place. Here "disparity" is not meant to be taken in an absolute sense. The two agreement payoffs q_1^o and q_2^o may well be closer to one another arithmetically than are the demands q_1 and q_2. The ratio of the two arbitrated agreement payoffs, however, is likely to be farther from the predicted ratio than was the ratio of current demands. For example, Figure 11 represents a perfectly symmetric bargaining problem; since it is symmetric, the model in the previous chapters would suggest a symmetric outcome: $q_1 = q_2 = \frac{1}{2}M$. At point D in Figure 10, however, the ratio $q_1/q_2 = .25$, and the corresponding range of arbitration points will give ratios q_1^o/q_2^o ranging from .06 to .26. Therefore the ratio of payoffs in the arbitrated agreement is likely to be much smaller than the ratio of the demands represented at D, while the latter is already smaller than the predicted ratio of unity.

We recognized in Chapter IV that as long as the payoff expectations of the parties do not satisfy our equilibrium relationship initially, they will not do so at the time of agreement either. The reason is that, even without arbitration, a settlement is bound to be reached before the adjustment is completed. Thus some asymmetry will be preserved. Nevertheless, this asymmetry is far smaller than that which will occur if arbitration takes place. Consider the example which we used at the end of Chapter IV (the case in which C_1 and $C_2 = 0$). Figure 13 represents this example on a graph whose axes represent payoffs to the two parties respectively. The initial demands, $q_1 = 5$, $q_2 = 8$, are amenable to arbitration, the possible range of outcomes being given by the heavily drawn portion of the payoff frontier. The point of agreement from the bargaining process was determined in Chapter IV to be $q_1 = 4.813$ and $q_2 = 5.187$. This outcome is represented by the point P in the figure. The point N is the predicted (Nash) outcome. It can be seen from the figure that the arbitration range does not include P and, in fact, it appears entirely on the "wrong" side of P (the side away from N).

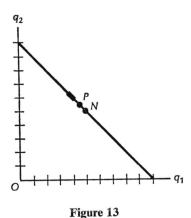

Figure 13

If the arbitration makes use of the simple rule of splitting the difference, we can expect disparities in demands to be intensified quite significantly. In part, this is simply a matter of arithmetic. Suppose that $q_2 > q_1$ and we achieve agreement by subtracting a quantity Δ from each demand. The resulting settlement ratio

$(q_1 - \Delta)/(q_2 - \Delta)$ is necessarily smaller than the original demand ratio q_1/q_2.[3] In addition, the dynamic properties of arbitration will lead to agreement points biased away from our predicted equilibrium solution. For example, we argued that "splitting the difference" will be an effective rule whenever the parties' demands fall within the triangular area M_2QM_1 in Figure 12. Suppose that the demands are outside this triangle, that concessions take place (moving us generally toward the Nash point), and that soon after we move into the triangle, the negotiation is arbitrated. In this case, as our derivation has shown, the settlement will be found near the outer edge of the arbitration range, away from the Nash solution.

Generalizing the Model

All of the conclusions in the preceding sections were derived from a very specific example in which utility functions are linear and in which the bargaining costs, C_1 and C_2, can be neglected. These restrictions arose largely as a matter of necessity, more general cases appearing to be much too cumbersome to be treated easily. Nevertheless, there is no reason why the consideration of more general cases should change the tenor of our conclusions; indeed, the consequences of generalizing the model are quite straightforward. For example, with any given set of current demands, positive bargaining costs will increase the likelihood of an early arbitration, simply because the higher are the bargaining costs, the greater is the saving which arbitration affords. We would expect the presence of diminishing marginal utility to have roughly the same prospects for increasing the likelihood of early arbitration, because each party is then more willing to forego a few marginal units of expected payoff in order to save the entire costs of negotiation.

It is easy to show further that the usefulness of "splitting the difference" is greater, the higher are the recurring costs of bargaining (C_1 and C_2). This, of course, is a reflection of the generally higher willingness to accept arbitration when such costs are high. Solving equation (28) for the point where the first party is just willing to accept a split-the-difference outcome, we obtain essentially the same solution as before:[4]

$$\frac{q_1 + q_2 - M}{q_1 + C_1/af} = 1.5936$$

Solving this for q_2, we obtain:

$$q_2 = .5936q_1 + M + 1.5936\frac{C_1}{af} \qquad (32)$$

Equation (32) only applies to the case in which $q_2 > q_1$. When the reverse is true, we must solve for the demands which leave the second party marginally willing to accept arbitration. This gives us a relation similar to (32):

$$q_1 = .5936q_2 + M + 1.5936\frac{C_2}{b} \qquad (33)$$

In Figure 14 we have graphed some representative examples of equations (32) and (33), using values for C_1/af and C_2/bg of

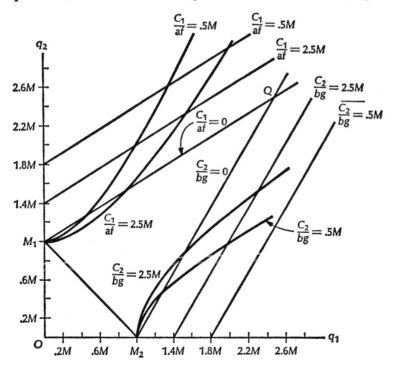

Figure 14

.25 M and .5 M. These are the straight lines with slopes equal to the slopes of the sides of the triangle M_1QM_2. As we expected, the range of conditions under which splitting the difference will lead to a satisfactory arbitration agreement expands as the recurring bargaining costs increase.

Limits on the Skewness of Payoff Demands

We have been discussing Figures 10 to 14 as though the parties' demands could conceivably fall anywhere within the positive quadrant. Intuitively, however, it seems quite unlikely that we would ever find situations in which one party is demanding an enormous payoff while the other expects very little. The latter player may conclude that although his demand is "optimal," it is still not worth the wait and therefore he may refuse to negotiate altogether. This can only occur when the recurring bargaining costs are positive: the discount process alone can never reduce the value of a payoff below zero.

We can determine the point at which a party will break off a negotiation by considering a case in which the present value of an optimal demand is equal to zero. Of course, this is given by equation (27) with zero substituted for the utility of the arbitration payoff. If we use our simplification in which the utility functions are taken to be linear, this becomes:

$$
\begin{aligned}
0 &= (q_1 + \frac{C_1}{af})e^{-\frac{q_1+q_2-M}{q_1+C_1/af}} - \frac{C_1}{af} \\
0 &= (q_2 + \frac{C_2}{bg})e^{-\frac{q_1+q_2-M}{q_2+C_2/bg}} - \frac{C_2}{bg}
\end{aligned}
\tag{34}
$$

These boundaries are drawn in Figure 14 for the same values of C_1/af and C_2/bg which were used to construct the arbitration boundaries for the split-the-difference rule. In the diagram they are the curved lines emanating from M_1 and M_2.

The Use of Substitutes for the Bargaining Process

Certainly the most prominent result which arises from the analysis in this chapter is the enormous range of demands which are susceptible to arbitration. Indeed, Figure 14 suggests qualitatively that if the recurring costs of bargaining are high, then it will be extremely unusual to have a negotiation in which (1) neither party has already decided that he prefers disagreement and (2) in which arbitration is not already possible. If this is the case, then why is the bargaining process used so frequently? Why is it not the relatively rare event that the preceding sections would seem to imply?

One answer could be that true bargaining *is* very rare, and that in most cases all we are observing is the *semblance* of bargaining, a sham which has been put up for the sake of good "public relations." Certainly there is some truth in such an argument; it seems to be widely believed, for example, that a good deal of false bargaining takes place during labor negotiations. This behavior is supposed to be a consequence of the participants' desire to impress and solace their "backers"—union members and stockholders—by appearing to "drive a hard bargain." Apart from this possibility, however, it is likely that our model has greatly overstated the possibility of applying principles of arbitration to some types of negotiations. Throughout this study we have made use of a particularly simple paradigm, a rather artificial example in which two individuals seek to divide a fixed quantity of some well-defined and perfectly homogeneous commodity. A model of this type is useful because it illuminates the fundamental symmetry of the bargaining process and because it simplifies exposition: an analysis of the decisions of one party may be applied directly and unaltered to the other party as well. Since such an example does seem to be a natural and appropriate one for the discussion of bargaining processes, it is rather surprising that negotiations of this type never seem to arise in practice, even when the technical preconditions are satisfied. The author must admit that he has never observed an extensive negotiation over a fixed quantity of a homogeneous good, whether it be a cake or even a large sum of money. Instead, the bargaining that we see occurring around us always seems to be concerned with a multitude of incommensurable issues all at once or with *indices* of one sort or another, indices which allocate a value which is itself very difficult to measure. For example, it is hard to call to mind any historical examples of negotiations which have taken place over the division of sums of money, but it is easy to think of cases of negotiations over prices—wage rates, tariff rates, prices under bilateral monopoly, and the like. The distinguishing characteristic of these latter cases is that enormous difficulties arise in any attempt to quantify the real values which are to be distributed by the negotiations, and this makes the application of simple arbitration principles nearly impossible.

Our analysis in this chapter has suggested that we will rarely see negotiation over homogeneous commodities simply because these disputes are so easy to arbitrate. When the parties are dividing a cake or a fixed sum of money, there is obviously no possibility that either one could get more than the whole sum, and most bargainers, even at first, would probably expect a relatively equal division. If M is the total amount to be divided, then we *always* expect to find $q_1 \leqslant M$ and $q_2 \leqslant M$. It is, of course, possible that expectations are highly optimistic and the two parties are making explicit demands $q_1 = M$ and $q_2 = M$ simply because M is the most that they could conceivably get. It is much more likely, however, that both of the parties recognize very well that they will not receive as much as M, and that each will estimate the other's concession rate with this in mind. Thus we will generally find $q_1 < M$ and $q_2 < M$. Referring again to Figure 12, this means that any pair of demands will fall within the triangle M_1QM_2. Thus the negotiation can immediately be arbitrated by splitting the difference. It follows that the reason we do not in general observe extended negotiations over the division of any fixed, homogeneous commodity is that the parties can always make use of a simple, widely accepted division rule which each finds preferable to the bargaining process. There are only two possible exceptions to this result: (1) expectations of concession rates may be so optimistic that at least one of the parties would demand more than M if it were possible, and (2) splitting the difference may not provide a strong enough focal point for one or both parties, so that negotiation over the arbitration point breaks out. For the vast majority of practical division problems, neither of these possibilities seems to be very likely to arise.

It is also very likely that many negotiations which are in fact arbitrated are misinterpreted as examples of bargaining. Unlike the bargaining process, arbitration rules cannot be implemented without knowledge of the limits to the range of possible settlements. If one is to arbitrate a dispute one must estimate the "real" demands of the two parties before it is possible to split the remaining difference between them. Suppose that two parties are negotiating over the price of a house for which the seller recently paid $15,000 and for which the buyer is willing to pay no more than $20,000. A split-the-difference rule would determine a price of $17,500. If the seller had originally paid $10,000, however, the same arbitration scheme would lead to a $15,000 price, quite a different result. Naturally, then, whenever arbitration is to be used, each party will take a great deal of care to ascertain that the limits of the bargaining range are correctly defined, or at least that they are not biased against himself. In fact, much more emphasis will be placed on these issues than will be the case during the bargaining process itself. Thus the normal case of a negotiation which is resolved by arbitration will very likely include some discussion and debate between the parties concerning the "facts" of the situation. It appears from this analysis that the term "bargaining" is popularly applied to two entirely different situations: (1) the bargaining process as we have defined it, a process which takes a considerable amount of time and in which discussions between the parties emphasize current demands, the benefits to be gained from specific concessions, the relevance of calendar time, and so on; and (2) the arbitration process which is characterized by quick agreement and in which the parties studiously avoid making specific demands and instead emphasize the "facts" which determine the limits of the bargaining range. As a practical matter, these two phenomena appear to be quite easy to distinguish empirically.

The bargaining process will be used only when arbitration cannot easily be implemented, and we can identify three separate circumstances under which this will be the case. First, for one of a variety of reasons, the third agent which is required for arbitration may be missing. If the payoffs are multidimensional or highly qualitative in nature, a single-dimensioned, quantitative rule such as splitting the difference is simply not applicable, and therefore the parties can not arbitrate the dispute for themselves. Other focal points are possible (for instance, rivers make "natural" boundaries between nations), but if they do not happen to arise, arbitration without the assistance of a third party is out of the question. If there is no third individual whom both sides can accept as "impartial," then arbitration may never occur. As an example, the location of true "neutrals" is indeed a formidable task in the case of international disputes, and therefore we rarely encounter arbitrated settlements in this area.

The second possible reason for the failure of arbitration is that even though early settlement is possible and a neutral arbitrator is available, the technical difficulties in identifying a mutually acceptable agreement point are so great that, for all practical purposes, such an outcome will never be found. This is especially true if, in contrast to our simple examples, the negotiation is concerned with several issues simultaneously (such as a labor negotiation concerned with wages, overtime, a guaranteed annual wage, retirement benefits, the company medical plan, allowable time off the job, grievance procedures, permission to perform union activities on company time, and a dozen other issues). In such cases, the arbitrator (unless he is a wizard) will almost certainly suggest a settlement point that is not Pareto optimal. Naturally, selection of a point inside the utility possibility frontier will tend to reduce the arbitrator's margin for error, so that even if the range of possible settlements is large relative to the distance between the negotiator's demands, it may be extremely small relative to the number of plausible options which present themselves to the arbitrator. In general, then, we expect that the more complex the issues are, the less likely it is that arbitration will take place, and hence the more likely it is that the bargaining process will have to be used.

The third circumstance which will require the use of the bargaining process is that in which arbitration itself is impossible. In the case of the division of a fixed quantity of some commodity, we can argue that the expectations of the players will be set "realistically" ($q_1 < M$ and $q_2 < M$) in which case arbitration (via splitting the difference) will be acceptable. In other situations, however, the limits of a bargaining range are not nearly so clearly defined, and it is quite likely that one or both of the parties will make demands which exceed these limits. In the case of wage rate negotiations or international disputes, one party is frequently heard complaining that the other side's demands are not only overoptimistic but totally impossible (although, of course, it is quite another matter to convince the second party of that fact). Moreover, examples abound (as in international negotiations again) in which, after protracted discussions, the parties have come to no agreement at all because none proved to be available. Thus it is frequently the case that demands do exceed the total capacity of the situation, and whenever this is true, it is perfectly possible that there is no room at all for arbitration; hence further bargaining is necessary before an outcome which is beneficial to both can be discovered.

The second and third points above emphasize the fact that bargaining can be a *productive* process. If the parties have not yet identified a range of potential agreements (as in the examples of international disputes), or if their current expectations are not yet efficient (in the sense of being on the Pareto optimal frontier), then further bargaining has the effect of creating value. Indeed, we expect most observed bargaining processes to have some benefit of this sort since, if their sole role were the distribution of a known quantity, they would be amenable to immediate arbitration. The benefit may not be worth its cost, of course, because of the overoptimism which characterizes disagreement, but the expense of bargaining is certainly not all dead weight.

Recognition of the productive element in the bargaining process introduces an important reason for avoiding the use of compulsory arbitration as a means of "resolving" disputes. It often appears that if one party demands X and the other wants Y, then some intermediate point would be acceptable, in the sense that the enforcement of such an outcome would involve little more than the loss of the parties' "bargaining rights" in what is essentially an exercise in *distribution*. If the dispute is imposing heavy costs upon some third party or the public at large, compulsory arbitration might appear to be worth this price. We now must recognize, however, that it may also impose a real loss of value upon the parties as well as a loss of "rights." Moreover, compulsory arbitration is also dangerous for a second reason. If it is true that the bargaining process is in use because overoptimistic expectations have led to demands which are outside the range of potential agreements, then there is no guarantee that the compulsory intermediate point is not also outside that range. It may be that the compulsory solution not only leaves one party worse off than he expected to be, but even worse off than he would have been with no agreement at all—with permanent disagreement. As a result, the conditions of such an artificial "settlement" would have to be enforced through some legal or political authority, and as soon as that authority was relaxed, the "agreement" would vanish. We will return to this matter in Chapter VIII.

Finally, as a general rule, we expect arbitration to be used at some point in *all* negotiations. It is unlikely that the bargaining process will ever be continued all the way to agreement, because as that point is approached, arbitration becomes increasingly easy. Eventually, an arbitrated settlement should not be at all difficult to implement, no matter how complex the issues are. As a consequence, the negotiation will require less time to reach a settlement than was suggested by the examples in Chapter IV. How much sooner it arrives depends, of course, upon all of the factors which have already been discussed.

▪ NOTES

1. Thomas Schelling, *The Strategy of Conflict* (Cambridge, Mass.: Harvard University Press, 1960), pp. 53–80.

2. Of course, compulsory arbitration is not usually used because it benefits the parties, but because further negotiation would impose losses upon other members of society. This issue is treated separately in Chapter IX.

3. Suppose $(q_1 - \Delta)/(q_2 - \Delta) > q_1/q_2$; then, multiplying out, $q_1q_2 - q_2\Delta > q_1q_2 - q_1\Delta$, which reduces to $q_1 > q_2$, which contradicts the original relation between the demands.

4. The solution technique is exactly the same as that used to obtain equation (31), except that $C_1 \neq 0$.

VI

▪ On the Use of Force, Threats, Promises, and Other Dirty Tricks

In Chapter I we suggested that within the bargaining problem one can distinguish three separate elements, dealing with, respectively, the bargaining process, the outcome of that process, and the choice of disagreement costs. Referring to the diagram in Figure 15, we may characterize these three as (1) the process of conceding along points on the utility frontier, (2) the determination of an outcome P on the frontier, and (3) the choice of disagreement point O which represents the payoffs to the two negotiators before agreement is reached. So far, our analysis has treated the disagreement conditions to be fixed, and we have considered only the first two of these dimensions; we shall now treat the third in more detail.

In this study we have always been concerned with negotiations in which an agreement beneficial to both parties is possible. Thus the origin of the utility possibility curve is always determined by the status quo *during* the bargaining process, and by no means may it be interpreted as "disagreement" in the sense of abandoning the negotiation altogether. In an attempt to keep attention focused upon this interpretation, we shall henceforth use the term *preagreement* rather than "disagreement" in discussing the state

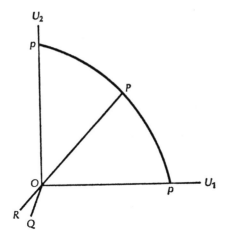

Figure 15

of affairs before a negotiation is concluded. In general, we expect preagreement costs to be higher than the disagreement costs: during the negotiation, the parties not only do not have a settlement (they are in "disagreement") but they also must bear the costs which are associated with the bargaining process itself (inconvenience, hiring of lawyers, emotional stress, temporarily foregone benefits of other forms of cooperation, and the like).

In practice a large portion of the preagreement costs are subject to the discretion of the negotiators: the use of violence, threats of violence, political and economic pressures, commitments, and assorted tactical devices are commonly treated as possibilities which may have a substantial influence on the outcome and which may or may not be used depending on the choice of the negotiators themselves. Indeed, many authors, by the proportion of their efforts devoted to these topics, seem to imply that "tactics" comprise the most important element in all of bargaining theory.[1] Despite the probable significance of this element, however, we shall resist any temptation to deal with it in isolation, because it is very clear that *an adequate analysis of the determination of preagreement costs is impossible without first providing a suitable theory of the bargaining process itself*. The impact on the outcome of a shift in origin from O to Q (see Figure 15) can be understood only in terms of the process of concession which translates those initial conditions into an outcome. As we shall see, even the *direction* of impact of some cost imposing actions may be ambiguous without such a theory.

These comments apply to the practicing negotiator as well as to the theorist. The party who indulges in the uses of force without sufficient knowledge as to how they may affect the point of agreement runs the certain risk of doing more damage than good to his own cause. A threat to burn down an opponent's house, challenge him in a primary election, or destroy his cities (or the carrying out of any of these actions) may well work to the threatener's own disadvantage, and it may require extensive experience and insight into the negotiation *process* to determine under what circumstances such uses of force can be effective.

In this chapter we shall examine a simple static model which associates alternative preagreement cost vectors with alternative outcomes, and which disregards the dynamic elements of cost changing decisions. Then, in the next chapter, we will be able to extend the model to one in which the problems of individual perception and expectations are explicitly considered. The need for a theory which permits the introduction of variable bargaining costs into the theory of negotiation was recognized by Nash himself soon after he formulated his basic outcome theorem. Moreover, it proves to be a relatively simple matter to apply the model which he developed for this purpose to our own somewhat more general case. An adaptation of the Nash approach, then, will provide the framework for our preliminary discussion below.

Notation

The negotiation costs with which we are concerned arise either as recurring costs (our per period utility costs C_1 and C_2) or as simple losses of utility which can be avoided only by contracting agreement. These latter costs have been used to determine the origins of the utility functions $f(q_1)$ and $g(q_2)$. Analytically, both kinds of cost may be seen to have the same influence on our model: from the point of view of player 1, for example, an increase in the discounted stream of costs C_1/a is entirely analogous to an increase in the utility of agreement $f(q_1)$.[2] Therefore, simply for the sake of convenience, we will represent all changes in our preagreement point by means of the variables C_1 and C_2, leaving the utility functions with their origins determined at whatever levels may be convenient. (Since we are only interested in cost changes, the absolute magnitudes of C_1 and C_2 are not relevant either.) Finally, since the discounted streams of costs $(C_1/a,$ $C_2/b)$ will be the objects of our discussion of preagreement, we will introduce variables z_1 and z_2 to represent these expressions.

$$z_1 \equiv \frac{C_1}{a} \qquad z_2 \equiv \frac{C_2}{b}$$

A Static Model of the Choice of Disagreement Costs

Nash constructed a simple model of bargaining "threats" to supplement his outcome theorem, and this provides a convenient starting point for us as well.[3] Despite our dependence upon Nash, however, our interpretation and use of the model will represent substantial departures from his work, and so the reader should not infer too much from their analytical similarity. In the first place, Nash was concerned only with the normative problem of choosing optimal bargaining costs, while we are attempting to deal with the positive aspects of the problem: we are as interested in deviations from his "optimum" (if, indeed, it is one) as we are with Nash's individualistic normative solution. Moreover, although the model which we will construct is essentially a static one, we do not intend to disregard completely the dynamic elements which we have already introduced. Consistent with his neglect of time dependent bargaining costs, Nash regarded his "disagreement points" simply as *alternatives* to agreement; hence it was quite proper for him to refer to such points as "threats." In contrast, we are dealing with preagreement: a situation which prevails until agreement is achieved, and much of whose cost is associated with the bargaining process itself. Threats in the usual sense may not even be relevant to a negotiation. They may not be believed, or they may be associated with a date which arrives long after agreement is expected to be reached. Threats, promises, and similar conditional actions may contribute to bargaining costs, of course, if they can be expected to be carried out before agreement, or if they are seen to increase the riskiness of a position (that is, if there is a danger that they will be carried out). In general, however, Nash's disagreement point has little in common with the preagreement point, and it would be inappropriate to apply the term "threat" to the origin of the diagram in Figure 15.

We concluded in Chapter III [from equation (13)] that the outcome of the bargaining process may be expected to occur at a point for which

$$\frac{dU_1}{dU_2} = \frac{U_1}{U_2}\frac{a}{b}\frac{r_1}{r_2} \tag{13}$$

which may be written:

$$\frac{U_1}{U_2} = \frac{dU_1}{dU_2}\frac{b}{a}\frac{r_2}{r_1} \tag{35}$$

where U_1 and U_2 are defined as the utility of the agreement to players 1 and 2, respectively (measured as increments from the point of preagreement), dU_1/dU_2 is the slope of the utility possibility frontier at the point of agreement, a and b are the two players' discount rates, and r_1 and r_2 represent, respectively, each party's estimate of the other's concession rate. Moreover, it was shown that the ratio r_1/r_2 can be determined by a dynamic equilibrium process, and that in the special case for which the two players are similar, we expect the ratio to equal unity and the outcome to coincide with the Nash point.

It is a significant property of this model that each of the three terms on the right hand side of equation (35) is completely independent of the level of bargaining costs. First, the equilibrium value of r_1/r_2 depends only upon the players' learning abilities, discount rates, and *marginal* utilities. Second, the discount rates a and b are constants. Third, the slope of the utility possibility frontier dU_1/dU_2 is determined by the marginal utilities $f'(q_1)$ and $g'(q_2)$, which are functions only of the final distribution of payoff. This independence property lends itself to a particularly convenient analytical device. Consider a negotiation whose outcome would normally occur at point P in Figure 15, and suppose that new costs, Δz_1 and Δz_2, are imposed on the two players. An agreement which previously yielded U_1 and U_2 would now be worth $U''_1 = U_1 + \Delta z_1$ and $U''_2 = U_2 + \Delta z_2$ to the two parties respectively. If the increments were chosen such that $U''_1/U''_2 = U_1/U_2$ at point P, *then the model of the bargaining process predicts that that same point P will be the outcome in both problems.* Referring again to Figure 15, if bargaining costs are imposed in such proportions as to maintain the preagreement point on the straight line RP, the outcome can always be expected to occur at P.

A whole family of straight lines such as RP can be constructed, each corresponding to a given outcome P_i. These we shall term "isosettlement lines," and such a family is depicted in Figure 16. These lines are all straight, and the slope of each is equal to $-(dU_1/dU_2)(b/a)(r_2/r_1)$ where the values of dU_1/dU_2 and r_2/r_1 are determined by the associated outcome P_i. In the Nash case, of course, this slope reduces to $-dU_1/dU_2$ at P_i.

Now imagine a set of actions which is available as options to player 1 and which imposes cost changes Δz_1 and Δz_2 upon himself and his opponent. These cost changes may be either positive or negative. The case of positive costs, for example, may arise from a threat of reprisals upon player 2 if agreement is not reached (Δz_1 is then determined by the cost of making plus the risk of having to carry out this threat), it may result from the temporary cancellation of other agreements with the same party, it may derive from an appeal for intervention from a third party, and so on. *Conciliatory* actions (Δz_1 and Δz_2 both negative) may equally be available: the formation of intermediate agreements, for example, may be found to increase substantially the outcome payoff to one of the parties. Whatever the signs of the cost changes, of course, if the new preagreement point lies upon the same isosettlement line as the old one, the outcome will not be changed.

By the very nature of this simple model, one must deal only

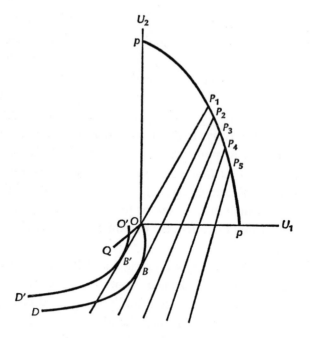

Figure 16

with the static relationship between the preagreement point and
the outcome. More specifically, since there is no variable describing the amount of time necessary to reach agreement and no
means for treating the dependence of total bargaining costs upon
the length of the negotiation, we must assume (following Nash)
that each party is indifferent among all negotiations which would
be concluded at the same point. In other words, player 1 will be
indifferent among all cost changing actions which would move the
preagreement point to the same new isosettlement line. For convenience, let us assume further that he will not take an action
which does not positively increase his payoff at agreement. Thus,
if an action involves positive costs ($\Delta z_1 > 0$, $\Delta z_2 > 0$), that action will be taken by player 1 only if the origin is shifted along a
line less steep than the isosettlement line:

$$\frac{\Delta z_1}{\Delta z_2} < - \left(\frac{dU_1}{dU_2}\right)_{P_i} \frac{b}{a} \frac{r_2}{r_1}$$

If an action is a conciliatory one ($\Delta z_1 < 0$, $\Delta z_2 < 0$), the reverse is true and the action will be taken only if:

$$\frac{\Delta z_1}{\Delta z_2} > - \left(\frac{dU_1}{dU_2}\right)_{P_i} \frac{b}{a} \frac{r_2}{r_1}$$

Naturally, the first party will always take an action which decreases his own preagreement costs while increasing those of his opponent ($\Delta z_1 < 0$, $\Delta z_2 > 0$).

Qualitatively, there is nothing at all unusual about such a model. If a party compares two conciliatory actions which give the same benefit to an adversary, he will prefer the one which benefits himself the most. He will only take that action, however, if his own utility gain is greater than that which he would receive if he simply waited for the normal bargaining process to move an equal distance toward the point of agreement (here "equal distance" refers to a given utility gain to the adversary, and "point of agreement" is defined before the conciliatory action). In the case of positive cost imposing actions, the reasoning is similar. A player will seek to take actions which impose cost upon his opponent at least cost to himself. The obverse of these statements is of some practical interest because it implies that a player is the more likely to use force the more benefit he can receive at agreement from a unit concession from the other party. For example, if an employer is indifferent between a particular wage concession and the granting of some degree of job security, and if the union much prefers the latter, there is more likelihood of a strike during negotiations over security than over wages. Moreover, this statement has nothing whatever to do with the magnitude of the disagreement—the "distance" between the negotiators.

Elaboration of the static model will continue along traditional lines of maximization theories. In general, a party has a whole series of actions available to him, each of which affects his and his opponent's bargaining cost to some degree. Some of these actions may be taken cumulatively—one can withhold foreign aid and refuse diplomatic recognition at the same time. Other actions have an exclusive property—in general, one cannot form intermediate trade agreements with an overseas nation and simultaneously blockade his ports. For the time being, we will restrict the analysis to the cumulative examples only, and introduce the problems of exclusive cases later. Suppose, further, that the available actions are predominantly of the cost increasing variety, so that the positive returns from any available conciliatory actions are more than matched by the cost imposing actions which are likely to be used. This presumably is by far the most common case in practice, although the reverse case could be treated by methods identical to those used here. Since, by assumption, actions can be cumulated, it is possible that some conciliatory moves can be combined with cost imposing ones so that Δz_1 is very small or even negative and Δz_2 is positive: this would represent a composite action that player 1 would always take.

Whatever actions he takes, player 1 will attempt to use those with the smallest values of the ratio $\Delta z_1 / \Delta z_2$. For example, his first action may be a composite one with $\Delta z_1 < 0$, $\Delta z_2 > 0$; his next action may be a somewhat less effective composite with $\Delta z_1 = 0$, $\Delta z_2 > 0$; his third move will have $\Delta z_1 > 0$, $\Delta z_2 > 0$; and so on. All of these cost imposing moves can be cumulated, and as the player adds more and more cost to preagreement, choosing the best actions first, he will find the actions to be subject to a sort of "diminishing marginal effectiveness"; that is, the values of $\Delta z_1 / \Delta z_2$ will increase as the use of force increases. If the set of actions is continuous, we can describe the resulting set of possible preagreement points by means of a curve such as *OBD* in Figure 16. By definition, no points below and to the right of *OBD* are available to player 1, although naturally if he were to choose a less effective action than he could, he might move the preagreement point to some location above and to the left of *OBD*. Finally, the "best" action or collection of actions is that which maximizes payoff at agreement. This appears on Figure 16 as point *B*, at which the locus of available preagreement points is tangent to an isosettlement line.

At point *B* the slope of *OBD* is equal to the slope of an isosettlement line, that is

$$\frac{\Delta z_1}{\Delta z_2} = - \left(\frac{dU_1}{dU_2}\right)_{P_i} \frac{b}{a} \frac{r_2}{r_1}$$

Substituting for z_1 and z_2, this becomes

$$\frac{\Delta C_1}{\Delta C_2} = - \left(\frac{dU_1}{dU_2}\right)_{P_i} \frac{r_2}{r_1} \tag{36}$$

Of course, both parties are likely to have a variety of cost imposing actions available to them. If it happens that both (1) the utility frontier is a straight line, so that all isosettlement lines are parallel, and (2) neither party's action influences the effectiveness of the other's actions (the cost changes Δz_1 and Δz_2 which result from a particular move of player 1 are not influenced by the moves of player 2), then each player can choose independently that action which is most favorable to himself, and the new preagreement point can be described without reference to any interactions between the two parties. In the absence of such a special case, however, we must consider the possibility that the most effective action for each party is affected by the moves of his adversary. Unfortunately, the analysis of such an interaction introduces a variety of new problems, some of which would take us far afield from our main topic and others of which are not subject to a satisfactory resolution at all. Thus we shall only propose a simple model, subject to a large number of additional restrictions, which will clarify the problems that can arise and will give a rough picture of the kind of solution that we expect to obtain.

The curve *OBD* was constructed by ranking (cumulatively) all the actions available to player 1 in order of their "effectiveness," where effectiveness is determined by the ratio $\Delta z_1/\Delta z_2$. We can make use of an index T_1 to reflect this ranking, low values of T_1 representing the use of only a few, very effective moves, and high values representing the more extreme uses of force (which also involve the use of marginal actions of lower effectiveness). Similarly, let us construct an index T_2 to reflect a ranking of actions available to the second party. The new costs associated with the preagreement point are now functions of the choices T_1 and T_2, and these functional relationships can be written $z_1 = \phi(T_1, T_2)$ and $z_2 = \varphi(T_1, T_2)$. Both of these functions are monotonically increasing: as T_1 and/or T_2 are increased, z_1 and z_2 increase. For the present we shall assume that these two functions are also continuous, although, as will be seen, this restriction involves a great deal more than ordinary analytical convenience. We must also assume that the rankings represented by increasing values of T_1 and T_2 are fixed: while the effectiveness of any given action may be altered, by an opponent's countermove, the ranking of actions will not change. Thus the additional costs, Δz_1 and Δz_2, which result from an incremental use of force on the part of player 1 may depend upon the value of T_2, but if the first party ranks an action (or combination of actions) A_1 as more effective than A_2, then nothing the second party can do will ever reverse that order. Similarly, we must assume that a marginal increase in force, ΔT_1, will always involve the addition of some new move, but it will never entail the *replacement* of any other moves which are already components of T_1.

In Figure 16 the proposed shape of the curve *OBD* suggests that whatever the value of T_2, there will always be some action T_1 which is optimal from the point of view of player 1. For example, if T_2 shifts the set of preagreement points available to the first negotiator to the locus *O'B'D'*, there is still an optimum preagreement point at *B'*. Of course, it is possible that the optimal action is no action at all, and $T_1 = 0$. Moreover, since the functions ϕ and φ are assumed to be continuous, and the solution equation (13) is also continuous, the general function relating an optimal action T_1 to any action T_2 is continuous as well.

This model is represented in Figure 17. The indices T_1 and T_2 depend only upon an invariant ranking of actions, and therefore they may be represented on the axes of the diagram. One may then construct the monotonically increasing curve I to represent the optimal move of the first party in response to any action of the second, and curve II to represent the optimal response of the second party to actions of the first. The special case in which neither negotiator is influenced by the action of the other would be represented by a vertical line I' and a horizontal line II' (the dashed lines). A case in which each party's action induces an intensified response ("escalation") is represented in curves which show increased T_1 for increased T_2 and vice versa (the solid curves in Figure 17). There is presumably a limit to the amount of force either party can use—there is only so much damage anyone can do to anyone else. We will represent these extremes by the values T_1^o and T_2^o.

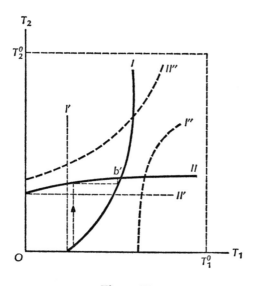

Figure 17

In general these force–reaction curves will intersect at a point such as b' in the figure. Moreover, as the curves are drawn, this intersection may be called an equilibrium: any T_1, T_2 combination not at b' will lead to reactions (such as those shown by the dotted paths) leading back to b'. Explosive escalation, however, is possible. For example, if neither party responded to minor uses of force, but reacted vigorously to more substantial costs, we could have the nonequilibrium case shown by the dashed curves I'' and II'' in Figure 17. In such cases the outcome would appear at T_1^o, T_2^o. It is possible that even in the "equilibrium" case the outcome would be at T_1^o, T_2^o. This would simply represent a situation in which the supply of cost imposing actions was physically limited (*not* a case in which the use of force is very expensive, which would simply involve the presence of *ineffective* actions).

Unfortunately, the question of whether or not a particular situation will be characterized by "equilibrium" or by "escalation" cannot be answered specifically in terms of our model. It depends upon the form of the functions $z_1 = \phi(T_1, T_2)$ and $z_2 = \varphi(T_1, T_2)$, and these in turn depend upon the particular circumstances and the range of opportunities which happen to present themselves to the parties, and not upon any deterministic mechanism within the problem. Nevertheless, Figure 17 does describe the "solution," in whichever form it may appear. There are, however, circumstances under which even this kind of result may be unobtainable.

The purpose of the continuity assumption and the assumption of fixed ranking order was to permit us to define the continuous reaction functions in Figure 17. Without these assumptions gaps might have appeared in the force–reaction functions, and, indeed, the figure itself could not have been constructed, since we would have had no consistent index which could be used for the axes. Suppose, for example, that T_1 can only take on discrete values in some range, as is shown in Figure 18. In this case it is clear that no solution point can be determined. In game-theoretic terms, this is an example in which no pure strategy saddle point exists.[4] As a game theorist Nash was able to avoid all such problems by permitting the use of "mixed strategies," that is, randomized combinations of actions whose use will guarantee the existence of continuous reaction functions.[5] Unfortunately, in the context of preagreement costs, the concept of mixed strategy is not applicable. It is essential to the effective operation of mixed strategies that a party's specific choice of action be concealed until after it has taken effect; the opponent must not be aware of a party's choice until after he has made his own choice (although each may know the relative *probability* with which each action may be taken). In our preagreement model, however, it may be possible to rescind an action after learning of an opponent's move, but before the latter has had any substantial impact. It would be senseless to try to conceal an action throughout the preagreement phase because then it could have no effect upon the outcome and that would be contrary to the purpose of taking the action in the first place. Thus the "mixed strategy" is a completely inappropriate device for this sort of problem, and it is the lack of any other solution which has led us to replace Nash's elegant model with such a clumsy and assumption-ridden one as we have.

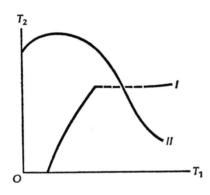

Figure 18

We have identified two sets of circumstances under which there may be no simple determination of the "optimal" choice of force. First, a case of "unlimited escalation" might arise, and we would then find each party using the maximum degree of force available to him (T_1^o and T_2^o). Empirically, such a case appears to be rather unusual. The second case is that in which the reaction functions in Figure 17 are not continuous. This possibility in turn can arise for any one of three reasons, each of which is quite plausible empirically. First, the ranking of actions in terms of relative effectiveness may not be constant (the "punishment must fit the crime"). An employer may prefer to use a lockout instead of an extensive public relations campaign so long as there is no strike, but if a strike occurs, these preferences might be reversed, destroying our simple ranking index. Second, the functions $z_1 = \phi(T_1, T_2)$ and $z_2 = \varphi(T_1, T_2)$ may not be continuous because T_1 and T_2 only take on discrete values—it may be hard, for example, to wage half a war (although great technological advances have been made in this direction). Third, our assumption that all actions can be taken cumulatively may not be appropriate. This last factor is probably the most important. If each party must choose between two strictly alternative actions, each may find himself going around in logical circles: "If I do A then he does X; if he does X then I should do B; if I do B then he does Y; if he does Y then I do A"; and so on. In these cases, without the possibility of using mixed strategies, we may be able to determine no solution at all.

The seriousness of discontinuous force–reaction functions may be reduced somewhat by two factors. First, the size of these discontinuities may actually be relatively small compared to the size (seriousness) of the actions themselves. Even a strike may be varied in intensity, depending upon who is permitted to cross picket lines, whether the strike is intended as a one or two day affair or as something to be in force until agreement is reached, and so on. Thus even if the choice of preagreement point is indeterminate because of discontinuities, it may lie within relatively narrow bounds. Second, even in a case in which the model fails to identify one preagreement point, dynamic considerations may constrain the possibilities to a significant degree. For example, suppose that a union would like to strike, that if the union strikes, the employer will call for government pressure, that if the employer calls in the government, the union would prefer not to have struck, and that without a strike the employer would rather not have political "assistance." The stage would then be set for the "if . . . then . . . but then if . . ." cycle which would never end. However, such things as strikes and political intervention are not easily revoked: once chosen, they tend to remain in effect until agreement. Thus if the union makes its move without regard for the possible response of the employer, preagreement will be characterized by a strike and government intervention, and this will be a stable state of affairs until the parties arrive at a settlement. Most examples with serious problems of discreteness are likely to have dynamic solutions of this sort, but, of course, unless the resulting preagreement point is reasonably close to our static equilibrium, any simple solution characteristics which we may formulate from the continuous model will not apply.[6]

Implications of the Static Model

As it stands, our simple theory is a highly idealized one; it is completely static, and it requires that both players anticipate the outcome of the bargaining process and understand something of the mechanism whereby it is obtained. Strictly speaking, it is hardly "realistic." On the other hand, it surely does point in the right direction: "experienced" negotiators, especially those who have had extensive contact with one another, must have acquired some ability to foresee the impact of various shifts in preagreement conditions, and they must be aware that they are subject to many of the influences revealed by our simple diagrams.

A matter of great interest to us is the extent to which a given shift in preagreement costs can influence the outcome of the negotiation. If a party imposes upon his opponent a recurring loss whose present value is $10 (if continued forever), by how much is that likely to reduce the payoff which the opponent will ultimately receive? Suppose player 2 imposes a loss Δz_1 upon player 1 and, in so doing, incurs a cost Δz_2 himself. We can determine dU_1/dz_1 by rewriting equation (13) with U_1 and U_2 defined *before* any additional costs have been imposed,

$$\frac{U_2 + z_2}{U_1 + z_1} = -\frac{dU_2}{dU_1}\frac{a}{b}\frac{r_1}{r_2}$$

and differentiating respect to z_1, remembering that z_2 is not constant as z_1 changes. Unfortunately, as the reader can see for himself, the resulting expression proves to be inordinately messy.

$$\frac{dU_1}{dz_1} = \frac{-\dfrac{dU_2}{dU_1} - \dfrac{dz_2}{dz_1}\dfrac{b}{a}\dfrac{r_2}{r_1}}{\left(1 + \dfrac{b}{a}\dfrac{r_2}{r_1}\right)\dfrac{dU_2}{dU_1} + (U_1 + z_1)\dfrac{d^2U_2}{dU_1^2}} \tag{37}$$

Here z_1 represents any costs which may already have been absorbed by player 1, and as usual, dU_2/dU_1 is the slope of the utility frontier, and d^2U_2/dU_1^2 is the rate of change of that slope (note that both of these expressions have negative signs).

Consider a simple problem which, according to the basic model of Chapter III, can be expected to produce the Nash point at agreement. To obtain this case, the players must have equal discount rates and equal learning rates, which, in equilibrium, leads to equal expected concession rates. Thus we have $(a/b)(r_1/r_2)$ $= 1$. For this example assume also that the utility frontier has a constant slope $[(d^2U_2/dU_1^2) = 0]$. Suppose first that player 2 takes an action which is entirely costless to himself $(dz_2 = 0)$. Expression (37) now reduces to a very simple relation, and the impact of the action upon player 1's payoff utility is given by $dU_1/dz_1 = -\frac{1}{2}$. Consider, for example, a case in which the parties are dividing a sum of money and the marginal utility of money is constant; then if player 2 imposed a cost of, say, \$1000 on player 1, the latter's payoff at agreement would be reduced by only half that much, or \$500.[7] If we had a similar case in which the action also imposed a cost on player 2, the impact would be even further reduced. For instance, suppose that $dz_2/dz_1 = \frac{1}{2}$: that is, that every dollar of cost imposed on player 1 involves a loss of \$.50 to player 2; then, according to equation (37), the impact of the \$1000 cost on player 1 will be to reduce his payoff at agreement by only \$250—one quarter as much! If diminishing marginal utility is present, the effectiveness of cost imposing action is reduced still further. This property is also reflected in Figure 16 by the tendency of the isosettlement lines to converge as we move away from the origin.

The practical implications of this quantitative relationship are quite important, since it suggests that cost imposing actions are potentially considerably greater in magnitude than are their consequences: we might expect to find long, costly strikes to take place over a few cents in a wage rate or international uses of force to appear greatly in excess of the values of their goals. Moreover, this conclusion contrasts quite sharply with the more traditional approach, which suggests that costs of threats need not be disproportionate to the payoff gains that they are intended to achieve. For example, the following "bimatrix" game has been presented by T. Schelling (the units in the boxes represent the utility payoffs to players 1 and 2 respectively):[8]

Figure 19

In this simple two alternative situation the "normal" solution would be the combination C', C_1, because player 1 always prefers C' to T, and given this fact, player 2 clearly benefits from choosing C_1 instead of C_2. Schelling introduces the possibility of a threat, however, which enables player 1 to achieve the outcome (C', C_2) instead. All that is required is for player 1 to threaten to use T_1 if player 2 chooses C_1. Now, since the use of T_1 would reduce the payoff of player 2 to zero anyway, he might as well accept (C', C_2), which yields a better return. Any similar situation in which player 2 receives a larger return from (C', C_2) than from (T, C_1) could be used for this example; that is, a threat which would impose a loss of D dollars upon a party can be used to shift the outcome D dollars away from him. In our continuous negotiation context, however, we expect the use of a threat of this magnitude to be far less effective and to be able to dislodge the payoff to player 2 only a little way from $2. A threat of a loss of $4 or more may be necessary to get the payoff of player 2 down by $1.

The possibility that during a negotiation the use of force must greatly exceed its objective brings up a further danger: suppose that player 1, following the reasoning of Schelling and others, *expects* his threat to induce the second party to concede from C_1 to C_2. Our analysis suggests that in this he is bound to be disappointed, and hence that the threat may have to be carried out. We may hypothesize that many examples of disrupted negotiations

—prolonged cases of labor hostility, military escalation, some cases of civil violence, and so on—are directly attributable to the failure of negotiators to respond according to an erroneous concept of "rationality," a concept derived from oversimplified discrete examples such as that given in Figure 19.[9]

When we move beyond the level of individual perspectives and consider the combined moves of both parties, we find the value of any particular cost imposing action reduced for quite a different reason. It is clear from Figure 16 that the equilibrium preagreement point B' is hardly desirable from the point of view of either negotiator. In fact, the natural preagreement point, with no cost imposing actions at all, lies on the same isosettlement locus as B'. In such a case, the only effect of the sequence of force and counterforce moves is to increase the cost of the negotiation to both parties. This problem cannot be discussed fully until we move from this static model to one in which the amount of time required by the bargaining process is taken into account explicitly. We can suggest, however, that this is certainly one area in which experience with the bargaining relationship may play a part; cost imposing tactics may be used as long as the negotiators are unfamiliar with their combined consequences, but as experience increases, and especially as a particular relationship between individuals extends over time, we certainly expect these tactics to be used less and less frequently.

An observation of some importance is that a particular threat or cost imposing action may not always operate to the benefit of its user. For example, the shift in preagreement point from O to Q in Figure 15 is composed of precisely the same Δz_1 and Δz_2 as the shift from O to Q in Figure 16, and yet in the first case the change operates to the advantage of the first party, while in the second case it improves the payoff to the second! This result can be explained by observing that the effectiveness of a given action depends upon the nature of the frontier of the outcome set as well as upon the cost changes Δz_1 and Δz_2. This tends to reaffirm our position that considerable insight and experience of the bargaining process is required before a negotiator can use force effectively. A device which was of great benefit to one party on one occasion may at other times prove to have a perverse influence. For example, a union may find a strike to be beneficial when negotiating over wages, but if it tries to use the same device at another time (for example, during negotiations dealing with items which threaten what management sees as its own prerogatives) it may find that the strike reduces rather than increases its own return.

Some Pitfalls and Prejudices

Before we elaborate on the theory any further, it perhaps is appropriate to discuss some dangers inherent in this sort of analysis, as well as to inform the reader of a few of the author's own prejudices. We pointed out in the introductory chapter that this study deals largely with nonpsychological, we might almost say "emotionally neutral," aspects of the bargaining problem. This is not the traditional approach at all; in fact, we are attempting to perform an economic analysis of an interpersonal relationship which is most frequently described in terms of purely psychological variables. Descriptions of particular negotiating sessions seem to make far more use of adjectives such as "aggressive," "friendly," "fearful," "angry," "hostile," and so on, than they do of our "outcome expectation," "discount rate," "cost," "payoff," or even "concession rate." It has seemed to the author that it is worthwhile to abstract from the psychological dimensions (except, of course, for our use of the learning process) in order to get at the more fundamental economic elements of the bargaining process. To abstract from these dimensions, however, does not mean that we may disregard them or *forget* them. If something occurs during a negotiation which seriously disturbs its psychological environment, we can hardly expect the predictive qualities of our theory to be left unimpaired. For example, we have already warned that retractions of offers during a negotiation may have an important impact upon an opponent's behavior—an impact, moreover, of considerably greater importance than would be implied by our simple model. The reason, of course, is that the retraction may generate resentment and reduce the opponent's willingness to cooperate at all: the players' preference systems may be altered drastically, and the corresponding utility possibility set distorted completely from its original shape.

The same danger arises in the case of cost changing devices which shift the preagreement point of a negotiation. It would be silly to argue that the use of a threat, a promise, force, or some conciliatory action would have no appreciable impact upon a party's preferences. It might be "rational" for a chess player to throw a game for me if I threaten to burn his house down otherwise, but it makes no sense at all to argue that he *will* do so, at least not without a more careful evaluation of changes in his preferences.

We might observe in passing that this problem of emotional reactions to cost imposing moves has often been ignored in the so-called theory of "strategic choice," and it is to be feared that this neglect has to a great extent vitiated any content which the theory might have had. The growing popularity of sophisticated game-theoretic techniques in the analysis of problems of social interaction has often been accompanied by an extraordinary naïvité in their interpretation. Certainly the preferences of individuals (often represented by the little numbers in the cells of bimatrix games, such as in Figure 19) cannot be expected to hold still while we indulge in threats, promises, commitments, or even random destruction, and work which disregards this fact cannot by itself be expected to produce usable insights.

Legitimacy

Our *caveats* concerning the relevance of psychological variables certainly cannot be ignored in this discussion of preagreement costs. Nevertheless, we would be taken far afield (and well beyond any pretense of qualifications) if we attempted to speculate further upon the nature of these interactions. To some extent, however, we may avoid the most serious difficulties by putting some further constraints upon the range of situations to which we expect the analysis to apply. Those devices which most seriously distort the preferences of the parties appear to be those which would be termed "unfair"—those which are not recognized as natural and appropriate to the situation. Many writers have dealt with this problem of legitimacy; for example, Kenneth Boulding has used the term to characterize uses of force which are accepted as part of the natural order of things.[10] (In Boulding's terms a party's "power" is increased if he has access to *legitimate* uses of force.) We may infer that "unfair" actions—those which tend to generate destabilizing emotional responses—are those which lack this particular property. If some form of force has already been accepted in the environment of a negotiation, relatively little hostility is likely to be aroused by its use. Thus, the operation of a union within a plant, or even the use of the strike mechanism, no longer engenders the widespread bitterness and resentment which once was the case, and the elimination of this adverse psychological reaction has greatly increased the economic usefulness of union membership to the employees. Again, it is legitimate in the political arena to threaten a representative with the possibility of a primary election, but not with the possibility of a physical assault. Each action may impose the same utility loss on him (net of psychological variables), but the two can hardly be expected to have the same effect upon his behavior.

We recognize that the introduction of legitimacy does not really "explain" anything. We are in no position to provide reasons why certain actions enjoy status as legitimate ones, nor can we make any predictions as to which actions will achieve that status in the future. On the other hand, some means are available for recognizing its existence: frequent use of a particular device throughout the history of one type of negotiation is a reasonable indicator that it has achieved legitimacy; and, of course, adverse emotional responses which indicate nonlegitimacy are generally easy to observe. It is interesting to note that occasionally legitimacy itself is subject to choice. Not only may the parties agree upon the "rules of the game" but often third parties are called into a negotiation to establish standards of "fairness" so that the negotiators may preserve some degree of emotional stability. The National Labor Relations Board, for example, is intended partly to serve this role in the area of labor negotiations, having as one of its chores the defining of "responsible" collective bargaining.[11] Despite such problems in explaining the presence of legitimacy, recognition of the property is sufficient for us here: we may feel reasonably confident that our preagreement model will provide satisfactory results as long as the cost changing actions which are used fall under this umbrella. "Unfair" actions may be used by the negotiators, especially if the payoff appears to be particularly high to the party using them, but we are under no illusions that any predictive qualities which may be found in our analysis could extend into these cases.

As long as they are correct, limitations which must be taken into account by the analyst are probably familiar to the experienced negotiator as well. Thus, contrary to what seems to be popular belief, nonlegitimized tactics can be expected to be used very sparingly. Fancy strategies and complex gimmicks appeal to the imagination, but not to the man who is motivated by the value of an agreement. Such devices are too likely to be interpreted as evidence of bad faith, and the objective of the bargaining process is, after all, cooperation. Even "legitimate" cost imposing actions would probably not be used without considerable caution. In the first place, as has been noted already, force and counterforce may largely negate one another, and once this is recognized by the two parties, cost imposing actions are likely to be less frequent. Second, any use of force at all will presumably have some psychological impact upon the course of a negotiation, and hence force would be avoided except when it is clearly worth its psychological price. For similar reasons, we expect conciliatory actions to be taken more frequently than would be implied by the simple static model.

Intermediate Agreement

Throughout this chapter we have treated the preagreement point as the *status quo* from which the bargaining process proceeds. It is nevertheless true that certain costs may contribute to the choice of outcome, even though they appear only in the form of possibilities: cost imposing actions which are never taken, and indeed which are never intended to be taken. By this we do not mean only unilateral threats of force—"if you do not concede, then I will . . ."—but the existence of alternatives which have been eliminated because the parties have already achieved some measure of cooperation. For example, we have already observed that the point B' in Figure 16 might become the preagreement point of the negotiation because the players would find that the moves which produce it simply cancel out, leaving both sides worse off during the bargaining process and improving the agreement payoff to neither.

Even if the equilibrium disagreement point strongly favors one of the two players, if the associated bargaining costs are very high, it would be to the advantage of both to avoid them by making use of some intermediate level of cooperation, and acknowledging that the possible equilibrium favored one party. A good example of this arises when we consider negotiations over the *renewal* of a previous agreement. In the vast majority of such cases (labor contracts, international trade agreements), the parties do not suspend agreement and return to some costly preagreement point; they generally maintain their previous level of cooperation and attempt to renegotiate *as if* they were starting all over again.

The notion that two parties can negotiate from a mutually acknowledged but nonoperative threat point introduces some tricky issues. If the potential preagreement point lies upon the same iso-settlement line as the existing origin, and if both parties have accepted the proposition that the related set of bargaining costs would benefit neither of them, then no particular problem arises. However, if the equilibrium threat favors one party, it is natural for the other to underplay its significance as much as he can, and it may become necessary for the first to refuse intermediate cooperation occasionally if he expects his opponent to respond to this higher level of costs. This is in keeping, for example, with Reder's interpretation of a strike as an *investment*—as something which will influence an employer's behavior for some time to come.[12] Furthermore, intermediate cooperation is potentially unstable, especially if the original preagreement point favors one party markedly. The agreement to negotiate from O rather than

B' (Figure 16) has many of the properties of the well-known Prisoner's Dilemma game: each party sees unilateral action as potentially improving his own payoff at agreement, and a great deal of sophistication and experience is required for him to foresee the true consequences of the action and to avoid them. It is also necessary, of course, that each player be able to make a reasonable estimate of the degree to which the original preagreement point would influence the outcome. If either feels that the outcome is likely to deviate from what he regards as a "fair" one, and if that observed deviation is large enough to justify incurring the necessary cost, then the intermediate cooperation will break down and the players will return to the original preagreement point.

Finally, it should be observed in passing that the existence of a previous agreement may itself change the costs associated with preagreement. The operation of a firm involves the establishment of plant and equipment, the training of management personnel, and often the attraction of a substantial labor pool. When employer–employee cooperation is disrupted by a strike, both parties incur costs which bear little or no resemblance to what they would have had to pay had there been no agreement in the first place. Similarly, international agreements may lead to trade patterns and financial interdependences quite different from any former state of noncooperation. Thus, unless a potentially dependent party is extremely farsighted, we might expect to find the distribution of the value of an agreement shifting away from him over time.[13]

The Definition of Bargaining Power

We mentioned early in Chapter II that we would encounter some difficulty if we attempted to apply any notion of "power" to the bargaining problem. Many writers have applied notions of "power" to the bargaining problem, but we said that, due to the difficulty of formulating a satisfactory definition of the term, we would avoid it altogether. The reasons for this difficulty are relatively easy to describe now that we have a more complete model to work with. As we stated earlier, it would be possible to interpret power purely in terms of outcome: if player 1 is able to shift the outcome from P_3 to P_4 (see Figure 16) he has some power, but less than he would have had had he been able to shift the outcome from P_3 to P_5. Such a definition would simply make "more power" synonymous with "better payoff." This seems to be an unsatisfactory interpretation, however, for it would render the frequent statement "he did better because he was more powerful" completely circular, and in fact, power would become the dependent variable rather than an independent variable (or a vector of independent variables). Nevertheless, this circularity does occur quite often in descriptions of bargaining relationships, and we suspect that references to ill-defined notions of power often represent attempts to conceal a fundamental inability to explain the distribution of payoff in an agreement.

It appears that if any useful concept of bargaining power exists at all, it must be associated with the variables with which the present chapter has been concerned: it must describe a player's ability to shift the costs of preagreement in such a way as to alter the outcome of the bargaining process. Moreover, although other variables might also enter into the definition, it would be desirable to exclude those which are related directly to payoff preferences. For example, suppose that one party is largely indifferent among various alternatives. If he makes changes in his demands which greatly favor the other party, we would not want to find ourselves defending the position that the second party is a very powerful one. The term "power" conveys the impression of an ability to overcome resistance, and one's power is surely not increased simply because his adversary is not interested in resistance. For this same reason, the definition of bargaining power should not depend upon whether or not cost changing ability is ever used. As we have already shown, if an action imposes positive costs on both players, its influence over the outcome depends upon the ratio $\Delta z_1/\Delta z_2$ and upon the relationship between $\Delta z_1/\Delta z_2$ and the slope of the outcome set. For example, in the situation described by Figure 9, the action OQ favors the interests of player 1, while in Figure 10 that same action would favor his opponent. With regard to the second case, it might seem rather unusual at first to assign some degree of "power" to player 1 because of a possible action which he does not take. The problem is that the choice of OQ depends upon the slope of the boundary of the payoff set, which in turn depends upon preferences. If we attempted to include this slope in the definition, making a player "powerful" only if he uses his cost imposing ability, then we would be including in the definition all of the variables which go into determining the outcome itself, and we would again be defining power simply as "better outcome."

The prime difficulty in associating "power" with the ability to influence bargaining costs rests in the need for quantification. Specific units of the parties' utility functions are not determined anywhere in our theory, and we have made no attempt to compare values of Δz_1 with values of Δz_2. The ratio $\Delta z_1/\Delta z_2$, for example, may take on any (positive) value we like, depending upon our choice of utility units. Moreover, the terms z_1 and z_2 have no natural origins, and hence even percentage changes are of no use to us. If we were willing to perform interpersonal utility comparisons, then we might argue that Bill is more powerful than Charles if he can impose a given cost on Albert at less (utility) cost to himself than Charles would have to pay, but this certainly is not consistent with the spirit in which our preference functions were constructed. Our recourse, then, must be to define "power" in terms of *real* variables rather than utilities. If Bill can force Albert to lose $1000 at a cost of $20 to himself, then Bill is more powerful than someone who must pay $100 to impose the same cost on Albert. This approach is awkward, for it means that "power" has as many dimensions as there are types of cost, and this in turn can give rise to a serious index number problem; but there seems to be no alternative.

Unfortunately, our power variable must have just twice as many dimensions as are implied by the above paragraph. Not only must we describe the *ratio* of costs which a given action imposes upon me and upon my opponent, but we must describe their absolute *magnitudes*. Is a negotiator more powerful when he can impose a loss of $1000 upon his opponent at a cost of $500 to himself, or when he can impose a loss of $100 at a cost of only $10? In terms of Figure 20, is player 1 more powerful if he can move to the point Q or is he more powerful if he can go to S? Which of these is *preferred* depends upon the slope of the payoff frontier. Q is preferred relative to the solid frontier, S relative to the dashed frontier. There is no reason, however, for arguing that one or the other represents a higher level of "bargaining power," and hence we are compelled to accompany every cost ratio with a cost magnitude (the distances OQ and OS) in our definition.

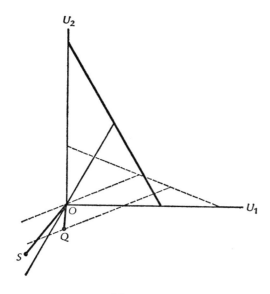

Figure 20

In sum, our attempt to define bargaining power leads us to a construct which must be represented with as many dimensions as there are variables in the original definition of bargaining costs. Certainly, we may use an aggregative notion of "more power" if every cost imposed on an adversary requires "less cost" to oneself, but for purposes of analysis, and even for empirical quantification, we are probably best off if we study the cost components themselves

Summary

The implications of the foregoing model may be combined into two major points. First, we are able to obtain a static model to describe the parties' choices of preagreement points, and, subject to certain rather severe approximations to reality, this model has a well-defined solution. Second, this simple model almost certainly overstates the amount of force which will be used in the bargaining situation. This second conclusion derives from three major factors: (1) the possibility of psychological and emotional reaction will tend to discourage the use of force (especially when one considers the relatively great amount of cost which may be necessary to achieve a given result); (2) the simultaneous use of cost imposing actions will tend to make both parties worse off, and awareness of this fact will lead them to withhold such actions, and even to make and maintain intermediate agreements; (3) the use of force is dangerous: many cost imposing actions may actually *reduce* a party's payoff at agreement, and these (generally less effective) actions will be avoided by all but the most experienced, and the most rash, of negotiators. In obtaining these consequences, we have not lost sight of the dynamic elements of negotiation, although time has not yet been explicitly introduced into the model. This we shall do in Chapter VII.

■ NOTES

1. The emphasis upon "strategy" bears ample witness to this proposition. See Thomas Schelling, *The Strategy of Conflict* (Cambridge, Mass.: Harvard University Press, 1960), Carl M. Stevens, *Strategy and Collective Bargaining Negotiation* (New York: McGraw-Hill Book Co., 1963), or Richard Walton and Robert McKensie, *A Behavioral Theory of Labor Negotiations* (New York: McGraw-Hill Book Co., 1965), Chapter III.

2. For example, the outcome of the bargaining model constructed in Chapter III [equation (11)] is described in terms of the sums $f(q_1) + C_1/a$ and $g(q_2) + C_2/b$.

3. John Nash, "Two Person Cooperative Games," *Econometrica,* XXI (1953), 128–140.

4. For a definition and description of a pure strategy equilibrium point, see R. Duncan Luce and Howard Raiffa, *Games and Decisions* (New York: John Wiley and Sons, 1957), pp. 56–68. Essentially, we have achieved a solution by obtaining all the necessary conditions to apply the Katutani Fixed Point Theorem. This is the same device that Nash used (*op. cit.*).

5. Mixed strategies are covered in more detail in Luce and Raiffa, *op. cit.*, pp. 68–76.

6. This is not the first model whose solution is made awkward by the presence of discontinuities. Discontinuities in economic processes (e.g., discrete plant sizes, etc.) can lead to discontinuous cost and profit functions. No model of oligopolistic markets seems to have been able to deal with such a problem very satisfactorily.

7. Recall that this cost may be either a net loss of utility which will be recovered only at the time of agreement, or a bargaining cost which recurs in every time period and whose discounted present value (if it were paid in perpetuity) would amount to $1000. The conclusion may be shown easily in graphical form. In Figure F–2 point e is the origin, and b is the Nash outcome. After the shift of origin to g the Nash outcome moves to c. We know that the slope of eb equals the slope of gc, which equals minus the slope of bc. The triangles abd and bcd are therefore congruent and hence $ad = dc$. But $ef = ad + dc = 2dc$. Since the triangle efg is similar to bcd, eg must equal twice the length bd. Thus the loss in U_2 in moving from b to c is half the loss in moving from e to g.

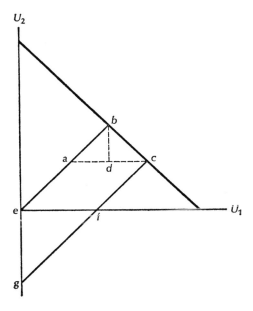

Figure F–2

8. Schelling, *op. cit.,* p. 126.

9. This is not meant to preclude the possibility that this analysis is also oversimplified and hence is misleading as well!

10. Kenneth E. Boulding, "The Nature of Political Conflict," delivered at the American Political Science Association Meeting, September 1965.

11. One is reminded of an example in which General Electric maintained that its negotiations were composed of too much unnecessary haggle, and, instead of negotiating, attempted to estimate beforehand what the outcome would be. It then made this as a final offer to the union. Whether or not its estimate was accurate proved to be irrelevant, since the National Labor Relations Board regarded the "tactic" itself as unfair. In the words of Clark Kerr, this is "almost" an unfair practice "for it denies the other party the opportunity of forcing some concession and thus claiming a victory of sorts." Clark Kerr, "Industrial Conflict and Its Mediation," *The American Journal of Sociology,* LX (1954), I 237.

12. Michael Reder, "Theory of Union Wage Policy," *Review of Economics and Statistics,* Vol. XXXIV (1952).

13. A related point is that force may *create* a bargaining range. A kidnapper intentionally shifts a preagreement point downward so that negotiation over ransom becomes possible. Before the use of force there was no potential agreement between the two parties which could make them both better off. Such examples could be discussed in terms of the foregoing model, but one must bear in mind that such uses of force universally fall outside the category of "legitimate" actions.

VII
The Dynamic Theory
of Preagreement Costs

Introduction

Decisions to use cost imposing or conciliatory tactics are necessarily made during a negotiation or even before any serious bargaining has taken place at all. Thus they are made without any prior knowledge of the outcome of the bargaining process, or perhaps even of the extent to which that outcome can be shifted by changes in bargaining costs. The static model in the last chapter, on the other hand, made considerable use of just such knowledge. Indeed, if we were to interpret it as a descriptive theory, we would have to require that each party be able to specify the quantitative relation between costs and bargaining outcomes. However plausible we may find its implications to be, we must recognize that such a model by no means reflects the negotiation as it is perceived by the individual participants. In this chapter we will discuss what amounts to an alternative theory of cost imposition, taking into account the fact that the parties perforce use current demands (or current payoff expectations) rather than ultimate outcomes as the independent variables in formulating their bargaining strategies.

The disregard of the dynamic properties of the bargaining process also leads the static model to overlook a possibility that high bargaining costs may actually be beneficial to both of the parties. The benefit arises because high costs tend to reduce payoff demands, which naturally lead to earlier settlement. If this saving in time is large enough to offset the increase in costs, then, of course, the players will have gained on balance.

When we formulate a model based upon the influence of bargaining costs on the amount of time necessary to reach agreement, we obtain a theory which is remarkably different from that discussed in the last chapter. In the terms of the static model, the whole chain of causality led from preagreement point to outcome: for each given outcome P_i there was a corresponding set of preagreement points on an "isosettlement" line, and the only way that the negotiation could arrive at P_i was to start from one of those specified points. From the point of view of our representative bargainer in the dynamic model, however, *any* outcome is possible. He needs only to be willing to wait long enough for his opponent to concede all the way to any desired payoff (as long as that outcome is in the payoff possibility set). A party demands a return q_1 simply because that is the most that he is willing to hold out for, given the expected pattern of concession behavior from his opponent. Thus when a player alters the costs of bargaining, he does so not primarily because he expects that action to alter the point of agreement, but because he expects it to affect the amount of time which must pass before any particular agreement can be achieved. Of course, once the time which must pass for any given outcome is altered, our bargainer may find it desirable to seek a different payoff; nevertheless, this is a secondary rather than a primary objective.

The discussion that follows must again be accompanied by a warning that we may easily overstate the case for deliberately changing the costs of bargaining. As we observed in Chapter VI, any attempt to impose higher costs upon the other party is likely to be interpreted as a sign of ill will, and this may disrupt the negotiation rather than accelerate it. In disregarding this element of the problem, our model is biased toward too favorable a treatment of strategies which make negotiation more uncomfortable. For this reason, this analysis could be interpreted as a determination of upper bounds to the effectiveness of cost imposing tactics, rather than as a positive theory.

The Influence of Bargaining Costs on Demands

We have just suggested that when a party makes a change in bargaining costs, his primary motive is to change the amount of time which is required to achieve any particular payoff. There are two ways in which this time saving could conceivably be generated: the parties could concede more rapidly when costs are higher, or they could concede just as before, but from smaller initial demands. We have already proposed (Chapters III and IV) that the latter is the more likely to be the case. In our dynamic model, concessions take place through the learning process: the negotiators recognize as time goes on that their expectations are overoptimistic, and the resulting downward revision in expectations leads to a downward revision in demands. Since there is no reason to expect learning ability to be influenced by changes in bargaining costs, there is no reason for these costs to alter concession rates.[1] Increases in bargaining costs, however, do increase the cost of waiting for any given payoff, and hence we expect the parties to be less willing to hold out for large returns—we expect higher bargaining costs to be associated with reduced demands.

We will again refer to our expression for the optimal demand of the first player [equation (6)]:

$$\left[f(q_1) + \frac{C_1}{a} \right] \frac{a}{r_2} = f'(q_1) \qquad (6)$$

In order to obtain the relation between changes in demand and changes in bargaining costs, we may differentiate equation (6) for dq_1/dC_1:

$$\frac{dq_1}{dC_1} = \frac{1}{r_2 f'(q_1) \left[\dfrac{f''(q_1)}{f'(q_1)} - \dfrac{a}{r_2} \right]} \qquad (38)$$

The bracketed term in the denominator of equation (38) is negative [from the second order conditions for an optimal demand—see equation (7)], marginal utility $f'(q_1)$ is positive, and the concession rate r_2 expected of the second player is also positive. Thus we have the expected result that, as bargaining costs rise, demands fall.

A similar relation describes the impact of a change in C_2 upon the second party's demand:

$$\frac{dq_2}{dC_2} = \frac{1}{r_1 g'(q_2) \left[\dfrac{g''(q_2)}{g'(q_2)} - \dfrac{b}{r_1} \right]} \qquad (39)$$

In the last chapter we concluded that an increase in bargaining costs would have a relatively small impact on the final settlement. Equations (38) and (39) suggest that bargaining costs do have a larger effect upon demands. Thus we can obtain dU_1/dZ_1 where U_1 is the utility which player 1 would receive from a settlement at his current demand by recalling our definition $Z = C_1/a$:

$$\frac{dU_1}{dZ_1} = f'(q_1) \cdot a \, \frac{dq_1}{dC_1} = \frac{a}{\dfrac{f''(q_1)}{f'(q_1)} \, r_2 - a}$$

In the case of linear utility functions, this implies that an increase in costs will be just matched by a decrease in demands; a threatened loss of $1 will induce an immediate concession of $1 and so on. If diminishing marginal utility is present, the impact of the threat will be smaller than this, but it will nevertheless be larger than the shift in outcome which was suggested by the static model. This is not a contradiction of our earlier conclusion: player 1 may reduce his demand by $1 now and only suffer a small loss at the time of settlement, so long as player 2 retains the same learning (and hence concession) rate.

The Expected Impact of Bargaining Cost Changes

Equations (38) and (39) summarize the dynamic impact of a change in bargaining costs upon a player's demands, but they do not necessarily reflect the response which his opponent expects.

It is possible that even though an increase in C_1 will not affect the concession rate of player 1, the second party thinks that it will. Hence player 2 may completely misinterpret the impact of his action, as well as the potential effectiveness of further increases in bargaining costs. For example, suppose that the discrete shift in q_1 which an increase in C_1 will occasion is interpreted by the second party as a great increase in the concession rate. Since this is a highly desirable result from his point of view, player 2 may decide to increase bargaining costs further, to increase q_2, or both, and the end result would probably be an even more costly negotiation than otherwise would have occurred.[2]

Our model could take a number of directions depending upon the nature of the expectations which we attribute to the parties. Indeed, it is very possible that in practice the form of the expectations varies, depending upon the character and tradition of the specific negotiation. We shall by no means discuss all of the possibilities, however; instead we focus upon one possibility which appears both to represent the nature of the problem well, and to be technically the simplest to deal with. This is the case in which each party has expectations of the "correct" form: each party will expect the other to respond to changes in bargaining costs with a corresponding change in demands, but with no change in concession rate. This hypothesis does seem to be a reasonable one, since it states essentially that each party expects his opponent to behave just as he himself would do under similar circumstances.

The Model

Suppose that the first party is considering whether or not to impose additional bargaining costs upon his opponent. Under most circumstances, this cannot be done without increasing his own costs as well. If this is the case, the new bargaining costs will alter *both* parties' demands, each demand falling in accordance with our earlier formulation [equations (38) and (39)]. Thus the first party must take into account four consequences of his cost imposing action: (1) the loss of utility associated with the reduction in

his own demand, (2) the time saving associated with his own reduced demand, (3) the increased bargaining cost which he has
imposed upon himself, and (4) the time saving resulting from his
opponent's reduced demand. Algebraically, these four factors are
summed in equation (40) with the first two factors combined in
brackets:

$$dU_1 = \left[\frac{\delta U_1}{\delta q_1} + \frac{\delta U_1}{\delta w} \frac{\delta w}{\delta q_1} \right] \frac{\delta q_1}{\delta C_1} dC_1 + \frac{\delta U_1}{\delta C_1} dC_1 + \frac{\delta U_1}{\delta w} \frac{\delta w}{\delta q_2} dq_2 \quad (40)$$

Here q_1 is itself determined by an optimization process, since the
first player has already selected a utility maximizing demand. This
optimum is characterized by the fact that any change in payoff
utility which results from a change in demand is just offset by the
change in the amount of time required to reach agreement. Thus
we have $\delta U_1/\delta q_1 = -(\delta U_1/\delta w)dw/dq_1$ for an optimal q_1. This
implies that the bracketed expression in equation (40) is equal
to zero, and hence that, in considering the impact of a marginal
change in bargaining costs, player 1 needs to consider only two
of the original four factors: the disutility of the increased cost itself, and the time saving realized from player 2's reduced demand.

We can determine the expressions $\delta U_1/\delta C_1$ and $\delta U_1/\delta q_2$ from
the equation in Chapter III which gives the total present value of
the negotiation from the point of view of player 1:

$$U_1^* = \left[f(q_1) + \frac{C_1}{a} \right] e^{-aw} - \frac{C_1}{a} \quad (5)$$

Differentiating this partially with respect to C_1:

$$\frac{\delta U_1^*}{\delta C_1} = -\frac{1}{a}(1 - e^{-aw}) \quad (41)$$

As expected, equation (41) implies that to increase bargaining
costs decreases the present value of the negotiation. Similarly,
we may determine the present value to player 1 of a change in
the opponent's demand, q_2. As we have already suggested, this
quantity is not derived from a change in expected payoff, but

from a reduction in the amount of time which is expected to pass before agreement is reached. This reduction is determined by differentiating equation (5) partially with respect to w and using the fact that $w = (q_1 + q_2 - M)/r_2$:

$$\frac{\delta U_1^*}{\delta q_2} = \frac{\delta U_1^*}{\delta w}\frac{\delta w}{\delta q_2} = \frac{-a}{r_2}\left[f(q_1) + \frac{C_1}{a}\right]e^{-aw}$$

From the expression for the optimal q_1 [equation (6)] this becomes:

$$\frac{\delta U_1^*}{\delta q_2} = -af'(q_1)\,e^{-aw} \qquad (42)$$

Throughout this discussion of bargaining costs we have been using the variables C_1 and C_2 as proxies for whatever specific cost changing actions the parties may take. It should not be forgotten that, although these are proper independent variables for us to consider, their values are not directly observable by the negotiators themselves. The costs C_1 and C_2 represent quantities of utility which cannot be measured in dollars or other physical units. Thus when the first party takes an action which increases preagreement costs, he knows the value of C_1, but he is unable to quantify the change in C_2. He may be well enough acquainted with the nature of his opponent's preferences to know when he is increasing C_2, but he cannot know precisely by how much. For his purposes, however, the magnitude of the change in C_2 is irrelevant, since his concern is with the extent to which he is able to change q_2, not with the amount of discomfort which he causes. Moreover, as long as our assumption that the parties' expectations take the "correct" form is satisfied, the impact of any of his actions upon q_2 is immediately observable, because the second party responds to the higher cost with a single, one-time shift in his demand. The first party is therefore able to determine how much it "costs" him to induce a given shift in his opponent's demand—he can observe dq_2/dC_1.[3]

Is There Any Solution?

It would now be natural for us to construct a model in which the first party makes increasing use of the cost imposing moves which are available to him until a point is reached at which further increases place more of a burden upon him than is justified by the associated reduction in the other's demand. There is, however, an unexpected difficulty with such a model: it is clear from equations (41) and (42) that maximizing behavior of this kind could lead to continuously increasing use of force as the negotiation progresses. As agreement draws nearer, for example, w approaches zero, so that the discount factor, e^{-aw}, approaches 1. This implies, from expression (41), that the disutility of any given increase in C_1 declines. The reason for this is apparent: C_1 describes a utility loss which recurs in each time period, and naturally we expect the influence of such a cost to be reduced as the time lag to agreement is reduced. For the same reason, we see from expression (42) that the value of any given reduction in an opponent's demand increases as time passes. This property also has a simple explanation, although it is not so obvious from the equations themselves. As the bargaining process nears agreement, the expected concession rates, r_1 and r_2, become smaller; thus a cost induced concession appears increasingly valuable as negotiators come to recognize the length of time which is required for an equivalent concession to come about naturally.

Equations (41) and (42) indicate not only that the utility of cost increases will grow as the negotiation progresses, but also that there is danger of a kind of "escalation" in cost changing decisions. Whenever C_1 and C_2 are increased, the parties' demands fall, and, again, w declines. This in turn is likely to increase the perceived desirability of further increases in costs, so that we may find bargaining costs increased virtually without limit. In part, this is neither an implausible nor an unfamiliar phenomenon; it is actually only a form of the principle of "getting the matter over with as quickly as possible." After all, if costs are so high that further bargaining is intolerable, then those costs may not have to be borne at all. It is tempting to conjecture that military escalation is often a consequence of considerations such as these. A nation may accelerate its application of force, not because it is afraid that it will "lose" otherwise, but because with the added force it can win *sooner*.

There is a striking similarity between the phenomenon of escalation as it appears here, and the process of arbitration. Indeed, the use of such high costs that agreement occurs immediately may prove to be beneficial to both sides for the same reason that arbitration is beneficial to them: each party finds the immediate agreement to be preferable to further negotiation, even if the resulting settlement yields him a payoff smaller than that which he was originally demanding. It is possible that if both parties indulged in cost imposing tactics, the outcome of the escalation would be little different from that of voluntary arbitration. More will be said on this point in a subsequent section.

Despite the suggestion that bargaining costs are subject to a serious escalation problem, most negotiations are not characterized by the unlimited use of force. There are two considerations which tend to limit cost imposing action. The first is simply the danger, which we have already mentioned, that such actions may antagonize the other party and disrupt the whole process. The use of force is generally not compatible with voluntary cooperation, and hence the object of the negotiation may be sacrificed if one side resorts to what the other would regard as an act of hostility. If this is indeed the effective constraint upon bargaining cost increases, and if a party makes his decision by weighing the gains from the increased use of force against the hostility which that force arouses, then, of course, our model is constructed from the wrong variables, and we would need to introduce more psychological inputs before we could construct a predictive theory.

There are many situations, however, in which the psychological factor does not appear to be the constraining one. Despite the adverse effect of such actions upon the tempers of negotiators, we find that strikes and lockouts do play a well-established part in labor negotiations, that price wars do take place in industrial disputes, that tariffs are encountered which seem to have been established largely for bargaining purposes, and so on. In these cases, unlimited escalation seems to be forestalled only by restrictions upon the supply of reasonably effective actions. This supply may be limited by the environment itself; for example, during an international dispute one nation may refuse to trade with another any longer, but after this action is taken there may simply be nothing left to do. Ultimately, however, most such restrictions are probably set culturally; that is, the set of "legitimate" actions is relatively small, and as a party attempts to compound the bargaining costs which he imposes upon his opponent, he finds the effectiveness of these actions declining rapidly. In this case the escalation problem is avoided (the second order conditions can be satisfied), and we can proceed to construct a model of "optimal" bargaining cost decisions.

The Optimal Use of Force

If each party has available a set of possible cost imposing actions, and if these actions can be ranged in order of decreasing "effectiveness" (as defined in the last chapter), then we may utilize equations (41) and (42) to determine how much force will be used. The first party will increase the costs of bargaining until the benefits which he derives from earlier settlement are matched by the increased costs themselves. That is:

$$\frac{\delta U_1^*}{\delta C_1} \, dC_1 + \frac{\delta U_1^*}{\delta q_2} \, dq_2 = 0$$

Substituting from equations (41) and (42), this may be rewritten:

$$\frac{dC_1}{dq_2} = af'(q_1) \, \frac{e^{-aw}}{1 - e^{-aw}} \tag{43}$$

As w approaches zero, e^{-aw} approaches 1, and by equation (43), dC_1/dq_2 becomes indefinitely large.[4] This is simply a restatement of our earlier observation that as agreement nears, the bargainer becomes increasingly willing to incur costs in order to obtain concessions from his opponent.

As we pointed out in the last section, the first player is never able to quantify the actual bargaining cost which he has imposed upon his opponent because this variable is defined in utility units; he is able to observe only the change in the second player's demand. There is a relation between the change in C_2 and the change in q_2, however, as given by equation (39). We may substitute this relation into equation (42), and obtain the marginal ratio of bargaining costs which is implied by player 1's action:

$$\frac{dC_1}{dC_2} = \frac{af'(q_1)}{bq'(q_2)} \frac{1}{\left[\dfrac{r_1\,g''(q_2)}{b\,g'(q_2)} - 1\right]} \frac{e^{-aw}}{1 - e^{-aw}} \qquad (44)$$

To simplify our discussion of the problem, we shall restrict our analysis to a case of linear utility functions. This restriction not only eliminates second order terms, but it implies that the frontier of the agreement possibility set is a straight line whose slope, dU_1/dU_2, is equal to $f'(q_1)/g'(q_2)$, whatever the values of q_1 and q_2 are. Thus equation (44) reduces to the following:

$$\frac{dC_1}{dC_2} = -\frac{a}{b} \frac{dU_1}{dU_2} \frac{e^{-aw}}{1 - e^{-aw}} \qquad (45)$$

where dU_1/dU_2 is the slope of the linear boundary of the utility possibility set.

Comparison with the Static Model

Considering the differences in their premises, it is not surprising that the static and dynamic models will, in general, provide different conclusions regarding the extent to which the parties will deliberately change the costs of bargaining. The contrast is very similar to that between the (static) Nash theory and our dynamic model of the bargaining process in Chapter III. It is a little more difficult to compare these two descriptions of cost imposition, however, because the dynamic model suggests that the use of force will increase over time, rather than maintain some stable value. This is a reasonable result—as expectations change, for example, we certainly expect a party to change his choice of tactics—but it leaves us with no satisfactory standard of comparison. The best we can do, then, is to describe those circumstances under which the dynamic model predicts that more force will be used than was indicated by the static model, and those in which less will be used.

Suppose that the conditions necessary for the Nash outcome are met; that is, the parties' discount rates and learning rates are equal. Then the static model [equation (36) in the last chapter] provides the equilibrium condition $dC_1/dC_2 = -dU_1/dU_2$, while equation (45) gives $dC_1/dC_2 = -(dU_1/dU_2)e^{-aw}/(1 - e^{-aw})$. These two are equivalent when $e^{-aw}/(1 - e^{-aw}) = 1$, or when $aw = 0.69315$. This is a relatively large figure; for example, if the discount rate is 25 per cent, w is equal to almost 2.8 years at this point. When the bargaining process is expected to take less time than this, *more* force will be used than is indicated by the static theory.

It is worth noting in passing that when $e^{-aw}/(1 - e^{-aw}) = 1$, then if the first party has the higher learning rate, he will use more force than is indicated by the static model, while if he has the lower learning rate, he will use less.[5] Similarly, when the discount rates are not equal (but learning rates are), the party with the lower discount rate will tend to use more force than is indicated by the static model, and vice versa.[6]

The Cost of Bargaining and Arbitration

We have already suggested that there is a similarity between the effects of large scale cost imposition and arbitration. In each case the parties find that the benefits of early settlement can outweigh losses from reduced payoffs and/or higher bargaining costs. Since cost imposition generally entails much larger losses than does arbitration, we expect it not to be used as readily as arbitration. Fortunately, it is not difficult to compare these two methods of bringing about an early settlement. Suppose we regard as "expensive" any use of force beyond that suggested by the static model. Such high cost imposition will occur whenever we have $e^{-aw}/(1 - e^{-aw}) > 1$; this occurs whenever $aw < 0.69315$. We may reduce this condition to a statement about the parties' demands by solving equation (6) for r_2, and substituting this into the definition of w.

$$\frac{(q_1 + q_2 - M)f'(q_1)}{f(q_1) + \dfrac{C_1}{a}} < 0.69315$$

We are still dealing with the case of linear utility functions ($U_1 = fq_1$), and so this relation may be rewritten as below:

$$q_2 < M + 0.69315 \, C_1/af - 0.30685q_1 \qquad (46)$$

Equation (46) is readily compared to equation (32) in Chapter V, which establishes the boundary within which splitting the difference will be acceptable to the first party as an arbitration scheme.

$$q_2 = M + 1.5936 \frac{C_1}{af} + 0.5936q_1 \qquad (32)$$

Whenever the inequality in (46) holds, the first party is certainly willing to accept arbitration to end the dispute. This tends to support the position that extreme cost imposition can serve to substitute for arbitration; that is, that whenever arbitration is not practicable (because there is no neutral third party, or because the issues to be negotiated are so complex that the arbitrator cannot identify an acceptable settlement point), then the parties may make use of high bargaining costs to achieve the same result.

In this regard there is an interesting practice which arises especially in cases of international bargaining, that of placing a firm deadline upon the negotiations which, if exceeded, puts an end to the process and leaves the parties in permanent disagreement. This can be interpreted as a bargaining cost which will become very large as time passes (whenever w is greater than the time left before the deadline date, the value of the agreement falls to zero). This device may be viewed as a voluntary means for making costs very high so as to prevent the negotiation from taking an enormous amount of time. It has the same effect as arbitration.

■ NOTES

1. It is possible that there are second order changes in marginal utility resulting from the smaller demands. Referring to equation (7), it is clear that this can have an influence on concession rates.

2. In practice, negotiators are certainly conscious of the possibility that one-time concessions would be interpreted as large increases in a concession rate, and, as a consequence, they would probably break down any large shifts in their demands into a series of small moves, simply to avoid this misinterpretation. Further discussion along these lines would bring us into the area of bluffing, a dimension which we wish to treat separately in the next chapter.

3. Of course, all this depends upon our elimination of the possibility of bluffing. If the second party deliberately misrepresents his payoff expectations in any way, it will be much more difficult for player 1 to estimate the extent of his influence over q_2 accurately.

4. The second order conditions which would confirm that U is indeed a maximum are extremely messy. We require $d^2U_1{}^*/dq_2{}^2 < 0$ where

$$
\frac{d^2U_1{}^*}{dq_2{}^2} = -\frac{1}{r_2} e^{-aw} \left[\frac{dC_1}{dq_2} - f'(q_1) \right] \left(\frac{dq_1}{dC_1} \cdot \frac{dC_1}{dq_2} + 1 \right)
$$

$$
- af''(q_1)e^{-aw} \frac{dq_1}{dC_1} \frac{dC_1}{dq_2} - \frac{1}{a}(1 - e^{-aw}) \frac{d^2C_1}{dq_2{}^2}
$$

In addition to the usual signs, we have $dC_1/dq_2 < 0$ and $d^2C_1/dq_2{}^2 > 0$. All of these terms are positive except for the last, and the coefficient of this negative term approaches zero as the negotiation nears agreement. This, of course, is the problem which we have discussed in the text.

5. Equation (44) is independent of our learning rates, α and β. Equation (36), however, through its dependence upon r_1 and r_2, is not. Suppose $\alpha > \beta$. As we have shown, this will lead, at equilibrium, to $r_1 > r_2$. From equation (36), this implies a smaller value of dC_1/dC_2; thus equation (45) indicates a greater use of force.

6. We showed in Chapter IV that when utility functions are linear, equilibrium would provide $r_1/r_2 = \sqrt{A/B}$ [equation (17)]. Since $\alpha = \beta$, this reduces to $r_1/r_2 = 1/\sqrt{a/b}$, and substituting this into equation (36) we obtain $dC_1/dC_2 = -(dU_1/dU_2)(a/b)^{1/2}$. When $a < b$, this gives a smaller value of dC_1/dC_2 than is indicated by equation (45): the static model thus underestimates the amount of force that player 1 will use.

VIII

▪ Bluffing

Introduction

As it has been developed so far, our theory has dealt only with what we have termed the "pure intransigence" component of the bargaining process. That is, we have assumed that the two parties simply put down their payoff expectations as explicit demands without any embellishments. As long as this assumption is satisfied, any incompatibility between demands reflects a fundamental divergence between expectations, and not simply the effects of verbal overstatements. The preceding chapters have provided some justification for the conviction that this is an extremely fruitful simplification to make. In dealing with bargaining problems, it is very easy to get bogged down in questions of strategy and tactics and, in so doing, to overlook the variables and relationships which underlie the whole situation. Moreover, although bluffing strategies may have an effect upon the bargaining process, they surely will not alter its fundamental character, and the insights which we have obtained from analysis of our pure intransigence model should apply reasonably well to all cases.

One of the impediments to an analysis of the general negotiation problem is the large number of qualitatively different strategies which the players may employ. The term "bluffing" is commonly applied to a wide variety of phenomena, many of which have absolutely nothing to do with one another beyond a

166

common property of involving something other than sheer forthrightness. Many of these, moreover, deal with special opportunities for misrepresentation which do not lend themselves particularly well to generalization. For our purposes, we shall distinguish two classes of bluffs: bluffs which are intended to distort or influence an opponent's perception of preagreement and disagreement, and bluffs which distort the payoff demands themselves.

Even this distinction does not bring the phenomena much closer to generalization, because each of these two types of distortion can appear in a variety of ways. For example, there are at least three entirely different ways of influencing preagreement. First, one of the parties may make a threat which he never intends to carry out, or he may promise to do something which he intends—or is forced—to do anyway. These are cases of actions which are falsely represented as being conditional upon some move or concession from an opponent, and, of course, this is the sort of bluff which can be "called." The object of these tactics, of course, is to influence an opponent's valuation of preagreement or simply to alter the perceived risk of prolonging the negotiation. A second type of bluff which is aimed at influencing preagreement is that in which one party conceals certain unfavorable outcome possibilities, or at least conceals their properties. For example, a shopkeeper may be aware that the same goods which he is selling can be obtained more cheaply across the street, but he is quite unlikely to inform his customers of that fact. In a third case, a bluff may consist of the understatement of certain potential preagreement costs. For example, if a firm stands to lose a profitable contract in the event of a strike, and if it feels that the loss would damage the company more than it would the union, that information may be carefully withheld.

The difficulty in handling these types of bluffing is essentially one of quantification rather than principle. If we are able to quantify their impacts upon opposite parties, taking into account variations in plausibility, then bluffs of this class can be introduced into theory via the model of cost imposition which we have already described. The technique for performing the analysis would be little different from that which follows for a second class of bluffs.

The second class of bluffs is associated with distortions of payoff expectations themselves. If we may dismiss the possibility that the parties will ever deliberately understate their expectations, then this is the case in which the apparent magnitude of the disagreement exceeds the divergence between expectations. We are particularly interested in this type of "bluff" for several reasons. In the first place, this strategy does not require the presence of any special circumstances or opportunities before it can be implemented. It is possible to inflate one's demands in any negotiation, regardless of the situation. Moreover, it seems to be the case in practice that demands are often increased to levels which exceed expectations by substantial amounts, and furthermore that most participants, as well as observers, *expect* demands to be inflated. Second, *a priori* considerations lead us to expect the parties to overstate their expectations, at least in the early stages of the bargaining process. Any negotiator with even minimal experience must have learned that he will very likely have to make some explicit concessions of his own. It is natural for him to try to avoid having to make any "real" concessions by building these expected sacrifices into his demands at the start, intending to give them up at whatever times seem propitious to him. Third, the popular notion of "bargaining in good faith" seems to require the making of some concessions if one is to retain the good will of the other party, and it might, therefore, be a good idea to leave enough "room" in one's demand to permit downward revisions, even when no change in expectations has taken place. Finally, each party probably recognizes that his own behavior can influence the demands of his opponent, and it may be believed that high demands will have a favorable influence.

Restricting the analysis of bluffing to cases in which payoff demands exceed payoff expectations still leaves room for a wide variety of particular bluffing strategies. For example, a player's bluff may consist of a demand for an exceptionally favorable outcome, this demand being maintained until the other player concedes to some desired payoff level. Alternatively, a player may demand a large payoff initially, and reduce the magnitude of his bluff gradually, either in proportion to the passage of time or in proportion to changes in his expectations. As a third case, the player may bluff by coordinating his concessions with his opponent's behavior, in an effort to "reward" certain actions and "punish" others. These and similar kinds of bluffing strategy can be introduced into the model which we have already analyzed. It would not be fruitful for us to devote much space to an extensive discussion of all of these, however. Instead we shall concentrate first on drawing some general conclusions, and then on giving a short illustration of one strategy in order to demonstrate how such behavioral assumptions can be introduced into our theory.

The analysis of the role of bluffing in the bargaining process would be very difficult if we attempted to take into account the wide variety of expectations variables which seems to be relevant. So far, our study has had to deal with only one such variable, the concession rate which each party expects to obtain from the other. If we attempted to deal with the *motives* for bluffing, however, we would have to consider several others in detail. First, there is the extent to which one party expects his own demand and concession rates to affect those of his opponent.

Second, if the parties were also engaging in cost imposing tactics, we would have to determine how each party estimates the impact of his actions upon his opponent's demand, and how that party takes into account the possibility that his opponent's demand in itself is a misrepresentation. Third, if any of these relationships were nonlinear, then, of course, we would encounter still more parameters which the parties must estimate before settling upon the appropriate bluff.[1] Since each of these relations is a question of expectations, each would have to be explained within the framework of a *learning* process. The number of variables required for such an analysis would very likely leave the model completely intractable. Indeed, it is not certain that such a model could even be constructed in principle, since most of the relevant learning processes would have to be related to the same observation (the opponent's actual concession rate); hence it would be impossible to determine which expectation needed to be changed. Did the second party concede less than expected because his concession behavior is nonlinear, because the first party has not made a convincing bluff, or simply because the first party has over-optimistic expectations? As it happens, as long as we are willing to investigate the nature of bluffing in a fairly general way, it may be quite unnecessary to perform such a complicated analysis as this suggests. This is so because we can show in general that over-stating one's demands will not improve one's payoff at agreement at all!

A player's optimum demand is given by expression (6) in Chapter III:

$$f(q_1) + \frac{C_1}{a} = \frac{r_2}{a} f'(q_1) \qquad (6)$$

We have already discussed the fact that the q_1 so determined is not a function of q_2, but only of r_2, the rate at which the second player is expected to concede. The second party may make what-ever demand he likes; as long as q_2 is not so high that the first party refuses to negotiate altogether (because the expected value to him of the negotiation is zero or less), there will be no change in q_1. It follows that it is simply not possible to reduce an op-ponent's expected payoff by inflating one's own demand. Indeed, if player 1 is also bluffing, it is likely that the magnitude of his bluff is determined in part by the value of q_2; thus the higher q_2 is, the higher q_1 may be.

If the second party wishes to behave in such a way as to bring about a small payoff demand from player 1, his strategy must be one which will induce a small value of r_2. This variable, however, is not determined by the level of q_2, *but by its rate of change.* That is, the second player will induce the first to make a small demand only by convincing him that his own concession rate is small. Now, whenever the second party demands a payoff larger than that which he expects, he will at some point have to make conces-sions in order to reach the intended outcome. This naturally will increase (or fail to decrease) the first player's estimate of r_2, re-sulting in a *less favorable* outcome for player 2. The best strategy, then, would be to minimize one's own concession rate, and this can be accomplished by demanding the payoff which one expects anyway. In the last analysis, the best bluff is no bluff at all! It should be borne in mind that, in terms of this model, concessions are *always* a sign of weakness, and hence that it is always a bad strategy to take steps which are likely to require additional concessions of one's own.

This conclusion is not altered if both players are bluffing, although it can happen that the bluffs cancel one another out so that the outcome point itself is not changed from what it would have been without any bluffing. Nevertheless, both parties will be made worse off, because their exaggerated demands have added to the amount of time which is required to reach agreement, and thus have increased the cost of reaching their settlement.

A Model of Demand Exaggeration

In this section we shall give one simple example to support the generalizations in the foregoing section, and also to demonstrate how considerations of bluffing behavior can be introduced into our bargaining model.

Consider a bargaining situation in which each party adds to his payoff expectation enough leeway, in the form of an inflated demand, to enable him to counter the expected concessions of his opponent with some "concessions" of his own. Naturally, the magnitude of this bluff would be decreased as agreement approached, partly because there would be less need for such "leeway" and partly because the existing bluff would be "used up" as time passed. It is desirable, from the point of view of simplicity of our model, to make this bluff as uncomplicated as possible, and hence we will suppose that each party demands an outcome which is greater than his expectations, according to some fixed proportion of the distance between his opponent's current payoff demand and his own expectations.

Anyone engaging in a strategy of inflating his own payoff demands would certainly be on the lookout for similar behavior on the part of his adversary. It is therefore necessary for us to consider each party's estimate of the extent to which the other is also distorting his demands. In general, the greater the difference between the two players' demands, the more bluffing each is likely to attribute to the other; let us again keep the model simple by assuming that each player estimates the magnitude of his opponent's bluff as a linear proportion of the distance between them. Let us define the following terms:

q_1^e = player 1's actual payoff expectation

q_1 = player 1's payoff demand

q_2' = player 1's estimate of player 2's actual payoff expectation

We may define q_2^e, q_2, and q_1' similarly from the point of view of player 2. The distance between player 1's outcome expectation and his opponent's demand is equal to $(q_1^e + q_2 - M)$, and hence, using simple linear rules, we can derive the first party's demand and his estimate of his opponent's "actual" expectation,

$$q_1 = q_1^e + \lambda_1(q_1^e + q_2 - M) \qquad (47)$$

$$q_2' = q_2 - \eta_1(q_1 + q_2 - M) \qquad (48)$$

Here λ_1 and η_1 are positive constants, with η_1 always less than 1. Note that we could have used the distance between the first party's expected payoff and his opponent's demand to obtain the estimate q_2' instead of the total distance $(q_1 + q_2 - M)$. This would have no effect upon the structure of the model: indeed, we would simply be using a different parameter $\eta_1^o = \eta_1 (1 + \lambda_1)$.

Similar expressions can be used to describe player 2's demand and his estimate of player 1's actual expectation:

$$q_2 = q_2^e + \lambda_2(q_2^e + q_1 - M), \qquad (49)$$

$$q_1' = q_1 - \eta_2(q_2 + q_1 - M), \qquad (50)$$

where λ_2 and η_2 are positive constants, and η_2 is less than 1.

Although there are no *a priori* restrictions on the magnitude of

λ_1 and λ_2, some peculiar problems can arise if they are very large. Suppose, for example, that one party followed the simple rule of inflating his own demand by an amount equal to the difference between his own expected payoff and his opponent's demand; that is, suppose $\lambda_1 = 1$. This would seem at first to be a reasonable strategy, because it permits concessions from the other party to be matched by concessions of one's own with no loss in expected return. However, if both sides were to make use of such a bluff, or if they were to bluff even more than that, it would be possible for demands to escalate without limit. Every time q_2 was increased by one unit, q_1 would also be increased by one unit, and this in turn would lead to a further increase in q_2, and so on. In practice, there are constraints which prevent λ_1 and λ_2 from equalling or exceeding unity over a very wide range. In the upward direction, there are bound to be limits beyond which demands would become patently absurd, depriving any further bluff of its value. In the other direction, no one would ever ask *less* than his expected payoff: thus it is impossible for demands to contract without limit. Since we must have $\lambda_1 < 1$ and $\lambda_2 < 1$ for both very large demands and very small demands, our linear approximations must retain these values throughout.[2] This ensures that when q_2 is increased by one unit and q_1 increases as a consequence, q_2 increases further, but by an amount less than one unit.

Eliminating the $(q_1 - M)$ term between equations (48) and (49), we can compare player 1's estimate, q_2', with the actual payoff expectation of player 2 (q_2^e):

$$q_2' = q_2(1 - \eta_1 \frac{1 + \lambda_2}{\lambda_2}) + q_2^e \eta_1 \frac{1 + \lambda_2}{\lambda_2} \qquad (51)$$

From equation (51) it follows that player 1's estimate is correct $(q_2' = q_2^e)$ whenever $\eta_1 = \lambda_2/(1 + \lambda_2)$. Similarly, player 2 will correctly estimate the value of q_1^e whenever $\eta_2 = \lambda_1/(1 + \lambda_1)$. We shall call the bluffs "successful" whenever $\eta_1 < \lambda_2/(1 + \lambda_1)$ and $\eta_2 < \lambda_1/(1 + \lambda_1)$.

Suppose that at some point during a negotiation, player 2 revises his expectations downward by an amount Δq_2^e. This will lead to a reduction in his expressed demand, and this in turn will lead to a fall in the demand of player 1 as well, since he now will reduce the magnitude of his bluff. In response to the drop in q_1, of course, player 2 may reduce his demand further, and so on. We will therefore find *both* demands reduced, with

$$\Delta q_1 = \lambda_1 \Delta q_2$$

$$\Delta q_2 = (1 + \lambda_2) \, \Delta q_2^e + \lambda_2 \Delta q_1$$

Solving these two so as to eliminate the Δq_1 term, we can find the total change in the second party's demand which results from the change in his payoff expectations.

$$\Delta q_2 = \frac{1 + \lambda_2}{1 - \lambda_1 \lambda_2} \, \Delta q_2^e$$

Since λ_1 and λ_2 are both positive and less than one, their product is also positive and less than one. Thus we still have the reasonable result that when q_2^e falls, q_2 falls as well. This expression may be combined with equation (51) to give us the change in q_2' which results from the change in expectations.

$$\Delta q_2' = \left[1 - \frac{(1 + \lambda_1)(1 + \lambda_2)}{1 - \lambda_1 \lambda_2} \left(\eta_1 - \frac{\lambda_2}{1 + \lambda_2} \right) \right] \Delta q_2^e \quad (52)$$

If the second party's bluff is successful, then expression (52) states that $\Delta q_2'$ is greater than Δq_2^e; that is, player 1 will *overestimate* the magnitude of the concession.

Expression (52) can be introduced into any version of our bargaining model, putting q_2' in wherever q_2 appeared before. Under most circumstances—all cases in which the second player is not actually increasing his demands—the learning process will lead player 1 to form optimistic estimates of r_2 and hence to concede more slowly than he would otherwise. If the second player's bluff is successful and the first player either does not bluff or fails to fool his opponent, then at agreement the ratio r_1/r_2 will be smaller than it would otherwise have been. From equation (13) in Chapter III it follows that the bluffing player will be made worse off by his own strategy.

Besides moving the agreement to the favor of the player who is not bluffing successfully, a strategy of overstating demands will lengthen the amount of time which is required by the negotiation. This, of course, is simply due to the fact that bluffing leads to overestimates of concession rates, and these lead to reductions in actual concessions. This is especially true if both parties are overstating their demands. Even if the bluffs cancel out in the sense that the outcome is unaffected, the time cost will still be very large.

Naturally, bluffing is another factor which must be taken into account before we could predict the Nash solution as the outcome of a negotiation. Specifically, besides our original conditions (identical learning abilities, identical discount rates, and symmetric utility functions), we must require that influence of bluffing be the same on both players. Referring to equation (52) we note that the extent to which the players overestimate one another's concession rates will be equal whenever:

$$\eta_1 - \frac{\lambda_2}{1 + \lambda_2} = \eta_2 - \frac{\lambda_1}{1 + \lambda_1}$$

The magnitudes of the players' bluffs (given by λ_1 and λ_2) need not be equal, but the "success" of the bluffs must be. The fact that one of the parties is overstating his expectations does not affect the outcome except insofar as the other party fails to appreciate it.

Other Bluffing Strategies

If we know that our simple bluff of overstating demands fails to produce any benefit for the bluffer, it is tempting to start searching for other strategies which will work better. Basically, there is only one other class of devices for overstating one's demand. We found that the policy outlined in the last section led to a worsening of one's payoff because it required that one produce relatively large concessions before an agreement is possible. It might appear that a more effective device would be to choose some payoff q and insist upon it, come what may, until the other party conceded entirely (or, what is basically the same thing, to demand a payoff q until the other party conceded to a point q', and then to jump to agreement).[3]

Using such an approach, the bluffing player would have to appraise his opponent's willingness to concede and then insist upon (or plan to jump to) some outcome which justified waiting for his opponent to concede to it. This, however, is precisely the mode of behavior which we have been attributing to each player all along! That is, in our model each player selects and demands a payoff from which he has no intention of conceding. In fact, concessions occur only when the basic data upon which he based his choice of payoff appear to have been changed.

It is, of course, possible for our player to bluff by demanding the outcome q permanently, even if, in the light of increased information (due to his learning behavior), this demand no longer appears to him to be optimal. This procedure *may* in fact increase a player's expected return: it certainly increases his physical payoff, although it also can increase the time necessary to reach agreement so much that the player's overall expected return is reduced. The major difficulty with this strategy is the impossibility of choosing an optimal demand—that is, we have already assumed that the player uses all the knowledge which is available to him in formulating his demand, changing that demand only when his knowledge changes. There is no reason for him to believe that his first impression will determine a demand which is a good one to which to apply this strategy. Although payoff demands do exist which are better (from one player's point of view) than direct optimization under limited knowledge, there is no way to distinguish them from bad demands which are much worse.

Finally, we note that this policy of demanding some outcome permanently, regardless of expectations, would be the worst that a player could possibly follow if the other were doing so as well. In short, this extreme "all or nothing" approach does not appear to be a useful alternative to our original "best" bluff of no bluff.

Why Overstate Demands?

Our discussion has led to the rather surprising result that overstating one's payoff expectations will, in general, operate to the bluffer's own disadvantage. One is naturally led to wonder what the factors are which induce negotiators to engage in such strategies in practice. After all, experienced bargainers, not just novices, seem to practice bluffing in this form, and therefore one would hesitate to declare that such behavior has no real value.

We have attempted throughout this study to emphasize the "mixed motive" character of the bargaining process. Although we frequently have referred to the parties as "opponents," we have repeatedly stated that the fundamental purpose of a negotiation is to organize *cooperation*. If the atmosphere of cooperation is disrupted, or if the parties become so antagonized by one another that each comes to derive satisfaction from the discomfort of the other, the negotiation may cease to offer any potential gains to either one of them.

It is our view that one form of bluffing—the simple overstatement of payoff expectations—has the effect of deemphasizing the competitive element of a negotiation relative to the cooperative element. This, moreover, is taken to be true despite the possibility that one party's ill temper may vary positively with the magnitude of the other's demand. We have already mentioned one way in which bluffing has this effect: high demands make possible expressions of "good faith" in the form of concessions even when no change in expectations is taking place at all. Indeed, in the area of labor negotiations, the National Labor Relations Board has actually formalized this process by stipulating that failure to make concessions is contrary to the directive that the parties engage in "bargaining in good faith." At least in this field the making of concessions is now mandatory, and, of course, any negotiator will take this requirement into account in determining his expressed demand.

This same concern for the emotional stability of a negotiation has led to our position that retraction of a previous payoff demand is a highly undesirable action. Despite the fact that increases in demands are perfectly consistent with our theory, we expect them to take place only rarely, because of the destructive impact which they may have on the cooperative spirit of a negotiation. The overstatements of payoff expectations, however, have the very useful property of permitting a player to conceal the fact that he is raising his expectations. That is, bluffing makes increases in q_1^e possible without running the risk of antagonizing a future partner. Moreover, especially at the start of a negotiation, one may be sufficiently unsure of the opponent's willingness to concede to want a good deal of leeway for revising expectations in one's own favor. Bluffing introduces such leeway, since it enables one to change expectations without modifying an actual bid.

This last motivation for bluffing also leads to a conclusion which is quite similar to Siegel and Fouraker's observation that players with more information tend to be more modest in their initial demands. We may attempt to "explain" this observation by means of two remarks: (1) increased knowledge leads to more accurate (less optimistic) expectations, and (2) increased knowledge reduces the need for bluffing by increasing the likelihood that expectations will be confirmed, and hence reducing the likelihood that a player will want to retract.[4] It may be argued that the first of these was the sole cause of the observed behavior, but to do so would require the rather strong assumption that, at the start of the negotiation, the players expected very favorable payoffs (far above the mean of the payoffs in their tables) in situations in which they had virtually no knowledge. It seems more plausible to assume that the very lack of knowledge, coupled with Siegel and Fouraker's rule that no bid, once made, could be retracted, brought about initially high bids as a defense against uncertainty—that is, it stimulated bluffing.

Bluffing and Arbitration

We have discussed at some length the uses of arbitration as a substitute for the bargaining process itself. It is likely that certain kinds of "bluffs" are important, not because they influence the bargaining process, but because they alter the outcome which is generated by various arbitration schemes. Thus if a wage dispute is to be settled by splitting the difference, the union will be benefited if it manages to convince the arbitrator that it expects a settlement of $4.00 an hour instead of $3.00. Similarly, if an automobile dealer insists that a car cost him $2400 instead of $2200 he is likely to get a better price for it, even if the selling price is always found to be greater than either of these figures. If a split-the-difference rule is used, every $1.00 by which he overstates his cost will add $.50 to the final selling price.

Although bluffing which is intended to influence arbitration settlements provides clearcut payoffs, there are two equally clearcut disadvantages to it. First, it may lead to an arbitration proposal which is so heavily biased against the other party that he rejects it and the arbitration fails altogether. Second, such bluffing often will involve the making of such bald falsehoods that the probability of their discovery is very great, and an uncovered bluff is likely to be so disruptive that the potential for a mutually beneficial agreement is entirely destroyed. If the parties are nearing the end of a protracted negotiation, and arbitration is seen by both as a highly desirable alternative to further discussion, neither party is likely to risk failure by bluffing heavily. If, on the other hand, the negotiation is one which can easily be arbitrated right at the outset, there is a high payoff to any party who can effectively conceal the fact that he has misrepresented or distorted the limits of the bargaining range.

■ NOTES

1. We should admit here, with regard to expectations of nonlinear relationships, that we made an important simplification in our basic model by assuming that concession rates were expected to be constant. That assumption was not looked upon as a seriously stringent one because, no matter what concession behavior one party expects from the other, the basic mechanism of the model (demands changing because concessions are not found to correspond to expectations) will not be affected. The important

assumption was that the parties' expectations were taken to be *symmetric*, that each party expected the same type of concession behavior from the other. Suppose instead that Adam expected a constant concession rate from Bill, but Bill expected a nonconstant concession rate from Adam, anticipating that Adam would concede rapidly at first, and more slowly afterward. Such a situation could be introduced into our model, although it would certainly add complications.

2. In a nonlinear model, of course, we could have a range of $\lambda \geq 1$, but, due to the instability of the resulting model, demands would never be found in that range. They might begin very high (near the upper limits of plausibility), and contract for a while in a stable fashion; but as soon as the intermediate range was reached, demands would explode downward until we had $\lambda_1, \lambda_2 < 1$ again.

3. These two approaches are analytically identical because of our conclusion that the opponent's demand is determined by one's own concession rate, and not by one's demand.

4. If we look upon a player's outcome expectations in terms of a probability density, (1) refers to the mean of the distribution, while (2) refers to its variance.

IX

■ On the Control
of Disagreement

Introduction

It is frequently true that the direct participants in a negotiation are not the only ones who pay the costs associated with the disagreement. Indeed, it is often the case that the interests of people who have no part in the dispute are even greater than the interests of those who are directly involved. When the longshoremen, the teamsters, or the steelworkers go out on strike, whole economies may be disrupted, and jobs as well as profits may be lost by people who have only a very distant relationship with the industries concerned. A New York City transit strike, for example, not only leaves millions of citizens walking to work, but it may imperil the existence of thousands of shops and other business establishments in the area.[1] Similarly, while the "great powers" haggle over the particulars of a nuclear test ban treaty, nonnuclear nations can do little but sit back and wonder how much longer the atmosphere will continue being poisoned. Third parties who are affected in these ways often seek means either to influence or at least to accelerate the negotiations in order to reduce their own losses. Unfortunately, it does not seem to be common for their efforts to meet with a substantial measure of success. We have just devoted a considerable number of pages to an analysis of the bargaining process; it is proper now to see if that analysis sheds any light upon the difficulties which are encountered in attempting to influence the negotiations of others, and to see if we can reach any conclusions regarding the best directions for such efforts to take.

Parties who are not directly involved in a negotiation may nevertheless have three different types of interest in it. First, they may be sympathetic toward one of the sides. For example, if the Teamsters Union achieves a large wage increase in its agreement with the truckers, that fact can be used as a precedent in other industries, contributing perhaps to wage increases elsewhere. Thus members of other unions would like to see as large a settlement as possible for the teamsters. In this sort of a situation, it is most appropriate for the "outsider" simply to join forces with the favored participant in the negotiation. From the point of view of our theory, this does not represent much of a complication, since it requires no more than the substitution of an "alliance" for one of the sides in the dispute. On the other hand, the third party in this case may not participate directly in the negotiation, but may instead take steps to improve the bargaining position of one side —either by imposing costs upon the opposite side, or by sharing the bargaining costs of the favored party. Analytically, this situation can also be handled in a straightforward manner through the use of a model of cost imposition similar to that in Chapter VI.[2] Thus this case of "pure sympathy" is not really a complex one and is not of much interest to us here.

In a second case, it is possible that although the third party has no particular sympathy toward one or the other negotiator, he is concerned with corollary properties of the settlement. For example, a wage settlement which embodies significant inflationary potential is often regarded as contrary to the "public interest"; this is taken to be a sufficient justification for government intervention. Similarly, nations may negotiate to form trading blocs which exclude other countries. In this sort of situation the interests of both negotiators are more or less in opposition to those of the outsider. There is therefore no neutral way for the latter to gain his own ends; he must participate actively in the bargaining process itself.[3] This is really a case of three person bargaining, a problem which is not qualitatively different from the one which has been discussed in previous chapters. A short discussion of multiple player bargaining appears in Appendix E.

In this chapter we shall focus upon the third case of outsider interest: that in which the very existence of the negotiation imposes costs upon third parties, either because the dispute interferes with their own activities (as in the case of strikes), or because the settlement itself promises to bring them some new benefits. When this case arises in its purest form, the third party has no interest whatever in the specific nature of the agreement but only in the amount of time which will pass before the dispute is resolved.

We recognize that often, perhaps usually, the three types of concern which we have outlined occur in combination. It is possible that although a third party is primarily interested in an early settlement, he might like to influence the characteristics of the agreement as well, in spite of the fact that he is not really a party to the negotiation. This same qualification may be even more important in reverse: the third party may be very anxious *not* to influence the agreement. He may wish for an early settlement, but this desire may often be tempered by principles of propriety or equity, so that he refrains from any involvement at all for fear of influencing the outcome. Thus in labor disputes, even when the public has no obvious interest in the nature of the agreement itself, the government may often avoid interference with the bargaining process for fear of distorting some "balance of power." Whether this attitude is sensible or not is a question which need not concern us here: it arises often enough so that we will have to consider the extent to which various methods of third party intervention will bias the bargaining process and lead to outcomes favoring one or the other side.

Quite a number of ways have been suggested to reduce the amount of time required by the bargaining process. It is perhaps not surprising to find that by far the largest proportion of these, especially of the ones which have actually been implemented, have been designed to deal with labor–management negotiations. These disputes have become the natural targets of intervention for two reasons. First, the economic costs which they can impose upon the general public are very high. Indeed, it is difficult to find comparable bargaining situations in which the number of persons seriously affected by a conflict can be so much larger than the number of disputants themselves. Usually, of course, a strike does not last long enough to do extensive economic damage, but the potential is always there, and third parties can be expected to take whatever steps are available to them to prevent the realization of that potential. Second, most of the stratagems which can be used to accelerate the bargaining process require that the third party have some degree of influence over the negotiators; at the very least, they must be willing to listen and take suggestions from him, and for many purposes the third party must be able to bring substantial amounts of pressure to bear. This fact makes it quite difficult, for example, to find a practical means for small nations to accelerate negotiations among larger countries because there is rarely any way of exerting the necessary influence. In the case of labor negotiations, on the other hand, governments possess considerable amounts of legal and political influence over the participants, and this makes possible the use of a number of methods that generally could not be implemented effectively elsewhere. For these reasons, our own discussions will also be most relevant to the problem of containing labor disputes although, at least in principle, they could be applied to any negotiation.

We have already had occasion in this study to touch upon most of the issues which are to be discussed here. We shall, in fact, make use of only the variables which we have already introduced into our theory, treating each device for accelerating the bargaining process by analyzing its impact upon those variables. An incidental benefit of this approach is that this chapter will serve to summarize some of the most important features of our study as well as to evaluate modes of intervention. We shall not use the more obvious criteria to classify these strategies—such as treating them in terms of the amount of force they require, or according to the stage of the negotiation at which they are most effective—but instead we shall organize them with respect to the particular variables which they affect the most.

Changes in the Cost of Bargaining

A large proportion of the devices which have been suggested as means of bringing about an early settlement in bargaining disputes are really little more than attempts to impose costs or loss of payoff value upon the negotiators themselves, with the hope that this will give them an additional incentive to come to agreement quickly. These costs may be associated with the bargaining process itself, increasing the personal inconvenience of extended debate, or they may make the temporary state of disagreement more expensive. In either case, further delay of agreement becomes more painful than it was before. We have distinguished three forms which such costs could take: constant amounts which recur in each period of time, a deterioration in the value of a settlement, and costs due to the time preferences of the negotiating parties. We will concentrate upon the first of these in this section and treat the other two later.

The recurrent bargaining costs C_1 and C_2 have a rather special effect upon the model which we have constructed. Although they do influence the players' demands, they do not play any primary role in the mechanism of concession. We have repeatedly emphasized that concessions take place as a consequence of the learning process: expectations change through learning, and demands are altered in accordance with changes in expectations. Neither of these relationships is affected by the presence of recurrent bargaining costs, and therefore, barring second order effects, concession rates will take the same values that they would have otherwise. Demands, of course, are lower as these costs are higher [see equations (38) and (39) in Chapter VII] so that, given the unchanged concession rates, we can conclude that any action which increases C_1 and C_2 will necessarily bring about an earlier agreement.

Attempts by a third party to accelerate the bargaining process by increasing its costs may result in changes in the point of agreement for two reasons. The first stems from the earlier agreement itself. Recall that in Chapter III we discussed an important property of the dynamic model of bargaining: the presence of an equilibrium mechanism which tends to remove large asymmetries in the players' expectations. As a consequence of this mechanism, we argued that to the extent that there is enough time for this equilibrium to work itself out, the bargaining process will arrive at an agreement point which is independent of initial expectations. It is clear that increases in the recurrent costs C_1 and C_2 will reduce the time available for this equilibrium process as well as bring about an earlier settlement. Moreover, increases cannot accelerate that process since, as we have just noted, they have no influence over the dynamic properties of negotiation. We must conclude, therefore, that whenever C_1 and/or C_2 are increased, the importance of initial expectations in the determination of the outcome will be proportionately greater. A numerical example of this phenomenon was given in the last section of Chapter IV. Of course, if the third party who imposes the higher costs is interested only in an early settlement, this result is of no concern to him. If he feels bound by principles of noninterference with the point of agreement, however, this may lead him to hesitate before using such cost increasing levies.

The fact that inducing an early settlement will interfere with the equilibrium mechanism is probably of minor importance, however, compared to the possibility that the bargaining costs themselves will be levied unequally. If this second problem arises, then the point of agreement may be heavily biased in favor of the party who is least affected. The likelihood of this result is increased by the difficulty of identifying a "neutral" cost increase, or even of specifying it in principle. If we are to distinguish the distortions which are due to nonneutral costs from those which are due simply to the earlier settlement, then we must define a "neutral" increase in bargaining costs as one which would not influence the outcome *in the event that the equilibrium process had ample time to work itself out*. The equilibrium outcome of the bargaining process is given by equation (11) in Chapter III, and the cost increases, to be neutral in our sense, must not affect the agreement point described there. Hence, the cost increases ΔC_1 and ΔC_2 must satisfy the following equation:

$$\frac{\frac{\Delta C_1}{a}}{\frac{\Delta C_2}{b}} = \frac{f(q_1^o) + \frac{C_1}{a}}{g(q_2^o) + \frac{C_2}{a}} \tag{53}$$

Here C_1 and C_2 are the existing bargaining costs experienced by the two players, a and b represent their respective discount rates, $f(q_1)$ and $g(q_2)$ are their utility functions, the right hand term in the equation is determined by the equilibrium outcome of the bargaining process [equation (11) in Chapter III], and q_2^o and q_2^o are the equilibrium payoffs.

As a practical matter, it is very unlikely that one could devise bargaining costs which would not alter the point of agreement in some way. In the first place, to determine neutral increases from equation (53) would seem to be virtually impossible for all but the most extremely simplified situations, because it would require that one know ahead of time just what the outcome will be. Even if we did know the neutral values of ΔC_1 and ΔC_2, the outcome would be affected by them because of the reduction in time available for the equilibrium adjustment. The determination of cost increases which would not affect the outcome in any way at all would require a complete specification of the whole dynamic process, including the parties' initial expectations.

The third party may fail to impose neutral cost increases only because of the difficulty in determining them. The problem may be compounded, however, by a limitation in the supply of actions which he is able to take. After all, negotiators normally do not submit voluntarily to externally imposed increases in their bargaining costs. It is necessary that the third party have some authority over the parties if such increases are to be levied successfully, and the costs which are required to bring about an early settlement may very well exhaust that authority. Therefore, if the third party has more influence over one side than the other, he has no alternative but to impose his costs unequally as well, and this will contribute to a further distortion in the settlement. For example, it is widely believed that in the 1956 Suez crisis, the United States had far more influence over France, Britain, and Israel than it had over the U.A.R., so that its efforts to settle the dispute quickly led to an extremely favorable outcome for the U.A.R. Finally, it is quite possible that the extra burdens which are placed upon the negotiators are deliberately chosen to influence the outcome, not because of institutional limitations, but because the third party feels more sympathy with one of the sides. This is a relatively straightforward problem which, as we have already pointed out, could be handled within a framework similar to that in Chapter VI.

There is a rather severe weakness inherent in the use of bargaining costs to bring about an early settlement. We have argued that if a third party takes steps to increase the recurring costs of bargaining, he will succeed in reducing demands, but his action will have no effect upon the learning process. It follows that the players' expectations will remain optimistic even at agreement, so that if the cost increases are ever removed, demands will immediately increase back to their former levels. Even if agreement has already been reached, the bargaining process is likely to be resumed. Thus the threat of high bargaining costs may have to be in effect permanently if the agreement is to be preserved. Unfortunately, many cost imposing devices are strictly temporary in their effects, so that either their use will prove in the long run to have been ineffective, or some device must be found to maintain the settlement. This, of course, is one of the reasons for establishing binding contracts. It is possible to get an early settlement simply by refusing any lunch to the negotiators until they agree, but without the legal and cultural apparatus of a contract, the bargaining process would resume all over again as soon as they had eaten. If the enforcement of a contract is difficult, then many cost imposing devices whose effects are necessarily temporary lose their value as means for bringing about an early settlement. It is likely that this is true in the area of international agreements, for example, in which the contracts and treaties often do not have the permanence which is characteristic of domestic agreements.

Our use of the phrase "increases in bargaining costs" tends to obscure the very wide variety of actions which can be used to bring about earlier settlements by increasing the unpleasantness of the bargaining process. These costs are by no means all economic in nature. For example, actions are often taken which serve simply to increase the personal inconvenience or danger of disagreement. In 1948 President Truman threatened to draft the railroad engineers, and during the 1965 steel dispute, President Johnson brought the chief negotiators to the White House and was rumored to have refused them any meals until they came to an agreement. In more mundane cases the costs are basically economic: the United States may refuse economic aid to both sides in a dispute, or the customers of a corporation which is struck may actively seek new sources of supply. We have already discussed the possibility that the negotiators themselves may use methods of increasing bargaining costs in order to influence the outcome (see Chapters VI and VII), and occasionally it has been suggested that these same costs be used by third parties to hasten agreement. An interesting example of this is the so-called statutory strike.[4] The idea behind this device is simply that when a union goes out on strike, both sides (as well as the general public) suffer economic losses. Why not require the employees to stay on the job and then tax both sides in amounts equivalent to those losses? Economically, both sides would be in a position equivalent to that under a strike, but the rest of the economy would suffer a much smaller loss. An additional attraction of such a scheme is that it would preserve the initial balance between the two parties, and this, as we have already observed, seems to have been accepted as a desirable objective when dealing with labor negotiations.

Another very great advantage of the statutory strike is that if the legal or political authorization for the scheme is ever abolished, the agreement will nevertheless be preserved. The same costs will be incurred by the parties whether they are just taxed or are actually undergoing a strike. The problem inherent in other cost imposing actions, that elimination of the costs will revive the negotiation (because of unchanged expectations), does not arise here. To the author's knowledge, the statutory strike has never actually been put into effect. This is probably due to the practical impossibility of quantifying all of the losses and benefits which may accrue to the two sides from the strike. Many of these are not easily put in dollar terms. For example, the company may suffer some permanent loss of market, or, on the other hand, it may be pleased to be able to dispose of an unwanted inventory surplus. The employees may be happy to have an "unplanned" vacation. Unless such things can be measured, the statutory strike will not preserve the balance as it is supposed to do.

An interesting device, similar to the statutory strike, but perhaps slightly more practical, would be to permit the strike, and instead of calculating its economic cost to the participants, to estimate the dollar loss which it imposes upon the general public. This sum could then be levied upon the two participants *together,* leaving them to determine the allocation of the tax between themselves as part of the negotiation. The tax burden which would result from this strategy would be quite different from that resulting from a statutory strike. In cases in which the public cost of the strike is low (for example, in which only a portion of the industry is closed down and there are alternative sources of supply) the tax would also be quite low. In every case, however, the costs of bargaining to the participants would be higher than that under a statutory strike, and thus agreement would come sooner. There are two advantages to such a system. First, there is no need to accomplish the virtually impossible feat of discovering taxes which would simulate a strike. There are, indeed, difficulties in estimating the social cost of a strike, but a politically defensible minimum figure could be used without fear of distorting the outcome of the negotiation. Second, it would permit the parties to substitute tax burden for conditions of agreement. That is, it would be possible for one party to absorb a larger share of the tax in exchange for a policy concession from the other, leading to an outcome which both would prefer to one with fixed tax shares. This same device has one rather curious drawback: once the parties have entered into a strike phase, they must be prevented from ending the strike until after they reached agreement upon the distribution of the tax burden. Any other method for enforcing the tax payment would necessarily involve costs (or threats) which were not related to the negotiation and which, of course, would not preserve the "balance of power" between the negotiators.

We should note, finally, that the costs which are incurred by the two sides in a strike are largely a matter of happenstance. Insofar as this is true, there is no clear reason (other than political necessity) why an authority whose only concern is with an early settlement should seek to reproduce those costs. Indeed, if it was felt that for institutional reasons one side had an undue advantage over the other, unequal costs could be imposed so as to "redress" the balance. This, of course, simply leads us back to the case in which the third party is sympathetic toward one of the sides.

Changes in the Cost of Disagreement

The discussion in the last section applies to any change in the recurring costs of bargaining. Nevertheless, we must be careful to distinguish between policies which alter the costs of the bargaining process itself and those which alter the character of permanent disagreement. In many cases, especially those involving labor negotiations, actions which increase the costs of delaying agreement do not permit the parties to "agree to disagree," giving up their entire cooperative enterprise and thus saving themselves all further bargaining costs. For example, the taxation schemes described at the end of the last section share this property. Whenever this is true, it becomes possible for one or both of the parties to wind up with an agreement payoff which is inferior to the original point of disagreement. In the case of a simple increase in bargaining costs (personal inconvenience, and so on), this sort of thing is impossible—neither party will ever concede beyond a point which yields him no more of a return than does permanent disagreement. Such a party will simply break off negotiations and save himself further bargaining costs by settling upon no agreement at all. Once permanent disagreement is artificially made more unpleasant, the parties may be forced to concede even further, leading to settlements which did not appear at all in the original set of outcome possibilities. Naturally it is doubly true in this case that the resulting agreement must be permanently enforced, by contract or other device, if it is to be preserved at all.

Compulsory Arbitration

In principle, compulsory arbitration is really only an extreme form of a cost imposing device. After all, it would be impossible to dictate a permanent settlement to the parties unless it were possible to levy prohibitive costs upon both of them in the event that they adamantly persisted in their disagreement. The analysis of compulsory arbitration is therefore quite similar to the foregoing discussion of increased bargaining costs, except that its conclusions tend to be more extreme in nature.

The simplest means for terminating a dispute which imposes heavy losses upon a third party certainly is to specify a settlement somewhere between the current demands of the parties and to enforce it. In its crudest form, such an action would require of the arbitrator very little insight into the particular negotiation which is involved, and no sophisticated understanding of the bargaining process in general. It does not involve even a semblance of an attempt to resolve the original divergence of expectations between the parties. As a consequence, of course, even if the agreement point which is chosen corresponds precisely to the settlement which the negotiators would have achieved independently, it must be true that the associated payoffs are inferior to the expectations of at least one of the parties. The settlement, whatever it is, will be regarded with hostility by that party, and whenever an opportunity arises, he will naturally attempt to reopen negotiations. If the settlement is to be established for any length of time, it must be enforced either by the establishment of a contract or through permanent third party control. Compulsory arbitration can never contribute to a working out of the negotiators' differences; it can only delay the conflict until the time that the enforcement of the settlement is relaxed.

A further disadvantage of using compulsory arbitration is that there is no guarantee that the arbitrated outcome is a potential point of agreement at all. Indeed, there is a considerable danger that it is not. As we argued in Chapter V, many disputes are probably difficult to settle because the limits of the range of possible agreements are so indistinct as to permit current expectations to be highly unrealistic. If this is the case, compulsory arbitration based upon the players' demands (or upon some compromise of them) is likely itself to lie outside the range of possible voluntary settlements, leaving one of the parties worse off than he would have been with no agreement at all. This is, of course, the same problem which we brought up in the last section with respect to increases in the costs of disagreement. In the more extreme case of compulsory arbitration, this problem is likely to be exacerbated. For example, if the negotiation involves a large number of separate issues, so that the set of possible agreements must be defined with several dimensions, it is quite possible that a compulsory settlement would leave *both* parties worse off than they would be with no agreement at all, despite the presence of a number of agreement points beneficial to both sides.

The Influence of the Discount Rate and Other Time Costs

The second type of cost which we associated with the bargaining process is that due to the natural preference for present over future goods. The longer the agreement is delayed, the less the present value of any given payoff, the rate of loss of value being represented by the players' discount rates, a and b. We would expect this influence to be similar to that of any other bargaining cost, and, indeed, we have already observed a resemblance to the recurrent costs C_1 and C_2, since high values of a and b will be associated with lower demands, other things being equal.

In contrast to the recurrent costs, however, the discount rates also have an impact upon the dynamics of the concession mechanism. They do not influence the learning process, of course, but as we pointed out in Chapter III, they do affect a player's response to revised expectations; higher discount rates tend to decrease the size of the concession which results from a given change in expectations. Since high discount rates tend to be associated both with smaller demands and with lower concession rates, it is not obvious on the surface what their net effect will be. When we appealed to the more restricted examples in Chapter IV, we were able to get more specific results with respect to this question, and there we concluded the following:

1. Higher discount rates will indeed bring about an earlier termination of the bargaining process.

2. Increases in discount rates tend to stabilize the bargaining process, reducing the possibility that one party will concede while the other retracts back to a very high payoff.

3. Increases in discount rates tend to accelerate the equilibrium process, so that it is possible for the outcome to be even less dependent upon the players' initial expectations than it would be otherwise, despite the earlier settlement.

Thus, high discount rates have the property of inducing an earlier settlement for the bargaining process than do the other types of bargaining cost, but they have the added feature of contributing desirable dynamic properties as well. Certainly, if a third party wished to intervene in a negotiation by increasing the costs of negotiation, but in a way which minimized his interference with the outcome, he would do best to change the parties' discount rates! Unfortunately, of course, an individual's rate of time preference is not generally thought of as a variable which is subject to external influence; nevertheless, it is possible to devise bargaining costs which will *simulate* such changes, as follows.

The third form in which time imposes a cost upon the bargaining process, deterioration in the value of payoffs themselves, has a similarity to the other two types of cost which we have already discussed. As it happens, any action which degrades the present value of a payoff by some constant percentage for every additional period of time between the present and the time of agreement will have exactly the same effect as an increase in discount rates. Moreover, costs which affect a negotiation in the same fashion as discount rates often arise quite naturally; for example, if a labor negotiation has gone past the point of a strike, the company may find its market being eroded gradually by its competitors, with roughly the same fraction of its remaining loyal customers defecting each month. It is possible that other common methods of bringing pressure on negotiators have a similar effect. The mobilization of public opinion against the parties may operate in this fashion. This latter tactic, moreover, has an advantage to its user in that it does not require that the third party have extensive legal or political control over the parties, and as a result, it can be applied to a wide variety of situations. Even in critical international disputes—nuclear test ban treaties or even armed conflicts—the influence of public (international) opinion can be utilized. On the other hand, the amount of pressure which can be brought to bear in this fashion often is not very substantial.

Naturally, not every cost which varies over time has the same effect upon the dynamic properties of the bargaining process. Recall that the recurring costs have no effect upon concession rates or the stability of the process so long as they are constant. We have just observed that costs whose impact *decreases* as the expected length of the negotiation increases do influence these dynamic variables, reducing concession rates and contributing toward stability. Intuitively, one would expect the reverse to be true for costs whose impact increases over time. That is, if a negotiator suffered a loss equivalent to $10 for the first day, $20 for the second, $30 for the third, and so on, we would find concession rates increased.[5] Indeed, it would appear on the surface that costs which were levied in this way would be the most effective because this would bring about the highest concession rates of any such device. However, if one is at all concerned with permitting the equilibrium to work itself out as far as possible and with preventing instability, this would be the worst pattern one could choose. Concession rates are by no means the best indicators of the effectiveness of cost increasing devices.

Mediation

Thus far we have discussed only the more "unpleasant" means that a third party may employ in order to hasten the conclusion of a negotiation. It is true that techniques which increase bargaining costs are often the first to come to mind, and it is also true that they are the most certain to work: high costs are *bound* to have some effect. Nevertheless, it is worthwhile to consider actions which will tend to oil the machinery of bargaining, as well as those which simply attempt to bring about an early settlement through the use of brute force. There are several reasons for preferring such an "oiling" approach to the cost imposing one. In the first place, if the bargaining process is permitted to work itself out, there is no problem that unresolved differences in expectations remain submerged in an enforced agreement. As we observed, if an early settlement is achieved through the use of cost imposing devices, at any time that those (potential) costs are removed, the disagreement will break out again and the whole negotiation will be resumed. It would certainly be preferable if the negotiation had been permitted to come to a natural conclusion, so that permanent enforcement of the agreement would not be necessary. A further potential advantage of any policy designed to accelerate the bargaining mechanism is that the third party would find himself much less vulnerable to the criticism that he distorted the outcome by imposing unequal costs. A third benefit is that these actions could be much easier to apply, because they do not require the third party to be able to exert much pressure upon the negotiators. He must, indeed, have enough influence over them to be permitted to involve himself in the negotiation, but he need not have the power to impose substantial losses on either.

It is natural for us to look first at the influence of possible changes in learning rates, since learning has played a central role in our bargaining theory. Moreover, although we have treated them as parameters, the learning rates are not really unalterable characteristics of the bargaining process. Disagreement is a consequence of incompatible and hence *erroneous* expectations: the rate at which those expectations are modified is certainly a function of the accessibility of the means to correct those errors; that is, of the accuracy, clarity, and credibility of the information which is transmitted between the two negotiators. Now it is quite likely that the use of various forms of bluffing as well as the expectation of bluffing from one's opponent will tend to interfere with efficient communication and hence with the learning process.

Even if one party were to describe his own expectations completely and accurately, it is unlikely that he would be believed. It is quite possible under these circumstances that, if we were to introduce a third party who enjoyed the trust of both sides and who was not expected to bluff, we might find the credibility of information passed between the two parties to be greatly increased. As a result, the learning process would be accelerated, and an earlier settlement would be brought about.

A third party whose activities are designed to improve the transfer of information in this way fills the role usually described as mediation. Mediation can be a very efficient mechanism for accelerating a bargaining process because it imposes no additional losses upon the parties, nor does it require the mediator to be a "powerful" individual. On the other hand, the problem of locating a really neutral mediator can be a serious one. If the third party who has an interest in an early settlement is known also to be concerned with the specific properties of the settlement, he will not be acceptable as a mediator himself, nor is it likely that he will be able to nominate another party who will be accepted as a neutral by both sides. In the area of international negotiations, for example, this seems to be a particular problem: it is astonishing how difficult it is to suggest, even casually, a true neutral in any major dispute between nations. If this is the case, then mediation of course ceases to be a practical means for bringing about an early agreement.

Increasing the speed of learning through mediation will, of course, have an influence over the dynamic properties of the bargaining process. For example, we noted in Chapter IV that high learning rates can contribute to instability in the bargaining process: rapid concessions in response to a quickened recognition of inflexibility in an opponent's position might only increase that inflexibility, or even encourage retraction of an offer. On the other hand, as long as the negotiation is stable, high learning rates have the compensatory advantage of accelerating the equilibrium mechanism as well, tending to reduce the dependence of the final outcome upon initial expectations.

Arbitration

Mediation or, in fact, any activity designed to accelerate and improve the flow of information between the negotiators will have another effect upon the bargaining process besides its impact upon learning. We arrived at the very striking conclusion in our study of arbitration that voluntary arbitration is virtually certain to take place if the limits of the range of possible agreements are well known and if there is some disinterested third agent who is able to suggest a settlement. The obstruction to early arbitration may be a simple matter of inadequate information concerning agreement possibilities: being unaware of the maximal available payoffs, the negotiators may make demands which exceed the potential of the situation. Again, it is the possibility of bluffing which brings this situation about. One's opponent is likely to insist that one's demand is "impossible" (that is, inferior to permanent disagreement from his point of view) whether or not that is true. If, through the intervention of a third party, the true limits of the bargaining range become known, a settlement may occur almost immediately. This conclusion is weakened in proportion to the number of issues being debated in the same negotiation: as we pointed out in Chapter V, the difficulty of identifying a settlement point which is acceptable to both sides increases rapidly as the number of dimensions in the problem increases.

Ideally, the purpose of "fact finding" should be to identify and quantify the subject matter of the negotiation, the objective being to simplify the process of arbitration. Unfortunately, this does not seem to have been the motivation of most "fact finding" efforts in the past; many of these seem to have been designed more to influence public opinion, or even to identify "guilty" parties, than to clarify the situation to the negotiators themselves. Potentially, however, efforts to quantify the subject of the negotiation for the participants' own use could prove to be the most influential of all methods for bringing about early agreement.

■ NOTES

1. See, for example, editorials in *The Wall Street Journal*, January 26, 1966.

2. The outside party would simply determine his own return from each possible point of agreement and then choose the set of bargaining costs which maximizes that return.

3. This of course requires that the third party be able to impose some costs upon or withhold some benefits from the others, so that his agreement will make a difference to them.

4. LeRoy Marceau and Richard Musgrave, "Strikes in Essential Industries: A Way Out," *Harvard Business Review,* XXVII (1949), 27.

5. Further discussion of this phenomenon is given in Appendix C.

X

▪ An Application to Economic Theory: Models of Oligopoly

Introduction

In this chapter we shall apply our negotiation theory to a specific economic problem. This involves a considerable departure from the substance of previous chapters, since the object of our discussion is no longer the bargaining process itself, but rather an economic situation in which such a process may be expected to occur. Our purpose, however, is not that of "solving" a new problem by proving that its answer lies wholly in the understanding of the bargaining process; we are really only interested in demonstrating how the model which we have constructed can be applied to specific problem areas in economics.

It is not at all difficult to find economic situations in which the bargaining process is relevant; indeed many of the most pressing problems in modern economics seem to involve circumstances in which only a few individuals are involved and in which, therefore, simple market models are not very satisfactory. In these cases, the assumptions which are commonly associated with both perfect competition and pure monopoly models not only seem to be unrealistic, but worse, they seem to neglect some of the most basic factors influencing the outcomes. It has become increasingly clear that oligopolistic markets, for example, are not merely quantitatively different from markets with numerous small competitors, but that they depend upon variables which were never relevant even in the most general analyses of competitive markets. Many of these markets (for instance, bilateral monopolies) can probably be approached through the direct application of a bargaining model, since it is clear that explicit negotiation between the parties actually is the means whereby the market decisions are made. In other situations, however, overt communication between the parties is either impossible or at least undesirable, and the use of our bargaining model, which depends upon such communication, would not be very reasonable without some further elaboration.

It is the purpose of this chapter to discuss these situations in terms of a model which will make the relevance of the bargaining process more explicit than it generally has been before. We shall conduct our analysis with reference to an oligopolistic market structure—a few firms buying inputs from purely competitive sellers and selling their outputs to competitive buyers—but the resulting paradigm should provide a good example of the approach one would use to deal with any situation in which two or more participants find possible variations in their joint returns (that is, the situation is "variable sum") and in which communication between participants is somehow limited.

Existing Theories of Oligopoly

It is worthwhile for us first to give a brief idea of the sort of work which has already been done in this area. The amount of material which exists on oligopoly theory is so enormous that any reasonably complete summary of it all would require an extensive treatise. We shall limit ourselves, therefore, to indicating our dependence upon the work of Fellner,[1] although some reference will be made to the works of Bishop,[2] Shubik,[3] Chamberlin,[4] and Stackelberg,[5] as well as the earlier theorists, Cournot[6] and Bertrand.[7]

It is only since the late 1940's that economists have begun to place much emphasis upon the bargaining process in their analysis of imperfect market structures. Formerly almost all of the thinking on this subject relied upon simple extensions of classical monopoly theory, treating the presence of other firms in the market as mechanically as possible. That is, the idea has always been to assume that each firm maximizes profit subject to some rigid assumption regarding the behavior of his competitors. Chamberlin[8] has classified these models under the headings "mutual dependence—ignored" (Cournot, Bertrand) and "mutual dependence—recognized" (Stackelberg, Chamberlin himself), depending upon whether or not the firms recognize the "indirect" effects of their policies—whether or not each firm recognizes that its competitors are likely to shift their positions in response to a shift in the firm's own position. Even these "indirect" effects, however, are often treated in too rigid a manner to be very realistic.

In general, these models can be described in terms of Stackelberg's familiar "reaction curves" for a duopoly model. In Figure 21, for example, we have diagrammed the quantity adjusting duopoly model. The horizontal axis measures the output of firm 1 and the vertical axis measures the output of firm 2. Given demand and cost data for the two firms, we can construct the dashed "iso-profit" or "profit-indifference" curves on the diagram. Consider, for example, the set of curves which are concave to the horizontal axis: each of these represents all the output combinations of the two firms which will yield constant profit to firm 1. As we move up, away from the horizontal axis, the "iso-profit" lines represent lower profit levels for firm 1. Similarly, the set of dashed lines which are concave to the vertical axis represent the iso-profit curves of firm 2. Now, imagine that firm 2 produces a fixed output of Q_2^o. So long as Q_2^o is not changed, firm 1 will produce an output Q_1^o—at the point at which a horizontal line from Q_2^o is tangent to an iso-profit curve—since this decision will produce the highest profit level which firm 1 can obtain, given Q_2^o. In this manner, for any value of Q_2, firm 1 can find an output which maximizes its profit. The set of all Q_2, Q_1 combinations which are generated in this fashion determines firm 1's "reaction curve"—technically the locus of the peaks of all his iso-profit curves. Similarly, of course, we can construct a reaction curve for firm 2. It is an important property of these curves that they are technologically fixed—they depend only on the profit functions of the individual firms (so long as factor supply and product demand conditions remain fixed).

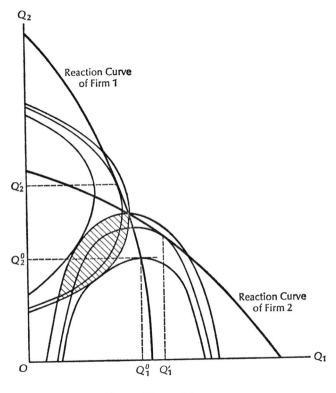

Figure 21

The Cournot solution is determined by the intersection of the two reaction curves—the point at which each firm has maximized its profit given the output of the other. It is well known, however, that this solution is not optimal from the point of view of the two firms—any point in the shaded area of the diagram would provide both firms with greater profits. In fact, many economists seem to believe that the outcome should be located somewhere on the locus of "Pareto optima"—the locus of points of tangency of the firms' iso-profit curves—because it is only at such a point that there are no further output adjustments that could increase the profits of both firms. A model due to Stackelberg comes closer to this result than does the Cournot model, but only at the great expense of assuming that each firm actually knows the reaction curve of his competitor. Thus in his theory, at least one firm will try to maximize his profit subject to the *reaction curve* of the other. In the diagram in Figure 21, for example, firm 1 will want to choose an output Q_1' where the reaction curve of firm 2 is tangent to an iso-profit line of firm 1. Unfortunately, as Stackelberg himself demonstrated, this approach is often completely unsatisfactory, because if each firm attempts to maximize against the reaction curve of his competitor, the model is likely to have no solution. In the case depicted in Figure 21, for example, firm 1 chooses Q_1' and firm 2 chooses Q_2' with the result that the outcome appears on *neither* reaction curve. If we construct our diagram such that one and only one firm prefers a point on his own reaction curve to a point of tangency between one of his iso-profit lines and his competitor's reaction curve, as is depicted in Figure 22, then this firm (firm 2) becomes a "follower," accepting the other's output as given and maximizing accordingly. Only in this case is the solution determinate.

As the example in Figure 22 suggests, it is always possible to avoid the Stackelberg dilemma by introducing leader–follower relationships into the assumptions of the model. In general, if one firm is accepted as a "leader," producing ultimately at a point of tangency between one of his iso-profit curves and the other's reaction curve, while the other—the "follower"—continues to adjust his output in the manner described by his reaction curve, the indeterminateness of the solution vanishes and we obtain a well-defined outcome. This sort of model, however, can only be used when it is clear how this asymmetry is to come about, that is, how the leader is chosen and what motivated the "leader" to lead and the "followers" to follow. Other than that shown in Figure 22, the only case in which this question is satisfactorily dealt with is that of a market dominated by one very large firm, with the rest of the market taken up by many very small firms. The small

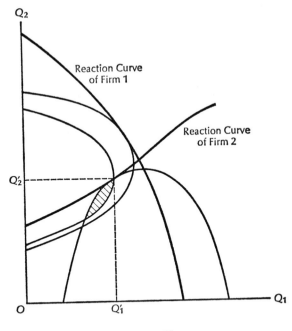

Figure 22

firms may be taken to behave competitively, and their resulting supply curve can be used as a reaction function against which the dominant firm maximizes profits. In duopoly markets, on the other hand, it is generally impossible to determine *a priori* who is to be the leader and who the follower in Stackelberg's sense.

Even the solution of the leader–follower model in Figure 22 is not optimal from the point of view of the firms themselves. All the output combinations inside the shaded area would generate higher profits for both of them. Moreover, it can be argued that firm 2 is making a mistake in accepting the role of follower; if instead it challenged the leadership position of firm 1, it might be able (through market bargaining) to win for itself an improved profit position. After all, firm 1 depends for its profits upon the acquiescence of its competitor.

The more recent "bargaining" models of oligopolistic behavior have introduced an important new dimension into this problem. Many of these theories recognized that it is not enough to point out that each firm is aware that its market decisions influence the operations of its competitor: an oligopolistic firm is also likely to be aware that the reactions of other firms can be *changed*. In this interpretation reaction curves are not permanently fixed by technological considerations; they must instead be treated as dependent variables in the analysis. When an oligopolist initiates a shift in his position or responds to a movement from another firm, the magnitude (and/or direction, if there is more than one variable) of his shift is certainly dependent, not only upon how he thinks the other will respond, but also on how he thinks his action will influence future reactions of his competitor. If these expectations change, then naturally his market actions will change accordingly, and these changes in turn will alter the expectations of the other firm. Thus the oligopoly problem, like the general bargaining problem, emerges as a matter of interacting expectations rather than simply one of maximizing against stationary constraints.

Unfortunately, many writers who have taken the "bargaining" approach to the oligopoly problem have never drawn out the full implications of this insight. For example, they have tended to focus their attention upon the set of efficient (Pareto optimal) outcomes to the problem without explaining how it is that the participants identify and achieve these outcomes. Thus both Bishop and Nash,[9] in their analyses, concentrate their attentions upon the Pareto optimal outcome alternatives, implicitly assuming throughout their work that both firms in a duopoly know the maximum possible profits and, in a sense, bargain over those profits. Bishop does construct "reaction curves," but these are "threat" and "warfare" curves designed to represent a firm's deliberate response to insufficiently cooperative behavior from another oligopolist. Surely this kind of approach looks at the problem from the wrong end. We have already pointed out the fact that neither firm knows nor has any way of knowing the locus of efficient outcomes beforehand, and it is hardly reasonable to construct a model in which two or more firms haggle over a set of alternatives of whose locations they are ignorant.

Fellner's analysis, on the other hand, does interpret a "reaction function" as the implicit object of a bargaining process, rather than a technologically fixed element in the theory. Unfortunately, Fellner has also made his analysis depend upon the asymmetrical concept of a "leader" and a "follower" in a duopoly, without explaining, in terms of his model, how this asymmetry is to come about.[10] Nevertheless, Fellner's basic construction will serve as a very useful starting point for a discussion which will repay (perhaps) part of this debt by making the conclusions of his model somewhat more concrete. In the following discussions we shall show how a pseudo-"leadership" condition may appear, even though it has far less relevance to the actual working of the market than it does in other analyses; and further we shall show that the model in fact may be expected to lead to a Pareto optimal solution, although only under very special circumstances may we expect attainment of the joint maximum.

Finally, the model which we will construct is meant to deal with a form of behavior rather than with a market having particular physical characteristics. It is true that complex oligopolistic interdependencies are possible only in cases in which there are only a few firms involved, but it is also true that even when this prerequisite is satisfied, the purely competitive or Cournot type of assumptions may be the relevant ones. Consider, for example, the political case of the United States and the Soviet Union, who at times have behaved as bitter competitors when a little implicit oligopolistic collusion would have been highly beneficial to both. Even when firms or nations are fully aware of their interdependence, our model may not be relevant: we are concerned only with the case in which each firm recognizes that its competitors may be induced to *modify* their responses over time so that it is possible for all to obtain increased profits through the resulting implicit collusion, and this is, indeed, a high order of awareness.

The Model

Just as in the general bargaining problem, we can distinguish three aspects of oligopolistic bargaining: the outcome, the mechanism of the market interaction which leads to the outcome, and the selection of market positions from which to bargain (the selection of "warfare" points). The last aspect is particularly important, because in the oligopoly example there is no obvious preagreement point which is in some sense "natural" to the situation. As usual, however, we must consider the mechanism of the bargaining process before we can discuss the matter of market warfare, and therefore we shall consider the negotiation to begin when the firms are at a particularly convenient starting point—the Cournot point.

Models such as Cournot's can be constructed in terms of price variables as well as quantity variables. Indeed, in the case of differentiated products which permit unequal prices to be charged by the firms, Figures 21 and 22 could have been translated into diagrams with prices on the axes with no loss in interpretation. This is frequently done by economists who feel that, although Cournot's assumptions are unrealistic in that any firm must realize that changes in its own behavior will cause its competitor to change output, they might not be so unrealistic when put in terms of price. That is, a firm may believe that changes in its own behavior will not cause its competitor to change its price. The resulting model would be similar to that of Cournot, although the outcome is not the same.[11] The formal structure of a model of oligopolistic bargaining could also be put in either price or output terms. Here we shall use a model expressed in units of output, because the resulting theory turns out to suggest the importance of market shares in oligopolistic bargaining, and this importance does seem to be reflected in the concerns of modern business management.

We have already outlined the bargaining model to be used. The "demands" of the firms are their reaction lines, and until the two parties agree on coincident demands it is impossible for them to move from the preagreement point. The "utility" to be derived from agreement is simply the profit which can be obtained from lower outputs and higher prices. Thus the parties never negotiate over the division of profits (just as individuals never bargain over utilities), even though higher profits are their ultimate objectives. The reaction curves in our model are just "reaction slopes": we use straight lines from the preagreement point, rather than more complex functions, because it would be a practical impossibility for one firm to communicate such demands to the other through the market place.[12]

Suppose that it is firm 1 which first attempts a movement from the preagreement point to generally lower outputs and hence higher profits. Thus it will reduce its output by some small quantity ΔQ_1. This quantity will be small partly because the firm is uncertain regarding the response of its competitor and partly because of the existence of various costs which are associated with large changes in output (such as setup costs). ΔQ_1 may prove to be a purely temporary contraction in output—if firm 2 fails to respond to this move, firm 1 will quickly restore its original output in order to avoid significant loss of profits. Suppose, however, that the second firm responds with a contraction of output, ΔQ_2. By doing so, firm 2 has established a demand—a "reaction slope" which indicates how firm 2 may be expected to respond to further output changes from firm 1.

The slope $\Delta Q_2/\Delta Q_1$ has implicit in it a certain expected profit level for firm 1; that is, in conjunction with the *status quo* point, it establishes a linear reaction curve for firm 2, and firm 1 can maximize his profits subject to this reaction curve. In the profit-indifference curve diagram in Figure 23, point A represents the preagreement point and point B represents the outputs after the two firms have reduced their sales by ΔQ_1 and ΔQ_2 respectively. Thus the straight line through AB is the demanded reaction slope of firm 2. If firm 1 were to accept this slope, it would maximize profits at point C. It may be that this profit level is satisfactory to firm 1, which in this case will try to move to the output level which is necessary to obtain this maximum. In general, however, we do not expect it to be satisfied with this, since firm 2 has probably "demanded" a reaction slope which is quite favorable to itself. Instead of accepting $\Delta Q_2/\Delta Q_1$ as the reaction slope, firm 1 may now establish its own desired slope by increasing this output level enough to set its *net* output decrease equal to $\Delta Q_1'$. This will communicate a "demand" or a reaction slope $\Delta Q_2/\Delta Q_1'$ to firm 2. Similarly, firm 2 will respond again with some $\Delta Q_2'$, and so on. Naturally, no permanent reduction in output will actually take place until the two firms manage to agree upon the reaction slope to be followed.

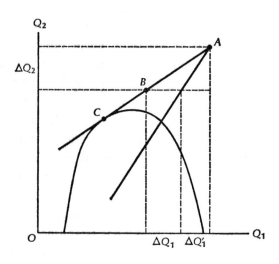

Figure 23

By this device of trial adjustments, each firm has indicated its "demand" to the other, and, in fact, we have developed a simple bargaining situation. Each slope $\Delta Q_2/\Delta Q_1$, given the original *status quo* point, yields a certain profit potential to firm 1, such that the greater is $\Delta Q_2/\Delta Q_1$, the greater is the profit. These profit figures are obtained for each firm by maximizing profits subject to the implied relative output levels. Of course, this procedure may not really be correct from the firm's own point of view because the other firm may refuse to maintain the value of $\Delta Q_2/\Delta Q_1$ all the way to the desired point of maximum profits. Nevertheless, as a first approximation, it is certainly a good assumption that each firm associates a given expected profit level with each value of the slope, and that this profit level is determined by this simple maximizing procedure.

Now suppose that agreement upon a reaction curve has not settled the problem because the absolute output levels at which the firms must produce in order to receive the expected profits are not the same. Indeed, this is likely to be the case in all but completely symmetrical situations with identical firms. With dissimilar firms, therefore, as the two contract their outputs along the agreed upon reaction curve, one will reach his optimum profit level first and then refuse to go further. For example, in Figure 24, firm 1 will refuse to contract output beyond point *P*. The second firm now has the choice of accepting the new outcome (which he certainly prefers to the old *status quo* point) or forcing a return to the old level. Even though the profit it receives at point *P* is inferior to its expectations, in general we expect the second firm to accept this outcome rather than attempting to re-open the bargaining process. The reason is that when the firm agreed upon the reaction slope *AP*, it compared the added expected profit which it would obtain from a more favorable reaction curve to the time cost which would result from a further delay in agreement, and found the cost to exceed the gain. This calculation has been disturbed by the failure to obtain even the profit which was expected from immediate agreement. Nevertheless it is reasonable to expect that, in the light of this new knowledge, the profits which would be expected from more favorable reaction curves are similarly reduced so that the reasons for reconsidering the decision to accept the present situation are not seriously strengthened. The total expected profit is reduced, but the marginal increment which can be realized from a more favorable reaction slope is not.

The possibility that one firm will reach an optimum profit level first and refuse to contract its output further introduces an interesting asymmetry into our model, but it is one which can be observed in practice, particularly in markets in which the relationship among the firms' prices is well established by technical considerations. In cases in which products are highly substitutable, for example, price adjustments must take place in equal proportions since the products must sell at common prices. When these prices are raised (and outputs are reduced) the final price is determined by the firm whose profits are maximized at the lowest price (and highest output)—all the other firms, many of whom may have already bid higher prices, must return to this level. To an observer it may easily appear that the situation is analogous to that shown in Figure 22; that is, the firm which thus fixes the

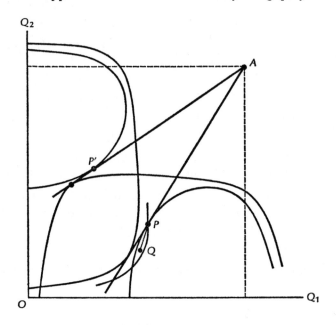

Figure 24

level is a "leader" in the market and the others are "followers." In our interpretation, however, the "leader" is not selected *a priori* as the firm which is to maximize profits subject to the reaction curves of its competitors; it is instead only the most efficient firm at the selected level of production (that is, it has lower marginal cost; its total cost, of course, may not be the lowest among the firms). It is, moreover, quite possible that if a different slope $\Delta Q_2 / \Delta Q_1$ had been agreed upon, a different firm would have emerged as "leader." For example, in Figure 24 firm 1 refused to move beyond point P when the reaction curve was AP. If, instead, the two firms had settled upon a reaction curve AP', it would have been the second firm that appeared to be a price leader.

The process of adjustment need not end permanently at the point selected by the leader, however. If the new levels of output are not Pareto optimal from the point of view of the two firms, then, by definition, further improvements in profits are possible for both of them. The new outputs can be used as the *status quo* point for a further bargaining process. Indeed, a new bargaining process may be initiated immediately as the less efficient firm attempts to extend the collusive agreement beyond the maximum profit point of his rival. Although the "leader" will refuse to move further along the agreed upon reaction slope, it is certainly willing to contract output further along some other line which will give it additional profits. Thus a new slope, $\Delta Q_2/\Delta Q_1$, will be selected, output will be reduced, and one of the firms will emerge as "leader" by being the first to refuse further contraction. This firm is not necessarily the same one which filled this role previously. From this new solution a third bargaining process may arise, and so on. This sequence of implicit negotiations will continue until both firms, contracting along a selected $\Delta Q_2/\Delta Q_1$, have maximized their profits at (approximately) the same point (as in point Q in Figure 24). By definition, moreover, such a point must represent a Pareto optimum from the point of view of the two firms.

The Characteristics of the Outcome

Applying what we have already learned about the bargaining process to the model of oligopoly bargaining, we can conclude the following:

1. Implicit oligopoly bargaining can lead the firms to a state of efficient collusion. This result does not require that any firm have knowledge of a competitor's profit or cost functions, and, further, no explicit communication is required beyond that already available through investigation of market data.

2. If the two firms are completely identical, having the same learning rates, discount rates, and profit functions, if the *status quo* point is symmetric, and if increasing returns to scale are not present, then the outcome will be symmetric ($Q_1 = Q_2$), and the firms will divide a jointly maximum profit equally. This is hardly a surprising conclusion, given the assumption of total symmetry. The requirement that returns to scale be constant or diminish is inserted to prevent instability in the bargaining process—that is, if we had increasing returns, any deviation from a symmetrical reaction curve would strengthen the insistence of the profiting firm for further gains while reducing the resistance of his com-

petitor. Thus increasing returns would tend to lead a duopolistic (or, in general, an oligopolistic) market into monopoly control: internal economies of scale are incompatible with stable oligopoly just as they are with perfect competition.

3. If the firms have similar learning rates and discount rates, the outcome of each individual bargaining process will tend to be the Nash solution—that is, the reaction curve which is chosen will maximize the product of the firm's expected profit increments over the *status quo* point. It does not follow, however, that the overall solution satisfies the Nash criterion: a series of small Nash solutions need not add up to a general Nash solution.

4. Firms with higher learning rates will tend to agree to less favorable reaction curves; that is, firms which are very sensitive to the rate of change of their competitor's "demands" are likely to give in relatively rapidly.

5. Firms with higher discount rates will also tend to agree on less favorable reaction curves. In general this may be expected, because firms with high time costs will be willing to sacrifice additional profit in order to hasten agreement.

6. Arbitration involving a third party is not likely to arise in the oligopoly situation. However, focal points may still be used by the firms to avoid the costs of extensive market bargaining, and, in this sense, we do encounter arbitration.[13]

The Nash Point

Our purpose in this chapter is to outline a dynamic mechanism whereby oligopolistic bargaining can take place. A few comments are in order, however, regarding the characteristics of the outcome itself. Suppose that the two firms in our market satisfy the necessary symmetry conditions, so that we can expect an outcome at the Nash point and retain the assumption that the pre-agreement point was the Cournot solution. It is interesting to investigate how variations in the firms' cost structures can influence the final division of the market. For example, it is easy to show that in the Cournot case the firm with the lower marginal costs produces the larger output. Defining Π_1 and Π_2 as the profits of firms 1 and 2, respectively, q_1 and q_2 as their outputs, and $C_1(q_1)$ and $C_2(q_2)$ as their costs, then we have:

$$\Pi_1 = Pq_1 - C_1(q_1)$$
$$\Pi_2 = Pq_2 - C_2(q_2)$$

The Cournot model has firm 1 maximizing Π_1 with q_2 assumed to be constant, and firm 2 maximizing Π_2 with q_1 assumed to be constant. Thus we have:

$$q_1\left(-\frac{dP}{dQ}\right) = P - \frac{dC_1}{dq_1}$$

$$q_2\left(-\frac{dP}{dQ}\right) = P - \frac{dC_2}{dq_2}$$

(54)

Here dP/dQ is the slope of the demand curve. Equation (54) implies $q_1 > q_2 \leftrightarrow dC_1/dq_1 < dC_2/dq_2$; that is, the firm with the lower marginal cost will enjoy the larger share of the market.

Perhaps surprisingly, the Nash solution will not necessarily lead even to the result that the lower cost firm will produce the greater output. The reason is that bargaining outcomes depend upon *total* rather than just *marginal* comparisons. The Nash solution maximizes the product $(\Pi_1 - \Pi_1^c)\ (\Pi_2 - \Pi_2^c)$ where Π_1^c, Π_2^c are the profits at the Cournot point; this product is always increased when a shift in outputs increases one firm's profit by a greater percentage than it decreases the profit of the other. Suppose an increase in q_2 increases the value of $(\Pi_2 - \Pi_2^c)$ by a large proportion, while the corresponding decrease in q_1 has only a small proportionate effect on $\Pi_1 - \Pi_1^c$. This condition may lead to a solution with $q_2 > q_1$ even though firm 1 is the lower cost firm in terms of both marginal and average costs.

In the case of two firms with constant costs, it is possible to show that the lower cost firm will always produce the greater amount of output, if the preagreement point is the Cournot solution. Maximizing the product $(\Pi_1 - \Pi_1^c)\ (\Pi_2 - \Pi_2^c)$ with respect to q_1 and q_2 we obtain the first order conditions.

$$[q_1(\Pi_2 - \Pi_2^c) + q_2(\Pi_1 - \Pi_1^c)]\frac{dP}{dQ} + \left(P - \frac{dC_1}{dq_1}\right)(\Pi_2 - \Pi_2^c) = 0$$

$$[q_1(\Pi_2 - \Pi_2^c) + q_2(\Pi_1 - \Pi_1^c)]\frac{dP}{dQ} + \left(P - \frac{dC_2}{dq_2}\right)(\Pi_1 - \Pi_1^c) = 0$$

Since we are assuming constant costs, we have $dC_1/dq_1 = m_1$ and $dC_2/dq_2 = m_2$. The first order conditions imply

$$\frac{P - m_1}{P - m_2} = \frac{(P - m_2)q_2 - \Pi_1^c}{(P - m_1)q_1 - \Pi_2^c} \tag{55}$$

Equation (55) can yield $q_2 > q_1$ only if

$$\frac{\Pi_1^c}{\Pi_2^c} < \frac{P - m_1}{P - m_2} \tag{56}$$

We know

$$\Pi_1^c = (P^c - m_1)q_1^c$$

$$\Pi_2^c = (P^c - m_2)q_2^c$$

where P^c is the market price at the Cournot solution and q_1^c, q_2^c are the corresponding outputs. We know $q_1^c > q_2^c$ because $m_1 < m_2$ and hence (56) can hold only if

$$\frac{P^c - m_1}{P^c - m_2} < \frac{P - m_1}{P - m_2} \tag{57}$$

Referring to Figure 22, the Nash solution must lie somewhere in the shaded area where $q_1 < q_1^c$ and $q_2 < q_2^c$, and hence where $P > P^c$. This, however, makes condition (57) impossible whenever $m_1 < m_2$. Thus the lower cost firm cannot produce the smaller output.

As a numerical example, suppose the demand is given by $P = 10 - q_1 - q_2$ and $m_1 = 1$, $m_2 = 2$. Then the Cournot solution has:

$$q_1^c = 3.33 \qquad q_2^c = 2.33$$

$$P = 4.33$$

$$\Pi_1 = 11.11 \qquad \Pi_2 = 5.44$$

and the Nash solution is:

$$q_1 = 2.57 \qquad q_2 = 1.70$$

$$P = 5.73$$

$$\Pi_1 = 12.14 \qquad \Pi_2 = 6.35$$

In this example, the market share of the low cost firm rises from 58.8% at the Cournot point to 60.25% at the negotiated settlement.

Market Warfare

There is no particularly compelling *a priori* reason for using the Cournot solution as the preagreement point for the market bargaining process. The *status quo* is particularly easy to alter in this situation, and so particular attention ought to be shown to its determination by the firms in an oligopoly.

The discussion in Chapter VII indicated, however, that in a dynamic context there is no unique "warfare point" which can be associated with a negotiation. As the bargaining process nears its conclusion, the benefits which the parties expect to receive from the use of force increase, and hence the complete theory requires specification of an optimal threat at each point in time. The static theory which was derived in Chapter VI does provide a convenient benchmark, however, and it does indicate how a party's decision to use more or less force is influenced by the various parameters of the negotiation. Our concern here, moreover, is not with variations in learning rates or discount rates, and how they influence the oligopoly model, because these issues have already been discussed in the general case. Instead we will focus on the relevance of different cost functions in the determination of an outcome. For this purpose the static model of Chapter VI is sufficient; it will not describe the optimal amount of force accurately (because it disregards the dynamic properties of the bargaining process) but it will indicate which party can use force most effectively and in what ways price warfare can alter outcomes.

Let us continue to accept the Nash solution as the outcome of the market bargaining process. The learning rates and discount rates in this case, and hence the slopes of the isosettlement lines, are equal in magnitude to the slope of the payoff frontier at each corresponding point on the frontier. Suppose that a straight line with slope $d\Pi_2/d\Pi_1 = S$ proves to be a reasonable approximation of the locus of Pareto optimal profit possibilities. Then the first firm attempts to obtain the most favorable isosettlement line it can by adjusting its output so as to maximize the value of $S\Pi_1 - \Pi_2$, given the value of q_2. Similarly, the second firm maximizes $\Pi_2 - S\Pi_1$ by adjusting q_2 for any given value of q_1. This provides the two warfare curves of the firm, and the most likely preagreement point for the negotiation is given by the intersection of these two curves.

It is interesting that the maximization of $\Pi_1 - \Pi_2$ is often suggested as a "good" warfare strategy for firm 1, although no very plausible justification for this device is generally given.[14] The model provided here will lead to the same result only in a special case, that of total symmetry. For this result, not only do we need parameter values that lead to a symmetric bargaining process (equal learning rates, and equal discount rates) but we require identical cost functions as well. Moreover, it is by no means implausible that the Nash solution should lead to asymmetric warfare functions when the costs of the firms differ. Compare two unrelated markets: A, in which the two firms have equal costs, and B in which firm 1 is more efficient than his competitor. In market A, firm 1 will maximize $\Pi_1 - \Pi_2$, while in B firm 1 maximizes $S\Pi_1 - \Pi_2$. Since $S < 1$, this implies that firm 1 uses more force in market B than it does in market A—a plausible result because in B the firm has much more to gain from a unit concession from his opponent (he can make a greater profit from a given Δq_1 in B, where he is efficient, than he can in A).

As we showed in the last section, we cannot make a general prediction that the firm with lower marginal or average costs will come out with the larger market share. In the case of constant costs, however, it is true that the more efficient firm always produces more than the less efficient one. Suppose that it is firm 1 which has the lower costs. Then the slope of the profit possibility curve must be less in magnitude than 1. Consider a movement along the profit possibility curve for which firm 2 loses an amount of profit $\Delta\Pi_2$. This could be accomplished by reducing q_2 by an amount $\Delta q_2 = \Delta\Pi_2/(P - m_2)$ and increasing q_1 by exactly the same amount so that P is not changed. This will produce an increase in Π_1 which is greater than $\Delta\Pi_2$ because of firm 1's lower costs. Movements along the profit possibility curve cannot make firm 1 worse off than this (by definition) and hence $d\Pi_2/d\Pi_1 > -1$. Now our warfare point has firm 1 maximizing the difference $D = S\Pi_1 - \Pi_2$ with respect to q_1, while firm 2 maximizes $-D$ with respect to q_2. The resulting first order conditions are:

$$PS - (Sq_1 - q_2)\frac{dP}{dQ} = m_1$$

$$P - (Sq_1 - q_2)\frac{dP}{dq} = m_2$$

By assumption, $m_1 < m_2$ and thus these two equations reduce to $Sq_1 > q_2$ which, since $S < 1$, implies $q_1 > q_2$. Therefore, at the warfare point the lower cost firm produces the larger output. We can use the same demonstration that was applied when the Cournot point was used for preagreement to show that after the negotiation, we will observe $q_1 > q_2$.

Referring again to our numerical example, where $P = 10 - q_1 - q_2$ and the marginal costs of firm 1 and 2 respectively were $m_1 = 1, m_2 = 2$, we obtain a warfare point:

$$q_1 = 4.953 \qquad q_2 = 3.485$$
$$P = 1.562$$
$$\Pi_1 = 2.787 \qquad \Pi_2 = 1.528$$

and the final negotiated outcome is:

$$q_1 = 2.635 \qquad q_2 = 1.644$$
$$P = 5.721$$
$$\Pi_1 = 12.43 \qquad \Pi_2 = 6.125$$

Market shares in this example are not markedly different from the case of bargaining from the Cournot point. Firm 1 supplies 58.7 per cent of the market at the warfare point, and 61.6 per cent at agreement.

Conclusion

This model as we have described it may seem to be unduly rigid in its assumptions. We certainly do not mean to suggest that oligopolistic bargaining is as cut and dried as we have described it. We do believe, however, that our highly simplified model does contain the essential characteristic of such negotiations; that is, the object of these bargaining processes is not really the final level of outputs, but the *response* behavior of the individual firms. This conclusion (assuming that the firms actually do reach agreement) is sufficient to ensure that ultimately the firms will produce somewhere on the locus of Pareto optima. We might add that the sort of implicit negotiation which we have described need not be confined to circumstances in which explicit communication is impossible. In many situations (as in international negotiations) individuals are not nearly so much influenced by what their opponents *say* as by what they *do*—communication is effectively diluted by suspicion and distrust—so that even explicit negotiation may well be supplemented by attempts to bring about desired physical payoffs even before agreement is reached.

▪ NOTES

1. William Fellner, *Competition among the Few* (New York: Alfred A. Knopf, 1949).

2. Robert L. Bishop, "Duopoly: Collusion or Warfare?" *American Economic Review*, L (December, 1960), 933–961.

3. Martin Shubik, *Strategy and Market Structure* (New York: John Wiley and Sons, 1959).

4. E. H. Chamberlin, *The Theory of Monopolistic Competition* (7th edition; Cambridge, Mass.: Harvard University Press, 1960).

5. See Fellner's description of the Stackelberg theory, *op. cit.*, pp. 98–119.

6. Augustin Cournot, *Recherches sur les principes mathématiques de la théorie de richesses* (Paris, 1838).

7. J. Bertrand, Review of Cournot, "Recherches," *Journal des Savants* (1883), p. 503.

8. E. H. Chamberlin, *op. cit.*, pp. 31–55.

9. John Nash, "Two Person Cooperative Games," *Econometrica,* XXI, (January 1953), 128–140. Of course Nash, dealing as he was with a purely outcome oriented theory, would not be faulted for disregarding this essentially dynamic problem.

10. Furthermore, although Fellner's hypothesis is one of "qualified joint maximization," the qualifications are so numerous and so convincing that one is tempted to conclude, that, in fact, no concrete predictions are being made at all. Moreover, the introduction of the "qualifications" tends also to reintroduce indeterminateness into the model regarding the final prices that the quantity adjusting oligopolists charge.

11. It is easy to show that such a model necessarily leads to greater outputs and lower prices than does that of Cournot.

12. In other words, they would have to resort to explicit verbal communication instead of relying upon price-output divisions to express their demands. Even if the demands are stated verbally, the simplicity of the linear reaction line would make it an attractive alternative to complicated reaction curves.

13. F. M. Sherer, "Focal Point Pricing and Conscious Parallelism," *Antitrust Bulletin* (Summer, 1967).

14. Bishop, *op. cit.*, uses this strategy exclusively, defending it only to the extent that it is plausible and illustrates the essence of the warfare problem effectively.

APPENDIXES

Throughout the preceding chapters a number of assumptions and simplifications have been made concerning the nature of the bargaining process itself. Several of these matters, such as our assumption of continuity in the outcome set, the restriction of our model to two person negotiation, and our use of an outcome set with only one dimension (so that all outcome alternatives are necessarily Pareto optimal) remain to be discussed. The following Appendixes contain a series of topical discussions devoted to the influence of several of these factors upon the general conclusions of our theory.

■ APPENDIX A

Payoff Deterioration

From time to time in this study, we have mentioned a third manner in which time may influence the bargaining process—the payoff alternatives themselves may change in value due to the influence of calendar time. This particular phenomenon may appear in many situations, of which the most familiar examples are probably labor negotiations in which extended strikes will last into peak business seasons, or, having started in such seasons, will last into periods of slack. In cases such as this, the utility which a player expects to receive from a negotiation depends not only upon his physical payoff and the time period over which he expects to have to wait for this payoff, but it also depends upon the *date* of agreement, $w + t$, where t represents the "present" date.

In more formal terms, we must introduce the variable $w + t$ into our expressions for the utility which player 1 expects to receive from the negotiation:

$$U_1 = f(q_1, w + t) \, e^{-aw}$$

where a is defined, as usual, as player 1's discount rate.

Player 1 will demand an outcome q_1 for which the marginal utility of an increase in demand is balanced by the marginal cost which results from the additional delay in agreement:

$$f_1(q_1, w + t) = \frac{a}{r_2} f(q_1, w + t) - f_2(q_1, w + t) \frac{1}{r_2} \qquad \text{(A–1)}$$

where

$$f_1(q_1, w + t) = \frac{\delta}{\delta q_1} f(q_1, w + t)$$

and

$$f_2(q_1, w + t) = \frac{\delta}{\delta(w + t)} f(q_1, w + t)$$

Expression (A–1) is comparable to the utility maximization expressions in Chapter III except that we now have the additional marginal cost term $f_2(q_1, w + t)/r_2$, representing the loss in outcome utility which results from the postponement of the *date* of agreement.

We observe immediately that if $f_2(q_1, w + t)$ is negative (that is, if the outcome utility does in fact *decrease* with increases in the calendar date), then the marginal cost of additional demands is always larger (for any q_1, w) than it would be in the absence of this phenomenon. As a consequence, our player will always tend to make *smaller* demands than he otherwise would. It follows that, *ceteris paribus,* the entire negotiation will tend to take less time, and the error in prediction of our equilibrium model may also tend to be larger.

We also note that since the optimal demand is now a function of the calendar date, it is perfectly possible for a party to alter his bid as time passes, even when no learning takes place at all. The specific form which these changes take depends upon the dynamic nature of the payoff deterioration; for example, we expect quite different patterns of concessions to arise depending upon whether the payoff deteriorates rapidly into nothing, dwindles asymptotically into nothing, or dwindles into only a fraction of its original value but never into nothing. Moreover, we should recognize that the payoff may lose value differently for the two parties; in fact one side may not observe any loss of value at all. These phenomena may be very complex, but they add no difficulties in principle to our theory. For example, we may determine the concession rate for player 1 by differentiating equation (A–1) with respect to time. In equation (A–2) we drop the arguments of the functions and use the notation $\dot{q}_1 = dq_1/dt$, and so on.

$$\left[f_{11}r_2 + f_{12} - af_1 - \frac{a}{r_2} f_2 + f_{21} + \frac{1}{r_2} f_{22} \right] \dot{q}_1 = -f_{12}r_2 + af_2 - f_{22}$$

(A–2)

$$+ \left[-f_{12} + \frac{a}{r_2} f_2 - \frac{1}{r_2} f_{22} \right] (\dot{q}_2 - wr_2) - f_1 \dot{r}_2$$

The second order conditions for equation (A–1) will ensure that the bracketed coefficient of $\dot{q}_1$ is negative. Equation (A–2) introduces a dependence of q_1 upon player 2's demand as well as upon time itself. Only when the expression $-f_{12}r_2 + af_2 - f_{22}$ equals zero will we have substantially the same model as before. This condition will be guaranteed by equation (A–1) whenever the payoff deterioration takes an exponential form with $f(q_1, w + t) = f(q_1)e^{-k(w+t)}$. In fact, we made use of this result in Chapter IX when we noted that bargaining costs (and payoff deterioration) could be made to simulate changes in the discount rate. That is, if the function $f(q_1, w + t)$ can be written in the form $f(q_1)e^{-k(w+t)}$, then the bargaining model which we have already studied can be applied using $(a + k)$ instead of a as the discount rate.

Except for the special case of exponential payoff deterioration, the complexity of equation (A–2) makes the model much more difficult to deal with in the simple terms we have been using for this study. In particular, it is very difficult to appraise the conditions under which the static model will be a useful description of the dynamic sequence of concessions. Naturally, we do not normally expect the Nash solution, indeed equation (13) (Chapter III) now takes the form:

$$\frac{dU_1}{dU_2} = \frac{a}{b} \frac{r_1}{r_2} \frac{U_1 - \frac{1}{a} f_2}{U_2 - \frac{1}{b} f_1}$$

(A–3)

The conditions necessary for the Nash solution are now that the players have equal learning and discount rates and, in addition, that the impact of time upon the value of any given payoff be the same for both of them. If the cake begins to get moldy, and the first party is more averse to this condition than the second, we no longer expect an equal division: the larger share will now go to the second party.

We can investigate the stability of the bargaining process with payoff deterioration by evaluating the slopes of the response functions, $q_1 = F(q_2, r_2)$ and $(q_2 = G(q_1, r_1))$, which were defined in Chapter III. These slopes, represented as $-A$ and $-B$ respectively, may be obtained from equation (A–2) and a similar equation constructed from the point of view of the second party. For example,

$$A = -\frac{dq_1}{dq_2} = \frac{f_{12} - \dfrac{a}{r_2} f_2 + \dfrac{1}{r_2} f_{22} + f_1 \dfrac{dr_2}{dq_2}}{f_{11}r_2 + f_{12} - af_1 - \dfrac{a}{r_2} f_2 + f_{21} + \dfrac{1}{r_2} f_{22}} \qquad (A\text{–}4)$$

where the value of dr_2/dq_2 is obtained from the learning function of player 1. In the models outlined in Chapter IV, $dr_2/dq_2 = -\alpha$. A similar expression is used to obtain B.

The bargaining process will be stable whenever $A < 1$ and $B < 1$. For example, suppose the value of a payoff declines linearly to nothing, all returns being valueless at a time T. Then $U_1 = f[q_1(T - w - t)]$. For simplicity, let us disregard the possibility of diminishing marginal utility so that U_1 is linearly dependent upon $q_1(T - w - t)$. Expression (A–4) now takes the form:

$$A = \frac{1 - \dfrac{a}{r_2}\, q_1 + \alpha(T - w - t)}{1 - \dfrac{a}{r_2}\, q_1 + 1 + a(T - w - t)}$$

Whenever $\alpha \leqslant a$ (which was our former stability condition), we will still have $A < 1$ and the bargaining process will be stable. In this case, however, we can have $\alpha > a$ and nevertheless find $A < 1$. Thus we may conclude that payoff deterioration of this linear form will generally contribute to the stability of the bargaining process.

■ APPENDIX B

The Case of Discontinuities
in the Outcome Set

In all of our discussion we have assumed that the outcome sets are continuously divisible. Since indivisibilities are often present in the payoff possibilities of bargaining situations, however, it would be a weakness in our theory if we were unable to deal with them. Analytically, of course, we could always transform a set of discrete alternatives into a continuously divisible outcome set by distributing the discrete payoffs through a system of lotteries with continuously variable probabilities. As this is virtually never done in practice, however, it would be more desirable to point out a means by which our present model can be adapted to treat such bargaining problems explicitly.

Let us consider a model in which there are only two outcome alternatives, P_1 and P_2, where player 1 prefers payoff P_1 to P_2 and player 2 prefers payoff P_2 to P_1. Suppose that at the start of the negotiation each party demands the outcome which he prefers. Assume further that player 1 expects player 2 to concede to P_1 after a period of time denoted by θ_2 and, conversely, that player 2 expects player 1 to concede to P_2 after a time θ_1. Player 1 demands outcome P_1 as long as the discounted utility of P_1 is greater than the utility which he would receive from immediate acceptance of outcome P_2. That is, as long as the following condition is satisfied:

$$f(P_1)e^{-a\theta_2} > f(P_2) \qquad \text{(B–1)}$$

The function f represents our usual utility function notation. Similarly, player 2 demands P_2 as long as the discounted utility to him of P_2 is greater than the utility which he would receive from immediate acceptance of P_1:

$$g(P_2)e^{-b\theta_1} < g(P_1)$$

As time passes, if neither player gives in, each player must eventually learn that his expectation is overoptimistic; hence θ_1 and θ_2 will increase in size until one party does finally concede. Suppose the one to do so is player 2. A necessary condition for this concession is that the discounted utility to player 2 of outcome P_2 is now no greater than the utility which he can receive from immediate acceptance of P_1; that is,

$$g(P_2)e^{-b\theta_1} \leqslant g(P_1) \tag{B-2}$$

Expressions (B–1) and (B–2) together imply the following formal condition:

$$f(P_1) \, g(P_1) > f(P_2) \, g(P_2)e^{a\theta_2 - b\theta_1}$$

The conditions $a = b$ and $\theta_1 = \theta_2$ will be sufficient to ensure that the concession by player 2 brings about a state of agreement at the Nash solution (it maximizes the product of the players' outcome utilities).

A similar analysis may be applied to a negotiation involving many discrete alternatives. In such a case, a player will demand the outcome which will yield to him the highest expected utility (appropriately discounted according to the expected time lapse between the present and the time of agreement). For example, if player 2 is demanding an outcome P_j, player 1 will demand the outcome P_i which satisfies the following condition:

$$f(P_i)e^{-a(i-j)\theta_2} \geqslant f(P_k)e^{-a(k-j)\theta_2} \qquad \text{for all } k \geqslant j$$

θ_2 is now player 1's estimate of the amount of time that it will take 2 to concede from any P_j to $P_j + 1$ (subscripts run in an ascending order from the outcome most preferred by player 2 to the outcome most preferred by player 1), and hence the expression $(i - j)\theta_2$ represents the expected time before agreement will be reached (i.e., this is the equivalent of our expression w). A similar analysis describes the demand of player 2.

It should be observed that we also need an assumption regarding the distribution of the payoff possibilities. In our continuous example it was possible for a player to demand outcomes of *any* desired magnitude within the limits of the bargaining process. If only a finite number of alternatives is available, however, it will generally be true that a demand of precisely the desired magnitude is unavailable to a player. Furthermore, it may happen that the utility difference to a player between an outcome P_i and its neighbor P_{i-1} is very large compared to the utility difference between other pairs of neighboring alternatives. At such a point, the player may be unwilling to concede for some time even though the bargaining process might lead him to concede part way in a series of smaller steps (were they available). As we will demonstrate below, this possibility presents no difficulty if we impose our assumption of diminishing marginal utility upon the payoff alternatives:

$$f(P_i) - f(P_{i-1}) \leqslant f(P_{i-1}) - f(P_{i-2}) \qquad \text{for all } i$$
$$g(P_j) - g(P_{j+1}) \leqslant g(P_{j+1}) - g(P_{j+2}) \qquad \text{for all } j \tag{B-3}$$

That is, the larger a player's demand, the smaller the utility increments (or decrements) which he receives from unit shifts in his demands. Given this assumption it is true that, if $a = b$ and $\theta_1 = \theta_2$ throughout the bargaining, the final agreement will take place at the Nash solution.* The proof of this statement is similar to the proof for the two-alternative case: suppose that it is player 1 who is the first to make a concession. We may express this by means of the pair of conditions:

$$f(P_i)e^{-a(i-j)\theta_2} \leqslant f(P_{i-1})e^{-a(i-1-j)\theta_2}$$
$$g(P_j)e^{-b(i-j)\theta_1} > g(P_{j+1})e^{-b(i-j-1)\theta_1}$$

If $a = b$ and $\theta_1 = \theta_2$, these two expressions imply a third:

$$f(P_{i-1})g(P_j) > f(P_i)g(P_{j+1})$$

It follows from this last inequality and assumption (B–3) above that such a sequence of concessions leads to an outcome P_k for which the product $f(P_k)g(P_k)$ is maximized.† Moreover, we can apply the same

---

* We are implicitly assuming that the subscripts refer only to relevant outcome alternatives—that is, player 1 will concede from P_i to P_{i-1} without ever skipping P_{i-1} in order to demand P_{i-2} immediately.

† Proof: We need to show that if $f(P_{i-1})g(P_j) > f(P_i)g(P_{j+1})$, then $f(P_{i-1})g(P_{i-1}) > f(P_i)g(P_i)$, since this would ensure that concessions always move from outcome pairs with lower utility products to pairs with higher utility products (i.e. no player will ever concede past the Nash point). Add the terms $f(P_{i-1})g(P_{i-1})$ and $f(P_i)g(P_i)$ to both sides of the given inequality and rearrange as follows:

$$f(P_{i-1})g(P_{i-1}) > f(P_i)g(P_i) + [f(P_i)g(P_{j+1}) - f(P_i)g(P_i)$$
$$+ f(P_{i-1})g(P_{i-1}) - f(P_{i-1})g(P_j)]$$

The term in brackets, which we call Z, can be factored to give

$$Z = f(P_i)[g(P_{j+1}) - g(P_i)] - f(P_{i-1})[g(P_j) - g(P_{i-1})]$$

It follows from assumption (B–3) that

$$g(P_j) - g(P_{j+1}) \leqq g(P_{i-1}) - g(P_i)$$

reasoning that we used in Chapter II to show that if the two players have equivalent learning abilities, there is a tendency for θ_1 to equal θ_2, whatever the initial expectations are. For example, suppose that $\theta_1 > \theta_2$ (player 1 expects 2 to concede from P_j to $P_j + 1$ in less time than 2 expects 1 to require in conceding from P_i to P_{i-1}). As time passes, neither party will concede, and player 1 will be the first to find that his expectations are overoptimistic; hence θ_1 must begin to rise sooner (or faster) than θ_2. Actual concessions will tend to reinforce this behavior, and eventually θ_1 will tend to approach equality with θ_2.

This model, then, is basically a duplicate of the continuous one which we have already studied. We could derive an explicit model similar to that of Chapter III by constructing a specific model of the players' learning behavior and solving the resulting dynamic system. We noted before that our continuous solution depended on second order derivatives of the utility functions. The counterpart in this model is the fact that the distribution of the outcome alternatives in utility space [the differences $f(P_i) - f(P_{i-1})$, and so on] will be relevant in the determination of θ_1 and θ_2 over time. If the utility differences are neither constant (utility functions linear) nor symmetric (in our special sense of Chapter II), we would not expect the values of θ_1 and θ_2 to tend to become equal, even if the players were otherwise identical.

---

or, rearranging

$$g(P_{j+1}) - g(P_i) \geqslant g(P_j) - (P_{i-1})$$

It is also true by definition of the utility functions that $f(P_i) > f(P_{i-1})$. Hence the expression Z is positive, and it follows that

$$f(P_{i-1})g(P_{i-1}) \geqslant f(P_i)g(P_i)$$

It should be observed that the assumption of diminishing marginal returns [assumption (B–3)] is only necessary to obtain the Nash solution in the case of a negotiation over discrete outcome alternatives. In the continuous model, we did not need this assumption until we came to the discussion of equilibrium expectations.

▪ APPENDIX C

A Utility Dependent Model

Our model has been constructed to represent bargaining situations in which each player formulates his demands and measures the extent of his opponent's concessions in terms of the actual payoff alternatives.

In some cases, however, this may not be possible. For example, if the alternatives are not strictly comparable, or if they are not measurable in common units, it is hard to define "concessions" in real terms. If this is the case, the parties are likely to use their own preference schedules as indicators of concessions, each side measuring the magnitude of an opponent's concession in terms of the increased utility which that concession would implicitly yield to himself.

Let us represent the utility which player 1 would receive from the outcome which player 2 is currently demanding by the term U_2; similarly, we define the utility which player 1 would receive from the outcome which he himself is demanding as U_1. We will use the term r_2 now to describe the rate at which player 1 expects his opponent to concede over his own *utility* scale U. In this case, the expected present value of player 1 of a demand for an outcome which would yield him U_1 is given by the expression U_1^* below:

$$U_1^* = U_1 e^{-a(U_1 - U_2)/r_2}$$

The expected concession rate r_2 operates in this model in a way similar to that in the model we have already discussed, except that in this case r_2 is modified in accordance with the rate of change of U_2 rather than the rate of change of player 2's actual demands. Player 2, on the other hand, is not really concerned with U_2, and in fact he probably does not even know its value. His object is to demand an outcome which at agreement would yield a utility for him of, say, V_2 which, assuming that we are only concerned at this time with Pareto optimal alternatives, is related to U_2 by some monotonic function $U = R(V)$. If the function R is linear, this model is no different from that in Chapter III, and a further analysis would produce all of the same conclusions that we have obtained before. If $R(V)$ is not linear, however, our results are changed in one respect. Specifically, if each of the players' utility functions displays diminishing marginal utility over successive outcome alternatives, we would expect an increased likelihood of instability in the bargaining process (rather than the contribution toward stability which we obtained from diminishing marginal utility in Chapter III). Suppose player 2 is demanding an outcome which gives him a large utility, V_2. The utility which this outcome would yield to player 1, U_2, will be fairly small. Compared to an example in which V_2 is smaller, a moderate change in player 2's demand will lower V_2 a small amount because of diminishing marginal utility. Similarly, the change in U_2 will be larger than it would have been, had V_2 been smaller. Thus we observe that a relatively small change in player 2's utility demand, V_2, will bring about a relatively large impact upon player 1's expectations and hence upon his demand. Of course the same analysis applies to an example in which player 1 is the one to change his demand. Thus if this model is to be stable, the players must possess lower learning rates or higher discount rates than those which were necessary for stability in our original model. It is a straightforward operation to obtain this conclusion formally if we make use of our linear model of learning behavior: $r_2 = \alpha(\dot{U}_2 - r_2)$, and so forth. We must first define the two terms. $D(r_1) = -d/dV R(V)$ at the point V_2 (V_2 is a function of r_1 only), and $E(r_2) = -d/dU \ R^{-1}(U)$ at the point U_1. The condition for stability in the bargaining process now takes the following form:

$$1 - ABD(r_1) \ E(r_2) > 0$$

Finally, the "solution" relationship between r_1 and r_2 is:

$$\frac{\dot{r}_1}{\dot{r}_2} = \frac{\beta}{\alpha} \frac{AE(r_2)}{BD(r_1)} \frac{r_2 - r_1}{r_1 - r_2} = \frac{r_1}{r_2}$$

Our conclusion that diminishing marginal utility tends to create instability is equivalent to the observation that diminishing marginal utility will make the product $D(r_1) \ E(r_2)$ greater than one until agreement is reached (when the product will equal one), and this in turn reduces the likelihood that, given the values of A and B, the stability condition is satisfied.

■ APPENDIX D

Pareto Optimality

The bargaining model which has been analyzed in this study has been restricted to deal only with Pareto optimal outcome alternatives. This is a consequence of our assumption that only one good was to be divided in the outcome: it was never possible to increase the payoff to one player (by giving him more of the good) without decreasing the payoff to the other. Since the discussion in Chapter V suggests that cases of multidimensional payoff sets provide the most important bargaining problems, and since there is reason to believe that in practice outcomes which are not Pareto optimal do occur, it is desirable to expand the set of possible outcomes of the model so that non Pareto optimal alternatives are included. This modification would also permit us to investigate whether our model is consistent with the Siegel–Fouraker observation that the bargaining processes tend to move to Pareto optimal solutions.

The addition of one or more goods to our original single good model introduces the possibility of substitution among the various goods which the players demand. In this situation it is tempting to use the approach which has become traditional in consumer theory. That is, player 1 may expect player 2 to be willing to concede in one of three ways: he may reduce his demand for good P alone at a rate of s_2 units of P per unit of time, or he may reduce his demand for good Q alone at a rate of r_2 units of Q per unit of time, or he may concede along both P and Q at a rate given by a linear combination of r_2 and s_2. This expectation is based upon the (correct) assumption that when player 2 formulates his demand, he would be willing to exchange some units of good P for some of Q in any proportion which would leave him indifferent among the demands. The expected ratio at which Q may be substituted for P would be given by s_2/r_2. Player 1 then would demand a payoff combination of goods P and Q which lies on one of his indifference curves at a point where the slope of the indifference curve is given by $-s_2/r_2$.

As much as a player might like to take this course (and as much as we might like to use such an analysis), it is beyond the capabilities of our tools, because it is impossible for either player to form usable estimates of the other's concession rates. In attempting to estimate player 2's rates of concession along P and Q, for example, player 1 is faced with a serious index number problem. We have represented an example of the situation in the figure below, where the axes measure the P, Q demands of player 2, p_2 and q_2.

Suppose that player 2 first demands an outcome (p', q') (we omit the subscripts for simplicity) but that after a time ΔT, he "concedes" to some point (p'', q'').

Player 1 expected player 2 to concede to some point on the line RR for which $p - p' = (q - q')s_2/r_2 - s_2\Delta T$. This line represents all the linear combinations of the points $p = p'$, $q = q' - r_2\Delta T$ and $q = q'$, $p = p' - s_2\Delta T$, and it may be described as an estimate by player 1 of one of player 2's indifference curves. Now if it happens that player 2 concedes such that $p' - p'' = 0$ or $q' - q'' = 0$ (for example, point A in the diagram), then player 1 is able to adjust his expectations as before. Thus if player 2 concedes to point A, player 1 has no cause to change s_2, while r_2 should be adjusted toward $(p' - p'')/\Delta T$. Similarly, if player 2 concedes along P alone there is no reason to adjust r_2, and so s_2 will be the only variable to change. However, if it happens that player 2 concedes along both P and Q, or if he

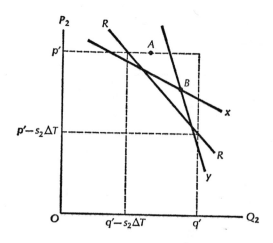

Figure D-1

concedes such that he demands more of one good and less of the other, then no such simple analysis applies. For example, a concession to point B could be accounted for by an infinite variety of r_2, s_2 combinations, of which the lines x and y provide only two examples. (The values of r_2 and s_2 which are implied by these examples can be determined from their intersections with the dashed lines $p = p'$, $q = q'$.) The possible "true" values for r_2 and s_2 are limited only by the condition that the indifference line for player 2 which they determine should have a negative slope.

Beyond these very limited qualitative conclusions, one can obtain no information from player 2's behavior. In general, a movement from (p', q') to (p'', q'') can be quantitatively accounted for by an infinite variety of r_2, s_2 combinations, and there are no means available for choosing one combination in preference over another. This information is certainly not sufficient to serve as the basis for a player's decision making, and hence it is reasonable to expect him to turn to some other measure of his opponent's behavior. The natural candidate and, in fact, the only other measure which is available is the player's own utility; that is, he must gauge the other's behavior by means of the potential utility which he would receive from the outcomes which the other demands. We are again reminded of Siegel and Fouraker's empirical conclusion that if one player shifted his demand even so as to retain the same potential outcome utility as he could have received from his previous demand (if he moves along one of his indifference curves by demanding more units of P and less of Q), and if it happened that the shift "conceded" a large amount of outcome utility to the other player, then the latter would respond markedly by increasing the utility value of the outcomes in his own subsequent demands. Thus, despite the neutrality of the first player's action, the second behaved as though a sizeable concession had been made. This strongly suggests that in Siegel and Fouraker's experiments, all of which were two dimensional, each player did use his own utility index to measure the magnitude of the other player's concessions.

Assuming that the players do measure one another's concessions in terms of their own utility functions, then it is appropriate to apply the model which we introduced in Appendix C to multidimensional bargaining situations. However, this approach reduces the players' payoff demands back to one dimension—utilities—and hence we have not explained *where* on an indifference curve a player places his demand. Once one party has decided to demand an outcome which would yield a utility U, he will attempt to demand a (p, q) combination to which his opponent will find it the easiest to concede. This is also clear from Siegel and Fouraker's conclusion that increasing the players' information (knowledge of one another's utilities) tends to increase the likelihood of Pareto optimal outcomes. (Demands on the locus of Pareto optima always minimize the utility concession which the opponent must suffer in order to reach a settlement.) As we have shown, however, it is impossible to find such a point precisely without complete knowledge, so the decision is essentially arbitrary. The most obvious course of action would be for a player to minimize the linear distance in $P \times Q$ space between his opponent's payoff demand and his own. This mechanism would tend to bring the bargaining process to a Pareto optimal point of agreement. This is, of course, only a suggestion; since we have no strong reason for expecting any particular mode of behavior in choosing the point to be demanded, this remains an empirical question. The empirical conclusion that bargaining processes do tend toward Pareto optima does indicate that some such mechanism must be in effect.

Unfortunately, we cannot describe our model completely in the multidimensional case because we do not know the form of the function $U = R(V)$ (see Appendix C): this function is dependent upon the procedures which the players use to determine their actual demands. The Nash solution may be "predicted" only in the basically uninteresting case in which the players' utility functions are linear. However, there is no reason to believe that our conclusions regarding the impact of various learning abilities and discount rates on both the actual outcome of the negotiation and the time required to reach agreement should be altered in this model.

▪ APPENDIX E
An *N*-Person Model

Conceptually, there is no reason why our theory cannot be generalized to cover negotiations.involving more than two bargainers: the basic mechanism of the analysis is left unchanged, and it is possible to apply the same kind of reasoning which we have used in the two person model to obtain a stable relationship between the players' expectations of the opponents' rates of concession. Such a model will not change any of the conclusions which have been derived before. Its usefulness may be somewhat restricted also by the scarcity of bargaining situations which involve more than two persons (or more than two "sides"). There are still several situations which are best interpreted as three person negotiations, however, such as labor–management disputes with a government desire for "noninflationary" settlements superimposed upon them, and therefore, we shall construct a general model to show how these cases can be handled analytically. This Appendix is not intended to be a complete mathematical restatement of the whole theory; it is confined to the model of the concession process (Chapters III and IV) and its major conclusions.

Assume that there are n players, the ith player demanding a quantity q_i. The ith player also has an estimate of the jth player's rate of concession, r_{ij} (we shall define $r_{ii} = 0$). Given these, the ith player can make an estimate of the amount of time w_i which will be needed before agreement will be reached, where

$$w_i \equiv \frac{\sum_i q_i - M}{\sum_j r_{ij}}$$

and M is the total amount to be divided.

The utility which player i expects to receive from a demand q_i is given by U_i^* below

$$U_i^* = f_i(q_i)e^{-a_i w_i}$$

As usual, a_i is the ith player's rate of discount. Maximizing U_i^* with respect to q_i and finding $\dot{q}_i$ by differentiation with respect to time, we obtain:

$$f'(q_i) = f(q_i) \frac{a_i}{R_i} \tag{E-1}$$

$$\dot{q}_i = \frac{A_i}{\alpha_i} \dot{R} \tag{E-2}$$

Equations (E-1) and (E-2) make use of a linear learning relation such as we used in Chapter IV, with α_i defined as player i's rate of learning:

$$\dot{r}_{ij} = -\alpha_i(\dot{q}_j + r_{ij}) \qquad \text{for all } j \neq i \tag{E-3}$$

We have also defined the following terms:

$$R_i \equiv \sum_{j=1}^{n} r_{ij}$$

$$\dot{R}_i \equiv \sum_{i=1}^{n} \dot{r}_{ij}$$

$$A_i = -\frac{\alpha_i}{\frac{f''_i(q_i)}{f'_i(q_i)} R_i - a_i}$$

Thus R_i represents the "concession rate" of player i's opponents taken collectively, while $\dot{R}_i$ is its rate of change. This model makes $\dot{q}_i$ a function of the rate of change of the opponents' demands taken collectively. That is, equation (E-3) implies

$$\dot{R}_i = \sum_{j \neq i} \dot{r}_{ij} = -\alpha_i(\sum_{j \neq i} \dot{q}_j + R_i)$$

and, substituting this into (E-2),

$$\dot{q}_i = -A_i (\sum_{j \neq i} \dot{q}_i + R_i)$$

Thus A_i is the slope of the "response function" which determines the rate of change of q_i as a function of the opponents' concession rates.

It is possible to solve for $\dot{q}_i$ and $\dot{r}_{ij}$ in terms of the r_{ij}'s by solving (E-2) and (E-3) simultaneously. First, we shall rewrite the response function:

$$k_i \dot{q}_i + \sum_{i \neq j}^{n} \dot{q}_i = -R_i$$

$$k_i \equiv \frac{1 - A_i}{A_i}$$

We have n such equations, one for each player, and the whole system may be described in matrix notation:

$$-\mathbf{K}\dot{\mathbf{Q}} = \mathbf{R}$$

where

$$\mathbf{K} \equiv \begin{bmatrix} 1 + k_1 & 1 & \cdots & 1 \\ 1 & 1 + k_2 & & 1 \\ \cdots & \cdots & \cdots & \cdots \\ 1 & 1 & \cdots & 1 + k_n \end{bmatrix}$$

$$\dot{\mathbf{Q}} \equiv \begin{bmatrix} \dot{q}_1 \\ \dot{q}_2 \\ \cdot \\ \cdot \\ \cdot \\ \dot{q}_n \end{bmatrix}, \quad \mathbf{R} \equiv \begin{bmatrix} R_1 \\ R_2 \\ \cdot \\ \cdot \\ \cdot \\ R_n \end{bmatrix}$$

It is possible to solve this system for $\dot{q}_j$:

$$\dot{q}_j = -\frac{R_j}{k_j} - \frac{\displaystyle\sum_{l=1}^{n} \frac{R_l}{k_l}}{k_j \left(1 + \displaystyle\sum_{l=1}^{n} \frac{1}{k_l}\right)} \tag{E-4}$$

Derivation:

Define $\mathbf{K}^n_i$ as the minor of the determinant $|\mathbf{K}|$ which contains the last $n - i$ rows and columns. Now, if we subtract the last row of $\mathbf{K}$ from the first, we find that

$$|\mathbf{K}| = k_1 \mathbf{K}^n_2 + (-1)^n k_n \begin{bmatrix} 1 & 1 + k_2 & \cdots & 1 \\ 1 & 1 & & 1 \\ \cdots & \cdots & \cdots & 1 + k_{n-1} \\ 1 & 1 & \cdots & 1 \end{bmatrix}$$

Subtracting the last row of this new determinant from the first, we find

$$|\mathbf{K}| = k_1\mathbf{K}_2^n
\begin{bmatrix}
1 & 1+k_3 & \cdots & 1 \\
1 & 1 & \cdots & 1 \\
\cdots & \cdots & \cdots & \cdots \\
1 & 1 & \cdots & 1+k_{n-1} \\
1 & 1 & \cdots & 1
\end{bmatrix}$$
$$+ (-1)^n k_n(-k_2)$$

which is the same as the previous determinant with rank diminished by 1. We can continue to subtract rows until we obtain:

$$|\mathbf{K}| = k_1\mathbf{K}_2^n + (-1)^{n-1} \prod_{i=2}^{n} (-k_i) = k_1\mathbf{K}_2^n + \prod_{i=2}^{n} (+k_i)$$

Similarly, we can find

$$\mathbf{K}_2^n = k_2\mathbf{K}_3^n + \prod_{i=3}^{n} k_i,$$

and so on, deriving finally

$$|\mathbf{K}| = \prod_{i=1}^{n} k_i + \sum_{j=1}^{n} \prod_{i=j}^{n} k_i$$

or:

$$|\mathbf{K}| = \prod_{i=1}^{n} k_i \left[1 + \sum_{i=1}^{n} \frac{1}{k_j} \right] \qquad \text{(E–5)}$$

Let us call $\mathbf{K}_{lm}$ the cofactor of the element in the lth row and m^{th} column of $\mathbf{K}$. Inspection of such a cofactor indicates that if we make $m - l - 1$ column interchanges, we can obtain a determinant exactly like $|\mathbf{K}|$ except for a missing m^{th} column and $k_l = 0$ (or, equivalently, a missing l^{th} column and $k_m = 0$). The expression for the cofactor, then, is the same as that for $|\mathbf{K}|$, multiplied by $(-1)^{m-l-1}$ (for the $m - l - 1$ column interchanges) except that it has no m term and $k_l = 0$. That is, every product in the expression for $|\mathbf{K}|$ must be zero except

$$\prod_{i \neq l,m} k_i;$$

so

$$\mathbf{K}_{lm} = (-1)^{m-l-1} \prod_{i \neq l,m} k_i$$

Finally, when we introduce the proper signs of the cofactors, we introduce a second sign factor $(-1)^{m-l}$ which makes all the off diagonal cofactor terms negative. It is obvious that $\mathbf{K}_{ll}$, a diagonal cofactor, is simply $|\mathbf{K}|$ with no l^{th} row or column. We shall call such a cofactor $\mathbf{K}_{-l}$. Note that the cofactor matrix turns out to be symmetric—it equals its own transpose.

Now we have

$$\mathbf{K}^{-1} = \frac{1}{|\mathbf{K}|} \begin{bmatrix} \mathbf{K}_{-1} & \prod_{i \neq 1,2} k_i & \cdots & \prod_{i \neq 1,n} k_i \\ -\prod_{i \neq 1,2} k_i & k_{-2} & \cdots & -\prod_{i \neq 2,n} k_i \\ \cdots & \cdots & \cdots & \cdots \end{bmatrix}$$

and we can solve for $\dot{q}_j$ using $\dot{Q} = -\mathbf{K}^{-1}R$.

$$q_j = -\frac{1}{|\mathbf{K}|} \left[\mathbf{K}_{-j} R_j - \sum_{l \neq j} \left\{ \prod_{\substack{i \neq l \\ i \neq j}} k_i R_i \right\} \right]$$

Simplifying, and putting in the expressions for $|\mathbf{K}|$ and $\mathbf{K}_{-j}$, this equation reduces to (E–4).

From (E–4) and (E–3) we can obtain $\dot{r}_{ij}$:

$$\dot{r}_{ij} = \alpha_i \left[\frac{R_i}{k_i} - \frac{\sum_{j \neq i} \frac{R_j}{k_j}}{k_i \left(1 + \sum_{j \neq i} \frac{1}{k_j}\right)} - r_{ij} \right]$$

$$\dot{R}_i = \frac{\left(\alpha_i 1 + \frac{1}{k_i}\right)}{1 + \sum \frac{1}{k_l}} \left[R_i - \sum \frac{R_l}{k_l} + R_i \sum \frac{1}{k_l} \right] \tag{E–6}$$

The sufficient condition for stability in the model is now $|\mathbf{K}| > 0$, and it can be seen from (E–5) that this is always true if $A_i < 1$ for every i: the same condition that we had in the two person case.

We can also use equation (E–6) to show that as long as the stability conditions are met, the learning process guarantees that at least one player will concede. Given the stability condition $0 < A_i < 1$ for all i, it can be shown from expression (E–5) that R_i must be negative for some i. Suppose this were not the case and all R_i were positive. Then the bracketed expression in (E–6) would be positive for all i, and summing these we obtain:

$$\sum_{i=1}^{n} \left[\sum_{j=1}^{n} \frac{R_j - R_i}{k_j} - R_i \right] > 0$$

But this expression equals

$$0 - \sum_{i=1}^{n} R_i$$

which must be negative by hypothesis. To avoid this contradiction, we must have at least one $\dot{R}_i < 0$ which, by equation (E–2), implies

$$\dot{q}_i < 0$$

In Chapter IV we discussed a tendency for the ratio r_1/r_2 to approach a value which would remain constant. That is, r_1 and r_2 would converge to a locus of points for which $\dot{r}_1/\dot{r}_2 = r_1/r_2$. The same tendency appears in the n-person case. Given an $\dot{R}_i < 0$, we can show from (E–6) that the ratio $\dot{R}_i/\dot{R}_j$ will tend to approach the condition

$$\frac{\dot{R}_i}{\dot{R}_j} = \frac{R_i}{R_j} \tag{E–7}$$

For example, suppose that (E–7) is satisfied and that we increase R_i alone. This tends to reduce $\dot{R}_i$ and increase $\dot{R}_j$ [from (E–6)]. Since both $\dot{R}_i$ and $\dot{R}_j$ are negative, this means that the high value of R_i had tended to increase $\dot{R}_i/\dot{R}_j$ so as to restore (E–7).

Writing out (E–7) in terms of R_i and R_j:

$$\frac{R_i}{R_j} = \frac{\alpha_i}{\alpha_j} \frac{1 - A_j}{1 - A_i} \frac{\displaystyle\sum_{l=1}^{n} \frac{R_l - R_i}{k_l} - R_i}{\displaystyle\sum_{l=1}^{n} \frac{R_l - R_j}{k_l} - R_j}$$

or:

$$1 = \frac{\alpha_i}{\alpha_j} \frac{1 - A_j}{1 - A_i} \frac{1 + \Sigma \frac{1}{k_l} - \frac{1}{R_i} \Sigma \frac{R_l}{k_l}}{1 + \Sigma \frac{1}{k_l} - \frac{1}{R_j} \Sigma \frac{R_l}{k_l}} \qquad (E-8)$$

Equation (E–8) can be used to derive the value of $R_i/_j$ for different values of the parameters. For example, suppose that the players are "similar" ($\alpha_i = \alpha_j = \alpha$, $a_i = a_j = a$ for all i, j) and the utility functions are linear, so that $k_i = k_j = k$ and $A_i = A_j = A$ for all i, j. Then (E–8) reduces to

$$\Sigma_i \frac{R_l}{R_j} = \Sigma_i \frac{R_l}{R_i}$$

implying $R_i = R_j$.

We have already established that under conditions of dynamic stability we must find some player conceding. In equilibrium, therefore, we must have all players conceding [all $\dot{R}_i < 0$ from (E–7)]. Finally, it follows from (E–6) that for all i:

$$1 + \sum_{l=1}^{n} \frac{1}{k_l} - \frac{1}{R_i} \Sigma \frac{R_l}{k_l} > 0$$

We observe that whenever $R_i = R_j$, the expression

$$\frac{1 + \sum_{l=1}^{n} \frac{1}{k_l} - \frac{1}{R_i} \sum_{l=1}^{n} \frac{R_l}{k_l}}{1 + \sum_{l=1}^{n} \frac{1}{k_l} - \frac{1}{R_j} \sum_{l=1}^{n} \frac{R_l}{k_l}}$$

equals 1 regardless of the values of the other R's. Moreover, since both numerator and denominator are positive, the condition $R_i > R_j$ implies that this fraction is less than one, and whenever $R_i < R_j$, the fraction is greater than one.

Suppose that the players have equal discount rates and linear utility functions, allowing us to avoid second order effects. Then if player i has a higher learning rate ($\alpha_i > \alpha_j$) we must have $(1 - A_i) < (1 - A_j)$ since $(0 < A < 1)$, and hence equation (E–8) implies $R_i < R_j$.

Similarly, if $\alpha_i = \alpha_j$, but the discount rates differ, we can derive the result $a_i > a_j => R_i > R_j$.

Using equation (E–1) for players i and j we can obtain an outcome equation analogous to equation (13) in Chapter III.

$$\frac{dU_i}{dU_j} = \frac{U_i}{U_j} \frac{a_i}{a_j} \frac{R_j}{R_i} \qquad (E\text{–}9)$$

Thus, we arrive at the same conclusions as before: a higher rate of learning, other things being equal, will be to the disadvantage of a player in terms of the final point of agreement; a rise in a player's discount rate favors him in terms of the relative expected rates of concession at agreement, although at the same time it acts against him in terms of his actual demands. The ambiguity with respect to the discount rate is the same as that which we observed in Chapter III. Finally, if $a_i = a_j$ and $\alpha_i = \alpha_j$, then $R_i = R_j$, and equation (E–9) predicts the Nash point as the outcome.

INDEX

245